BONHOEFFER

AND

CONTINENTAL THOUGHT

Indiana Series in the Philosophy of Religion

Merold Westphal, editor

Bonhoeffer and Continental Thought

CRUCIFORM PHILOSOPHY

†

EDITED BY

Brian Gregor & Jens Zimmermann

Indiana University Press

Bloomington & Indianapolis

This book is a publication of

Indiana University Press
601 North Morton Street
Bloomington, IN 47404-3797 USA

www.iupress.indiana.edu

Telephone orders   800-842-6796
Fax orders   812-855-7931
Orders by e-mail   iuporder@indiana.edu

© 2009 by Indiana University Press
All rights reserved

The paper used in this publication meets
the minimum requirements of American
National Standard for Information Sci-
ences—Permanence of Paper for Printed
Library Materials, ANSI Z39.48-1984.
Manufactured in the United States of
America

Library of Congress Cataloging-in-Publi-
cation Data

Bonhoeffer and Continental thought:
cruciform philosophy/edited by Brian
Gregor and Jens Zimmermann.
   p. cm. — (Indiana series in the philosophy of religion)
   Includes index.
   ISBN 978-0-253-35318-4 (cloth : alk.
paper) — ISBN 978-0-253-22084-4 (pbk.:
alk. paper) 1. Bonhoeffer, Dietrich, 1906–
1945. 2. Philosophical theology. 3. Philosophy and religion. 4. Continental philosophy. I. Gregor, Brian. II. Zimmermann,
Jens, date
   BT40.B57 2009
   230'.044092—dc22
                                    2009007058

1 2 3 4 5 14 13 12 11 10 09

CONTENTS

ACKNOWLEDGMENTS

In addition to our contributors, numerous people deserve thanks for their help in realizing this project: Merold Westphal, who believed in its merits enough to include it in his series; Barry Harvey for reviewing, critiquing, and recommending the first draft of the manuscript; Clifford Green and Ernst Feil for their advice and support; Dee Mortensen, Laura MacLeod, and their staff at Indiana University Press, as well as Carol A. Kennedy for her fine editorial work; Richard Kearney, whose help with the Ricoeur essay and general support was greatly appreciated; Michael Boddy and Ruth Tonkiss Cameron for their generous assistance with the Bonhoeffer Collection at Union Theological Seminary; the Canadian government's SSHRC and CRC (Canada Research Chairs) program, the Ernest Fortin Memorial Foundation, and the GSA at Boston College for financial support; and Elisabeth Fallon, without whose assistance we would have never finished the index. Finally, thanks to our wives—Margaret Gregor and Sabine Zimmermann—for their patience.

ABBREVIATIONS

AB DBWE 2: *Act and Being: Transcendental Philosophy and Ontology in Systematic Theology,* trans. H. Martin Rumscheidt (Minneapolis: Fortress Press, 1996).

CC *Christ the Center,* new trans. Edwin H. Robinson (New York: Harper and Row, 1978).

CF DBWE 3: *Creation and Fall: A Theological Exposition of Genesis 1–3,* trans. Douglas Stephen Bax (Minneapolis: Fortress Press, 1997).

D DBWE 4: *Discipleship,* trans. Martin Kuske and Ilse Tödt (Minneapolis: Fortress Press, 2001).

E DBWE 6: *Ethics,* ed. Clifford J. Green, trans. Reinhard Krauss, Charles C. West, and Douglass W. Stott (Minneapolis: Fortress Press, 2005).

FTP DBWE 7: *Fiction from Tegel Prison,* trans. Renate Bethge and Ilse Tödt (Minneapolis: Fortress Press, 2000).

LPP *Letters and Papers from Prison,* enlarged ed., ed. Eberhard Bethge (New York: Simon and Schuster, 1971).

NRS *No Rusty Swords: Letters, Lectures and Notes 1935–1939 from the Collected Works,* trans. Edwin H. Robertson and John Bowden (London: William Collins Sons, 1966).

SC DBWE 1: *Sanctorum Communio: A Theological Study of the Sociology of the Church*, trans. Reinhard Krauss and Nancy Lukens (Minneapolis: Fortress Press, 1998).

TF *A Testament to Freedom: The Essential Writings of Dietrich Bonhoeffer*, rev. ed., ed. Geffrey B. Kelly and F. Burton Nelson (San Francisco: HarperCollins, 1995).

WF *The Way to Freedom: Letters, Lectures and Notes 1935–1939*, ed. Edwin H. Robinson, trans. Edwin H. Robinson and John Bowden (New York: Harper and Row, 1966).

Dietrich Bonhoeffer Werke

DBW 1 *Sanctorum Communio: Eine dogmatische Untersuchung zur Soziologie der Kirche.*

DBW 2 *Akt und Sein: Transzendentalphilosophie und Ontologie in der systematischen Theologie.*

DBW 3 *Schöpfung und Fall.*

DBW 4 *Nachfolge.*

DBW 5 *Gemeinsames Leben* und *Das Gebetbuch der Bibel.*

DBW 6 *Ethik.*

DBW 7 *Fragmente aus Tegel.*

DBW 8 *Widerstand und Ergebung.*

DBW 9 *Jugend und Studium: 1918–27.*

DBW 10 *Barcelona, Berlin, Amerika: 1928–31.*

DBW 11 *Ökumene, Universität, Pfarramt: 1931–32.*

DBW 12 *Berlin: 1933.*

DBW 13 *London: 1933–35.*

DBW 14 *Illegale Theologenausbildung: 1935–37.*

DBW 15 *Illegale Theologenausbildung: 1937–40.*

DBW 16 *Konspiration und Haft: 1940–45.*

BONHOEFFER
AND
CONTINENTAL THOUGHT

Dietrich Bonhoeffer and Cruciform Philosophy

BRIAN GREGOR & JENS ZIMMERMANN

With this collection of essays we want to introduce Dietrich Bonhoeffer as a philosophical theologian. It is our conviction that Bonhoeffer's writings have a great deal to offer the contemporary philosophical scene—particularly given philosophy's recent "turn to religion." This suggestion often comes as a surprise to those who are not used to thinking of Bonhoeffer as a philosophical theologian: "Bonhoeffer? Isn't he the Lutheran pastor who was killed by the Nazis at the end of World War II?" In the popular imagination, Bonhoeffer ranks alongside such religious figures as Gandhi, Martin Luther King Jr., and Desmond Tutu as a spiritual thinker who made brave sacrifices and left behind a powerful testimony of political action with his involvement in the anti-Nazi resistance movement. Among those who have read some of Bonhoeffer's more famous texts, he is known as the author of *The Cost of Discipleship* and *Life Together,* and often *Letters and Papers from Prison,* which have a wide lay readership because of their profound spiritual insights. Yet underwriting Bonhoeffer's work in these texts is a deep engagement with not only theological but also, and most notably for our concerns in this volume, *philosophical* thinking.

Bonhoeffer's interest in philosophy was in keeping with his overall commitment to finding the best available resources for thinking through theological issues. This commitment reflects his upbringing, which emphasized the importance of intellectual and cultural development. In keeping with family tradition, Bonhoeffer's university studies began with a year at the University of Tübingen.[1] There he embarked toward becoming a theologian—a goal he set for himself at fifteen.[2] But in Eberhard Bethge's account, during these early years of study Bonhoeffer's interest in theology was due more to philosophical curiosity than to personal religious involvement.[3] This posture would change dramatically later on, but during this year at Tübingen Bonhoeffer read widely, with a pronounced interest in philosophy. Epistemology was a prevailing concern for him,[4] and he took several courses with the philosopher Karl Groos, studying logic, the history of modern philosophy, and Kant's first *Critique*.[5] As Bethge recounts, when the theologian (and later Bonhoeffer's dissertation supervisor) Reinhold Seeberg met Bonhoeffer's father during a Berlin University Senate meeting in 1925, "he expressed his surprise and admiration at the young man's solid philosophical preparation and his extensive knowledge of contemporary philosophy."[6] After Tübingen, Bonhoeffer spent the next three years at the University of Berlin, where he began to focus more directly on theology. Nevertheless, along with this greater theological emphasis, he continued to read philosophy, imbibing the works of Weber, Hegel, Husserl, and also Heidegger.[7]

After concluding his doctorate at Berlin and qualifying for a university teaching post with his habilitation, Bonhoeffer spent 1930–31 studying at Union Theological Seminary in New York, where he encountered Anglo-American philosophical voices. He read almost everything by William James, whom he found "uncommonly fascinating," as well as Dewey, Perry, and Russell, whose radically empirical and uncompromisingly pragmatic orientation struck Bonhoeffer as remarkable: "Questions such as that of Kantian epistemology are 'nonsense,' and no problem to them, because they take life no further. It is not truth, but 'works' that is 'valid,' and that is their criterion."[8] Contrasted with Bonhoeffer's philosophical formation on questions of epistemology and logic, this way of thinking was new and "fascinating." In these thinkers—James in particular—he found a way to understand the many aspects of American existence that he found so surprising. Bonhoeffer even planned to undertake a major work on the influence of pragmatism in American philosophy and theology, but was unable to have his stay in the United States extended.[9]

Back at the University of Berlin, where he was now qualified to give seminars and lectures, Bonhoeffer continued his exploration of philosophical themes in his teaching: in WS 1931–32, "The Concept of Philosophy and Protestant Theology"; in WS 1932–33, "Dogmatics: Problems of a Theological Anthropology"; and in the summer of 1933, Bonhoeffer's last lecture course, "Dogmatics: Hegel's Philosophy of Religion."[10] The direct influence of philosophy is perhaps less explicit during the period of Bonhoeffer's involvement in the church struggle with the rising power of Nazism, but his philosophical interests never disappeared. This is evident from the list of books he read during his imprisonment during the 1940s, which includes—among numerous other works—Kant's *Anthropology,* Nicolai Hartmann, J. Ortega y Gasset, and Wilhelm Dilthey.[11] In short, philosophy, from detailed episte-mological and phenomenological concerns to a broader philosophy of culture, was a recurring influence in Bonhoeffer's theological explorations.

Methodology and the Place of Philosophy in Bonhoeffer's Authorship

Bonhoeffer's theological engagement with philosophy involved a good deal of methodological reflection regarding the long-standing tension between faith and reason in its various manifestations as revelation/reason, theol-ogy/philosophy, and so on, whose mostly oppositional, even dualistic for-mulations Bonhoeffer sought to overcome. This concern for a holistic un-derstanding of human existence appears straightaway in the opening of his dissertation, *Sanctorum Communio,* where he articulates a specifically Christian phenomenology of sociality, with the ultimate goal of a sociology of the Christian community—the *ek-klesia,* the church. It is worth con-sidering this discussion at length, because in it we find the beginning of a methodology that will continue to guide Bonhoeffer's engagement with philosophy throughout his works. What is striking about this methodology is Bonhoeffer's hermeneutic consciousness, that is, his awareness of how methodological prejudices and their embodiment in conceptual constructs shape our interpretation of phenomena.

In *Sanctorum Communio,* Bonhoeffer claims to employ a specifically Christian social philosophy and Christian sociology in his inquiry, but in order to avoid "a hopeless confusion of concepts," he takes care to differ-entiate between the distinct disciplines of social philosophy and sociology (SC 24–25). Social philosophy uncovers the ontological structures of fun-damental social relationships, which are then normative for empirical in-quiry into human community. Sociology is one such empirical discipline, since it builds on the concepts of social philosophy. Bonhoeffer's model of sociology is not, however, the social science we associate with surveys and other statistical research. In fact, he takes care to distinguish his model of sociology from the genetic and historical-causal orientations that typically characterize sociology, arguing instead for a phenomenological approach to the distinct structures of religious community (SC 30–31).

But in undertaking a phenomenology of Christian social existence, Bonhoeffer does not subscribe to Husserl's model of phenomenology as presuppositionless science. He does not pretend to offer a theologically neutral description. Instead, his phenomenology of sociality is distinctly and openly theological, since it proceeds on the basis of a Christian conception of sociality. His task is to understand, "from the perspective of social philosophy and sociology," the structure of Christ's church as a reality given in revelation (SC 33). Understanding the church as revelational *donatum* should not, however, permit the reduction of fundamental insights by philosophy and sociology to theological concepts; these insights are hardly "neutral," but they do have a currency and significance of their own. Bonhoeffer carefully employs these findings to think philosophically (and sociologically) while assuming the presuppositions of Christian theology. He maintains that Christian presuppositions remain indispensable for this task, because they derive from the phenomena themselves. Bonhoeffer thus rejects the possibility that a pure, neutral sociology of religion can properly understand the nature of the church. Such conceptions do not correspond adequately to the nature of the phenomenon. In order to understand the church, one must approach it from within: "Only those who take the claim of the church seriously—not relativizing it in relation to other similar claims or their own rationality, but viewing it from the standpoint of the gospel—can possibly glimpse something of its true nature" (SC 33). This is not to deny that an external examiner can study the morphology of the church as a "religious community" or "religious society" (SC 126). But the external perspective does not—and cannot—take seriously the reality of God's revelation in Christ, which constitutes the church. This is because the church of Christ "*establishes its own foundation in itself;* like all revelations, it can be judged only by itself" (SC 127). The concrete uniqueness of God's self-revelation cannot be adequately perceived by extra-theological categories and norms—for example, a phenomenology of "the holy" or a sociological categorization of "religions of revelation." Consequently, "the church can be understood fully only from within, on the basis of its own claim; only on this basis can we develop appropriately critical criteria for judging it" (SC 127).

No doubt Bonhoeffer's "Christian social philosophy" is specifically Christian. But is it genuinely *philosophical*? This is a crucial question given our concerns in this volume. Bonhoeffer acknowledges the difficulty of determining the relation between philosophy and theology, which he identifies as "the basic task and also the difficulty" of his dissertation (SC-A 22).[12] In a related passage Bonhoeffer mentions his aim of arriving at "a philosophical foundation for Christian thought" (SC-A 35). His use of the term "foundation" does not connote a neutral philosophical foundation for theological inquiry, let alone foundation*alism.* Given Bonhoeffer's explicit repudiation of such strategies, it is most accurate to understand "foundation" as referring to fundamental philosophical *frameworks,* rather than absolute philosophical *grounding.* Bonhoeffer is trying to find the appropriate philosophical conceptions for thinking Christianly about human sociality. Thus in the second chapter of his dissertation Bonhoeffer examines a series of philosophical conceptions of the person—running from Aristotle, through Stoicism, Epicureanism, and Descartes, to German Idealism—and evaluates them vis-à-vis the Christian concept of the person. Bonhoeffer employs a similar evaluative approach for philosophical conceptions of the human being in his *Habilitationsschrift, Act and Being,* with Heidegger as one of his most important interlocutors.[13]

Bonhoeffer's engagement with philosophy demonstrates his desire to take philosophy seriously and to make use of whatever insight he can glean. At the same time, Bonhoeffer balances the desire to take philosophy seriously with his commitment to the priority of God's revelation in Christ. On this point he shows the influence of Karl Barth, who insists that revelation does not need philosophical legitimation, insofar as the ultimate reality of God makes philosophical categories possible in the first place: "not because [they] are necessitated by the created order, but because they are presupposed and implemented by revelation, can we treat problems of social philosophy and sociology within a theological framework" (SC 65).[14]

How, then, should we think of the relation between these two commitments? The disciplinary hierarchy Bonhoeffer gives in *Sanctorum Communio* can be summarized as follows: If social philosophy is normative for sociology, the faith perspective of theology is normative for social philosophy. In other words, while sociology presupposes the normative guidelines of social philosophy, the latter presupposes the faith perspective of theology, which takes the revelation of Jesus Christ and his church as normative because the ultimate reality of all things coheres in Christ. The best way to describe Bonhoeffer's relation to philosophy is within the classical Augustinian model of human inquiry as *faith seeking understanding.*

His adherence to this model underlines the relevance of Bonhoeffer's theology for contemporary philosophy in two ways. First, he shares the basic hermeneutical premise of much contemporary continental philosophy. Not only post-metaphysical convictions in philosophy but also post-positivistic convictions in science have led to the general acknowledgment that the human quest for meaning is shaped as "faith seeking understanding."[15] As Adriaan Peperzak has recently formulated this renewed "faith" perspective in philosophy after the disappointment of metaphysical positivism: "Is it not time to retrieve the ancient and premodern meaning of philosophy? . . . Though not confined to any particular religion, such a philosophy is a form of *fides quaerens intellectum*."[16]

Secondly, Bonhoeffer remains faithful to this classical model's serious commitment to unfolding faith reflectively through philosophical inquiry. The understanding that faith seeks is not an insular, closed discourse in which theology unpacks its presuppositions with the occasional help from the handmaiden philosophy. Theology does not seek to obliterate philosophical discourse but rather to learn from its careful analyses of common human concerns and gain self-understanding in responding to them. Yet "faith seeking understanding" also entails faithfulness to the Christian character of truth as it unfolds with the help of philosophy. Here too Bonhoeffer's thought is genuinely philosophical (in addition to being theological) insofar as it explores the philosophical implications of Christian faith. What results from this approach, then, is perhaps best expressed by Charles Marsh as "Bonhoeffer's Christological redescription of philosophy."[17] Following Marsh's cue, we have chosen "Cruciform Philosophy" as this volume's title to underline Bonhoeffer's conviction that the incarnation—with its fundamental ontological structure of "being-for-the-other," in the self-giving nature of Christ's life, death, and resurrection—provides a challenge to philosophy in its dialogue with theology within a common human rationality.

Even if the hermeneutic nature of all human inquiry thus absolves Bonhoeffer of charges of privileging the irrational (theology) over the rational (positivism), does his well-known Christocentric focus not diminish any philosophy that is not Christologically oriented—especially given his emphasis on the way Christ undoes any attempt at neutral, autonomous philosophical understanding? For instance, consider the following passage from *Ethics*: "Ever since Jesus Christ said of himself, 'I am the life' (John 14:6; 11:27), no Christian thinking or indeed philosophical reflection can any longer ignore this claim and the reality it contains. This statement of Jesus about himself declares every attempt to formulate the essence of life in itself as futile and doomed from the start" (E 249). Similarly, Bonhoeffer rejects any attempt to understand the ultimate nature of reality in terms of "nature" or "life"—insofar as these denote neutral, autonomous metaphysical or philosophical concepts. Bonhoeffer's claim that there is only one Christ-reality created and unified by Christ has serious implications for the relation of philosophy and theology:

> There are not two realities, *but only one reality,* and that is God's reality revealed in Christ, in the reality of the world. . . . The world has no reality

of its own independent of God's revelation in Christ. . . . Hence there are not two realms, but only the one realm of Christ-reality [*Christuswirklichkeit*], in which the reality of God and the reality of the world are united. . . . There are not two competing realms standing side by side and battling over the borderline, as if this question of boundaries was always the decisive one. Rather, the whole reality of the world has already been drawn into and is held together in Christ. History moves only from this center and toward this center. (E 58)

If we are not careful in reading passages such as these, we might draw the mistaken conclusion that Bonhoeffer creates in fact a Christocratic model of human thinking, and condemns extra-Christian philosophy to utter futility while preparing the way for theological triumphalism.[18]

Bonhoeffer himself was fully aware of this danger and worked out the simultaneity of a unified Christ reality and genuinely hermeneutic epistemology in his discussion of the relation between *ultimate* and *penultimate* things.[19] For the Christian, the ultimate reality is creation as affirmed by the incarnation, as judged at the cross, and as promised full redemption in the resurrection of Jesus the Christ. This means that the world is unified in and contingent on Christ: "the world, the natural, the profane, and reason are seen as included in God from the beginning. All this does not exist 'in and for itself'" (E 59). Yet because creation is unified in and affirmed by the incarnate Word of God, all human thought and action has to follow the incarnational pattern set by God himself: "Just as the reality of God has entered the reality of the world in Christ, what is Christian cannot be had otherwise than in what is worldly, the 'supernatural' only in the natural, the holy only in the profane, the revelational only in the rational." Out of his consciousness of the unity of the world in Christ, the Christian has to bring this unity to life in his or her sphere of existence as interpretive application: "The unity of the reality of God and the reality of the world established in Christ (repeats itself, or more exactly) realizes itself again and again in human beings" (E 59). This reiteration of the world's unity in Christ occurs when we interpret this ultimate unity for every cultural situation anew, availing ourselves of the best thought available. "The reality of God," says Bonhoeffer, "is disclosed only as it places me completely into the reality of the world. But I find the reality of the world always already borne, accepted, and reconciled in the reality of God" (E 55).

In this interpretive effort, neither a simple affirmation of existent structures in the name of immanence or nature nor a complete dissolution of them in the name of eschatology adequately expresses the ultimate unity of reality in Christ. Bonhoeffer terms these false extremes *compromise* and *radicalism,* respectively. Radicalism—considered in terms of the relation between the secular and the sacred, philosophy and theology—denotes what is usually caricatured as the Barthian position, which denies the role of philosophy in shaping theological concepts. Compromise, on the other hand, denies the relativizing power of God's revelation—the radical challenge of divine possibility in the realm of the human. As Bonhoeffer explains in a short aphorism,

> Radicalism hates time, and compromise hates eternity.
> Radicalism hates patience, and compromise hates decision.
> Radicalism hates wisdom, and compromise hates simplicity.
> Radicalism hates moderation and measure, and compromise hates the immeasurable.
> Radicalism hates the real, and compromise hates the Word. (E 156)[20]

Bonhoeffer's refusal to concede the radical autonomy of either theology or philosophy—*because* all reality is defined Christologically—has important implications for contemporary discussions of post-secular philosophy.

The Religious Turn in Continental Philosophy: Surveying the Contemporary Scene

In recent years there has been a lot of talk about a "religious turn" in Western thought and culture. Religious questions and perspectives have returned to academic and intellectual endeavors from which they were once banished by the secularizing impulses of modernity and the Enlightenment. This turn has been particularly evident in Continental philosophy, the landscape of which is marked by a variety of positions regarding the meaning and possibilities of religion in the contemporary world.[21]

To note, however, that religious questions are no longer excluded to the degree they once were should not imply that Continental philosophers had at one point succeeded in expunging the religious from the philosophical. While many movements and thinkers may have been hell-bent on secularity or even downright anti-religiosity, the religious has been a constant influence in Continental philosophy. In particular this is due to the centrality of German philosophy in the Continental tradition, since so many of the key thinkers who shaped German philosophy were immersed in religious and theological matters. As Nietzsche famously writes in *The Antichrist,* "[t]he Protestant parson is the grandfather of German philosophy."[22]

Nietzsche, of course, was contemptuous of this parentage. But he was not alone in objecting to the way that philosophy's pedigree had been tainted by theological blood. This allegation became a common way of distancing oneself from one's philosophical forebears: whereas one's predecessors are actually theologians in disguise, one's own work is truly philosophical, since it is at last free from the unwelcome influence of religion. Only following this liberation is philosophy capable of true autonomy and intellectual purity. William Desmond illustrates this well when he writes, "Schopenhauer used this strategy against Kant; as Feuerbach and Marx use it differently against Hegel; as Marx uses it against others who have not 'overcome' theology fully."[23] Similar allegations arise from the Heideggerian camp, which dismisses the complex and varied synthesis of faith and reason in the Christian tradition as the simultaneously *unholy* and *un-philosophical* matrimony known as onto-theology.[24] This facile and erroneous equation of Christian theology with metaphysics now lends successive thinkers the air of liberators from the shackles of metaphysical objectivism: Heidegger calls Nietzsche the last metaphysician, while Derrida, in turn, levels the same charge against Heidegger.

Whatever the merits and defects of the debate over metaphysics, one of the most interesting developments to follow in its wake is the return of religion—and along with it a number of pressing questions. First: *Who (or what) comes after the God of metaphysics?*[25] Second: *What form should religion take after the strictures of secularity have been loosened?* And third: *How is reason to conduct itself in light of religion's return?* As Jürgen Habermas has recently formulated the third question, "how does modern reason, which has taken leave of metaphysics, understand itself in relation to religion?"[26] Habermas offers the important reminder that reason cannot understand itself without religion, and in the West this means Christian theology. That said, Habermas also stresses that it is "equally important" to maintain the "expectation that theology engages seriously with postmetaphysical thinking."[27] But the demand that theology take seriously post-metaphysical thinking may prove extremely difficult because it still implies that theology should follow rational guidelines; yet after the generally acknowledged breakdown of secular reason defined as logical positivism, how do we define "rational"? As a result of this unresolved question, contemporary philosophical discussions about God after metaphysics remain defined by a struggle for authority between theological doctrine and experienced faith. This struggle is characterized by a new openness to religion, which is, however, immediately limited by the simultaneous fear that Queen Theology could once again claim dominion in the realm of thought by declaring that all good philosophy is already fundamentally on the way to its consummation as theology.

This fear of theological imperialism principally informs the current division within continental philosophy's religious turn, which separates those who follow Heidegger in assuming that theological concepts must be bracketed from rigorous philosophical work[28] and those who believe in their integration into philosophy. The former position is championed by Dominique Janicaud, who identified and criticized the "theological turn" in French phenomenology, a term he applies to the work of such thinkers as Emmanuel Levinas, Jean-Luc Marion, Jean-Louis Chrétien, and Michel Henry.[29] Janicaud clearly voices his objections to a phenomenology of religion that stacks its hermeneutical cards in favor of theology. This "bad" phenomenology already has its mind made up to encounter the biblical God in the epoché. The "game is fixed," and "phenomenology has been taken hostage by a theology that does not want to say its name"[30] but can be easily identified: "All is acquired and imposed from the outset, and this all is no little thing: nothing less than the God of the biblical tradition. Strict treason of the reduction that handed over the transcendental I to its nudity, here theology is restored with its parade of capital letters." As a defender of a more neutral, less theologically biased phenomenology, Janicaud asks why biblical theology should install "itself at the most intimate dwelling of consciousness, as if that were as natural as could be?"[31]

In his essay analyzing this theological turn, Janicaud identifies Emmanuel Levinas as particularly responsible for these aberrations within the phenomenological method.[32] Levinas blurs the boundaries between phenomenology and theology "by installing the transcendence of the Other [*Autre*] at the heart of a phenomenology that can no longer quite be considered one, (and thereby) expressly divests the philosophical regard of the neutrality of which he ought, in principle, to make it his duty to protect."[33] Levinas compromises the methodological purity of phenomenology, and thereby opens the door through which subsequent phenomenologists, similarly compromised, proceed.

Janicaud asserts that he is not against theology as such, but against its contamination of interest-free phenomenology. Consequently he praises another French thinker with deep investments in phenomenology and theology, Paul Ricoeur, for his methodological restraint. Although Ricoeur's philosophy bears the undeniable influence of Christian texts and theology, Janicaud nevertheless commends Ricoeur's itinerary for phenomenology as "exemplary," since it is committed to treating "'the manner of appearing [*apparaître*] of things as an autonomous problem.'"[34]

Yet despite Ricoeur's scrupulous distinction between philosophy and theology, he shares neither Janicaud's zeal for a pure, rigorous, scientific phenomenology nor his opposition of phenomenology to hermeneutics.[35] Ricoeur's own departure from phenomenology's eidetic ideal stems from his conviction that phenomenology does not proceed outside of the hermeneutical circle. Phenomenological description is never immediate; rather, it is always already mediated by the symbols and texts that have shaped the phenomenologist's situated understanding. In short, all understanding is mediated by interpretation.[36] And so the transcendental ego's aspirations of absolute and ultimate foundation are frustrated by the hermeneutical nature of understanding. Ricoeur thus exposes as illusory Janicaud's own commitment to phenomenology as a neutral, autonomous science.

Based on his hermeneutical convictions, Ricoeur also rejects the commonly assumed possibility of a general, neutral phenomenology of religion that seeks to describe "the religious phenomenon grasped in its historical and geographical universality."[37] Ricoeur objects to the implicit assumption of an unmediated, direct encounter with universal structures. He does suggest the universal structure of "call-and-response" as a candidate for the most basic religious experience, but he insists that the structure of this phenomenon can never be intuited in its "naked immediacy," since it is always mediated linguistically, culturally, and historically.[38] Consequently, we must begin with a hermeneutic of religious phenomena (such as the call and the response) within a particular religious tradition. From that starting point one can engage other religious traditions analogically, seeking to understand both similarities and differences. Contrary to any pretensions to a neutral phenomenology, Ricoeur thus concedes a phenomenology of "Religion," but only if this "regulative ideal," which guides a principally hermeneutical encounter toward an "interconfessional, interreligious hospitality," in no way eliminates the particular characteristics of divergent theologies.[39]

Ricoeur's model of interconfessional and interreligious hospitality plays an important role in the work of his student Richard Kearney. While Kearney is less anxious than Ricoeur to keep philosophy and theology separate,[40] he shares Ricoeur's commitment to a deliberately hermeneutical approach to the phenomenology of religion. The centerpiece of Kearney's position is his hermeneutics of a "possible God"—a God who "neither is nor is not but may be."[41] Against the traditional metaphysical subordination of possibility to act and the consequent interpretation of God as pure, perfectly fulfilled actuality, Kearney seeks to retrieve a deeper sense of God's *posse*. Through his rereading of several key biblical passages and of such religious thinkers as Nicholas of Cusa, Kearney proposes a God for whom all things are possible. He is careful to note that this is a "hermeneutical wager"—which is not to say a Pascalian cost-benefit analysis, nor a disinterested contemplation of abstract possibilities, but an existential commitment to a God who *may* be, who inhabits the realm of the *peut-être*. This God does not appear within the metaphysical register of onto-theology, but eschatologically, coming from the future to transform the present. In this way God enables us to transform our world through the gift of impossible possibilities; when we respond, in turn, with acts of love and justice, we enable God to manifest in the world— and in some way to "be" God.[42]

Kearney's hermeneutics of God has generated considerable critical discussion[43] and is subject to theological critique insofar as he lacks Bonhoeffer's Christological and ecclesiological emphases, with their concomitant commitment to God's actuality and the importance of doctrine.[44] Kearney's challenge to the metaphysics of divine immutability is a welcome insight, but Bonhoeffer insists on the already accomplished reality of God reconciling the world to himself in Christ.[45] In Christ's death and resurrection, this reconciliation is already actual. To be sure, this "already" brings with it a "not yet"—but God's ongoing relation with the world has its basis in the finished work of Christ.[46] As a number of commentators have observed, Kearney's Christology and eschatology underestimate Christ's suffering and death on the cross as the *crux* of atonement.[47] Thus, while Kearney's project is laudably incarnational, from Bonhoeffer's perspective it is insufficiently *cruciform*. Nonetheless, this commitment to particularity, embodiment, and the incarnational set Kearney at odds with a common tendency in Continental philosophy to emphasize the utter transcendence of divinity, which appears only in the form of radical disruption.

This is one of the major points of contrast between Kearney's hermeneutical approach and those positions that bear the decisive imprint of Levinas. Kearney has criticized Jean-Luc Marion's phenomenology for being insufficiently hermeneutical in its apophatic stress on God's divinity *beyond* or *without* Being (*Dieu sans l'Etre*).[48] This emphasis in Marion's thought is due to the influence not solely of Levinas, but also of Christian thinkers who share Levinas's Neoplatonic proclivity to designate God as the Good beyond being—for instance, Dionysius the Areopagite. Nevertheless, Levinas has played an important role in Continental philosophy's increasing emphasis on radical alterity. Not only does Levinas's demand for ethics as first philosophy re-call philosophy to the personal transcendent categories of the Hebrew tradition, but his ethical philosophy remains marked by the radical transcendence of the *wholly other* God. In his attempt to shield human dignity against totalizing structures, Levinas's overemphasis on the disruptive, asymmetric and non-systematic, otherness becomes too unsayable, even traumatic, to allow for the necessary cultural and interreligious dialogue philosophy and theology have to pursue in our current cultural context.

This influence is especially apparent in the deconstructive approach to religion. Jacques Derrida, although both more at ease with the necessary ontological grounding of human reason and more conflicted about theological categories than Levinas, proposes a secular form of Levinas's ethical transcendence. Derrida suggests a radically open hospitality to the other,[49] indeconstructible justice, and structural messianic (as opposed to determinate messian*isms*) in which any substantive content other than the structure itself remains deconstructible.[50] John D. Caputo's theological appropriation of deconstruction for his "radical hermeneutics" demonstrates the dangers of this approach for theology. Much like justice or the messianic in Derrida, for Caputo God becomes "a name of an event, of I know not what, of a bottomless provocation, like the name of love and justice, and I am in no position to stop the endless chain of substitutions in which it is caught up."[51] Caputo perhaps demonstrates best how good intentions—the hermeneutic emphasis to combat fundamentalism, and the existential emphasis to counter merely abstract, socially unconscious theology—can be ruinous to the very object of its passion. By rigorously "suspending the question of the name or status of the caller in its ontic or ontological identity,"[52] Caputo's attempt to establish a radically unconditional, indiscriminate hospitality in effect closes the door—a rather inhospitable gesture—to the biblical God whose address occurred incarnationally and thus ontologically, and whose self-revelation invites a relational participation. And as in any human relation and friendship (and does not Jesus call his followers friends and brothers?), the name and identity of the caller is all-important.

Caputo's deconstructionist version of negative theology is also disconcerting because like a number of other contemporary approaches to salvage Christianity with the help of post-metaphysical philosophy, he emphasizes the weakness of God to the neglect of his incarnational presence. Caputo's God event is, however, modeled neither on the orthodox understanding of the scandal of the cross nor on Luther's theology of the cross, but on deconstruction's dogmatic refusal of presence.

Another, both philosophically and theologically more interesting, attempt to utilize the weakness of God is Gianni Vattimo's kenotic hermeneutic or "weak" ontology. By transcribing Christian incarnational theology primarily into Heidegger's history of being as the overcoming of metaphysics, Vattimo marries his philosophy of "weak thought" with theology, reconciling not only religion and philosophy but also nihilism with Christianity.

> I have begun to take Christianity seriously again because I have constructed a philosophy inspired by Nietzsche and Heidegger, and have interpreted my experience in the contemporary world in light of it. . . . The fact of the matter is that at a certain moment I found myself thinking that the weak reading of Heidegger and the idea that the history of Being has as a guiding thread the weakening of strong structures . . . was nothing but the transcription of the Christian doctrine of the incarnation of the Son of God.[53]

By qualifying Heidegger's *Seinsgeschichte* through the sacrificial *kenosis* of God in Christ, the process of secularization is no longer a threat to Christianity but has become its very essence, weakening all ontological structures progressively toward nonviolent coexistence: "secularization is the way in which *kenosis*, having begun with the incarnation of Christ, but even before that with the covenant between God and 'his' people, continues to realize itself more and more clearly by furthering the education of mankind concerning the overcoming of originary violence essential to the sacred and to social life itself."[54] With the incarnation as the driving principle of weak ontology, secularization is not the enemy of Christian revelation but its very substance.

For all its purported emphasis on the incarnation, Vattimo's argument that "postmodern nihilism constitutes the actual truth of Christianity" ends up pretty much in the same place as deconstructionist and post-Levinasian ethical philosophies, namely with the refusal of positive doctrine or relative consensus in the church's history of interpretation on the meaning of biblical texts. All such strong structures are continually weakened in the name of charity, yet what charity looks like is no longer clear, for that too, presumably, could change over time.[55] Vattimo's post-metaphysical theology cannot, in the end, uphold genuine transcendence, because he rejects any such idea as still too metaphysical, as he must since he follows Heidegger in equating theology with metaphysics.

Perhaps closest in spirit to Bonhoeffer's understanding of the mediating role of philosophy in theology is the British movement known as Radical Orthodoxy. Much like Bonhoeffer, Radical Orthodoxy (RO) wants to "reclaim the world by situating its concerns and activities within a theological framework."[56] The group "does see the contemporary, postfoundationalist context as a catalyst for the recovery of an unapologetically confessional theory and practice."[57] This perceived affinity between postmodernity and theology is "neither an identification of the two nor an accommodation of one to the other but rather the discernment of an opportunity afforded by the contemporary situation."[58] In mapping out a post-secular theology, RO recognizes already the defining aporia of immanence and transcendence in post-metaphysical thinking about religion. Embracing a hermeneutic ontology, they advocate the mediation of theology through culture, and reject approaches like Barthianism, for instance, because it "tended to assume a positive autonomy for theology, which rendered philosophical concerns a matter of indifference."[59] Similarly, RO denounces eliminative materialism as too reductive to capture either the fullness or the complexity of human life and meaning.[60]

Yet often enough RO's desire for theological categories leads all too quickly to the consummation of philosophy by theology, and by a participatory, Neoplatonist theology at that. Catherine Pickstock's assertion that eucharistic language "is the condition of possibility for all human meaning" could almost pass for a Bonhoefferian re-description of philosophy, but RO's treatment of philosophy is less patient than Bonhoeffer's.[61] As a consequence, Pickstock and RO in general are justly criticized for reading philosophy all too readily as theology so that philosophy becomes the theologian's shopping mall, or, as Laurence Hemming put it, consummation turns into evacuation.[62] It is not clear that philosophy has much to offer once theology has "consummated" it.[63]

Bonhoeffer himself becomes a victim of RO's consumptive reading practice. Instead of drawing on Bonhoeffer's participatory ontology and his ultimate-penultimate distinction as exemplary approaches to descriptions of Christian belief and its relation to culture, Milbank denounces Bonhoeffer (albeit "in his weaker more Lutheran dialectical moments") as fideistic. Following a common misunderstanding of Bonhoeffer's "religionless Christianity" as advocating absolute secular autonomy, Milbank charges Bonhoeffer with a reductive theology of the cross, "perhaps construing even this as the tragic presence of God in his secular absence."[64] This judgment is highly unfortunate since Bonhoeffer's participatory ontology in *Act and Being* together with this decidedly non-dialectical unification of secular and sacred in one Christ reality in the *Ethics* (incidentally constituting Bonhoeffer's rehabilitation of Luther's theology) should have appealed to Milbank's integrative thinking concerning theology and philosophy.

In the end, for all its good intentions, it is mostly likely that RO's theological self-understanding as a countercultural movement to secularism provides, on the one hand, a welcome argumentative edge, but blinds it, on the other, to alternative philosophical and theological positions on the nature of human existence. John Milbank captures the Barthian spirit of

RO when he writes that "if Christianity seeks to 'find a place for' secular reason, it may be perversely compromising with what, on its own terms, is either deviancy or falsehood."[65] Yet that its "own terms" are derived from philosophy, and hence inevitably must live with the tension of philosophical interrogation, seems often overlooked. As we shall see in the next section, Bonhoeffer's insistence on the relative autonomy of the penultimate, secular realm is much more radical than RO in seeking an ultimate unity of the secular and the sacred.[66]

We could also mention other thinkers who have made important contributions to this debate, such as the recent philosophical readings of the apostle Paul by Alain Badiou, Giorgio Agamben, and Slavoj Žižek; Hent de Vries's survey in *Philosophy and the Turn to Religion,* or in his earlier attempt to read Adorno and Levinas as offering "minimal" theologies;[67] Merold Westphal's work on overcoming onto-theology for the sake of ethical and religious transcendence;[68] as well as the work of Jim Olthuis, Kevin Hart, and John-Panteleimon Manoussakis. The list could go on, but we do not intend this survey to be exhaustive; instead, we mention these thinkers, movements, and positions in order to better appreciate the context to which Bonhoeffer has so much to offer.

Bonhoeffer's Contribution to the Contemporary Philosophical Scene

Given this new openness to matters religious, and the various approaches we have briefly outlined above, contemporary Continental philosophy is in a better position than ever before to appreciate the rich insights that Bonhoeffer has to offer. This should come as no surprise if we recognize that Bonhoeffer too struggled with the question of God and/or religion after metaphysics. Having read and digested Kant, Kierkegaard, Nietzsche, Dilthey, Heidegger—in short, the key figures who have shaped the current landscape in Continental philosophy—Bonhoeffer too tried to restate Christianity in more existential and less metaphysical or positivistic terms. His question is our question: "How do we speak of God—without religion, i.e. without the temporally conditioned presuppositions of metaphysics, inwardness, and so on?" (LPP 280). In this attempt, Bonhoeffer took cultural and philosophical objections to Christianity seriously. Rather than caricature philosophical accounts of human existence, Bonhoeffer argued for a Christian philosophy able to appeal to a culture accustomed to cherishing freedom of thought, in a world come of age—that is, in a world that is no longer afraid to use its own understanding:[69]

> I should like to speak of God not on the boundaries but at the centre, not in weaknesses but in strength; and therefore not in death and guilt but in man's life and goodness. As to the boundaries, it seems to me better to be silent and leave the insoluble unsolved. Belief in the resurrection is *not* the "solution" of the problem of death. God's "beyond" is not the beyond of our cognitive faculties. The transcendence of epistemological theory has nothing to do with the transcendence of God. God is beyond in the midst of our life. (LPP 282)

God does not show up like a *deus ex machina,* but emerges in the very rigor of thought, in the midst of the strongest arguments against him. Statements like these, and others like them, held great appeal for the radical theologians of the 1960s, who embraced Bonhoeffer as a forerunner to their own proclamations of the death of God.[70] But just as this movement could not withstand the scrutiny of theological scholarship, its reading of Bonhoeffer could not sustain itself once it became clearer how these later, provocative fragments belonged to the larger continuity of Bonhoeffer's life and thought. Subsequent scholarship has shown how superficial the radical theologians' interpretation of Bonhoeffer's Christology really was.[71] It turns out there was more to Bonhoeffer's "radical theology" than they anticipated.

With this example in mind, one of our guiding aims in this book is to encourage people to read Bonhoeffer's oeuvre as a whole—not only for the sake of reading him accurately and minimizing misinterpretations, but also because this will deepen the understanding of the philosophical and theological roots supporting his more popular writings, as well as his political witness. Any reading of Bonhoeffer as philosophical theologian has to recognize the centrality of Christology in his thinking. Overlooking this defining theological commitment in Bonhoeffer constitutes the cardinal error of the radical atheologians of the 1960s. It would be an equally misleading error for philosophers to pick up on particular themes—such as his critique of religion, his emphasis on embodied, this-worldly faith, or his emphasis on ethical alterity—in isolation from his deep Christological commitments. If philosophy is truly to hear and appropriate Bonhoeffer's "Christological redescription of philosophy," it will lead in the direction of a cruciform, Christian philosophy.

The key to Bonhoeffer's contribution to contemporary discussions of God after metaphysics is his incarnational Christology. Throughout his writings, Bonhoeffer insists on the inseparability of its three defining aspects. In the incarnation, the wholly transcendent other became identical with humanity, thus affirming his creation. At the cross, all of creation has been judged, and by his resurrection, humanity's redemption is completed in Christ, whose perfect humanity forms the present eschatological hope of creation's realized redemption, toward which all of reality is inexorably moving. As participation in Christ, the Christian life takes part in all three aspects at once: "Christian life means being human in the power of Christ's becoming human, being judged and pardoned in the power of the cross, living a new life in the power of the resurrection. No one of these is without the others" (E 159).

From Bonhoeffer's incarnational Christology flows a theological ontology that avoids some of the extreme positions we have outlined above. The "one Christ-reality" sounds indeed like Radical Orthodoxy's "consummation of philosophy"; however, since the holy is found only in the profane and the revelational only in the rational, and vice versa, Christian thinking is not a one-way street in which theology unilaterally appropriates philosophical terms. Similarly, Bonhoeffer can speak about the weakness of God, especially in his musings about religionless Christianity, but he does so without forgetting the resurrection and its power already at work in the church and every believer. To name only two concrete examples: While Bonhoeffer, like deconstructionists, champions the transcendence and radical hermeneutical nature of God, the incarnation and its reflective unfolding in the Christian tradition also provide an adequate, if not comprehensive, substantive expression of what the incarnation means. Bonhoeffer's sense of created orders as divine mandates for the good of humanity, in combination with his conviction that Christian interpretation of Scripture and culture must be structured—following the incarnation—as suffering with the world, was the very strength of his political resistance.[72] Bonhoeffer, in other words, *did* know what he loved when he loved his God. This is not to suggest a metaphysical posture that escapes finitude or the hermeneutical circle—as though he could know absolutely or certainly. But in surrendering Cartesian certainty one does not fall into sheer indeterminacy. Nor does this require that we relinquish conviction. It was not on account of agnosticism but *because* Christ was *also* the God of Abraham, Isaac, and Jacob who dogmatically demanded obedience that Bonhoeffer resisted Hitler to the death. It was because the Messiah had come and demonstrated love and justice on the cross that justice was worth dying for.

Bonhoeffer is equally careful to guard the personal transcendence of the incarnation. Contrary to Vattimo's philosophical appropriation of the incarnation, God is neither an indeterminate event nor a principle of weakening but the transcendent other whom one encounters existentially, and concretely as "the just one" or "the loving one." That, insists Bonhoeffer in one of his earliest texts, "must remain the ontological foundation of theological determinations of Being." To go behind this concrete transcendence to something more general "destroys the very heart of Christian revelation," because "the contingency of God's revelation as law and gospel is now twisted into a general theory of being with requisite modifications, thereby blocking the road to a genuinely theological concept of sin and grace" (AB 75). Vattimo's incarnational ontology, however, does exactly what Bonhoeffer warns against. By equating Christ with an impersonal, general historical principle of kenotic love that weakens strong structures, Vattimo turns God into a general theory of being and thus courts the same danger as Heidegger—whose alleged openness to Being, for all its pious talk, in effect determines how God may manifest himself.[73] Once Christian theology is deprived of its concrete doctrines and God loses his distinct face as Christ, who knows what may show up under his name after metaphysics, whether it is in the name of Being or even in the name of God?

Because of his intense engagement with idealist and existentialist German philosophy, Bonhoeffer already prefigures many of today's discussions about God after metaphysics. Yet unlike so many post-metaphysical thinkers, Bonhoeffer's incarnational Christology allows him to combine a number of elements that remain all too often opposed in current discussions: immanence and transcendence, ontology and ethics, reflection and existence, sameness and difference, full participation in the divine and yet the full ambiguity and risk of its hermeneutical unfolding in theology. As a consequence, we are convinced that much work is yet to be done in appropriating the thought of this immensely intuitive and deep thinker for the current conversation on post-metaphysical theology and philosophy.

The Aims and Scope of This Volume

This is not the first scholarly endeavor to identify the importance of Continental philosophy in Bonhoeffer's thought, nor is it the first to bring him into dialogue with other key Continental thinkers. In a recent survey of Bonhoeffer's scholarly reception, Stephen Haynes notes that there are studies comparing Bonhoeffer with such philosophical thinkers as Hegel, Feuerbach, Nietzsche, Marx, Dilthey, Heidegger, Camus, Sartre, Adorno, Levinas, and Rorty.[74] Scattered throughout a variety of journals, dissertations, and annual meetings of organizations such as the AAR and the International Bonhoeffer Society are numerous studies treating Bonhoeffer in relation to Kierkegaard, Nietzsche, Heidegger, and others. A good deal of work still remains in exploring these connections and intersections, but the task of the present book is not primarily historical or genealogical—that is, to locate and trace philosophical sources.[75] The question of influences does appear in a number of the essays herein, but it is subordinate to the larger purpose of exploring the implications of Bonhoeffer's theology for the contemporary philosophical context.[76]

The first section of essays has a meta-philosophical focus, discussing Bonhoeffer's account of philosophy's limits as well as its possibilities. Christiane Tietz opens the discussion by presenting Bonhoeffer on the uses and abuses, the possibilities and the limits, of philosophical thinking—both in the early thinking of *Act and Being* and in the later work of *Ethics*, in which Bonhoeffer's more developed Christology allows for a more refined affirmation and criticism of philosophy. The theme of limits also guides Paul D. Janz's contribution, which focuses on the limits of phenomenology. Janz argues that Bonhoeffer's fundamentally incarnational orientation entails a critique of any philosophical or theological position that fails to do justice to the genuine otherness of sensible, embodied reality. Here Janz draws our attention to the alliance between Kant and Bonhoeffer.[77] Consequently (but not surprisingly), idealism comes under fire, but also (and more surprisingly) such proponents of radical transcendence as Karl Barth and Emmanuel Levinas. Despite the merit and fruitfulness of the latter two thinkers, Janz locates in both a lapse back into idealism's propensity to grant priority to the mental. In the end, Janz leaves the reader with a large question mark regarding the compatibility of phenomenology—particularly if it is conceived as a fundamental source for theology—with a robustly incarnational theology like Bonhoeffer's.

In part 2 we consider Bonhoeffer in relation with two of his most important influences and interlocutors from German philosophers: Frits de Lange's essay discusses Bonhoeffer's engagement with Nietzsche, starting from his early lectures and sermons, and continuing through to his prison writings. Jean Greisch and Jens Zimmermann then bring Bonhoeffer into proximity with Heidegger. Greisch juxtaposes the lives and thought of Heidegger and Bonhoeffer, asking whether philosophers, qua philosophers, are able to offer political resistance that is not only effective, but oriented toward the good. Zimmermann explores both the influence of Heidegger on Bonhoeffer's theology and the implications of this theology for the issues Heidegger has bequeathed to Continental philosophy concerning self-knowledge and human identity.

Part 3 addresses Bonhoeffer's infamous notion of "religionless Christianity," which is particularly intriguing in light of the return to religion.

After all, was not Bonhoeffer writing about the meaning of Christianity in a world without a religious a priori, in which religion gives way to the secular?[78] Prima facie, it might seem that he leads us away from what is happening in contemporary philosophy: While philosophy is turning toward religion, Bonhoeffer takes us in the direction of something enigmatic called "religionless Christianity." But before we conclude that Bonhoeffer has nothing to say to this contemporary milieu, we must recognize that his critique of religion—and "religious" interpretations of Scripture—targets the temporally-historically conditioned presuppositions of metaphysics, the individualistic inwardness that passes for piety, and the stop-gap God who exists simply to solve human mysteries and problems.[79] What he is seeking is the meaning of Christianity after religion of this sort. In this regard his concern is not unlike those concerns that are central within the religious turn. But given Bonhoeffer's deeply Christological commitments, it should by now be clear why his religionless Christianity differs from attempts to do "weak theology," "minimal theology," or the deconstructive "religion without religion," which eschews religious determinacy.

Having said that, it is still no easy task to explain what the enigmatic notion of "religionless Christianity" actually involves or entails. Thus we devote an entire section of the present volume to that question. Ralf K. Wüstenberg begins by looking at its philosophical roots in Kant, Dilthey, and William James. This is followed by a lecture that Paul Ricoeur delivered in 1966.[80] Ricoeur's essay bears the influences of its time, specifically insofar as he organizes his reading of Bonhoeffer around the relation between law and gospel—a strategy that derives from Gerhard Ebeling's influential interpretation of Bonhoeffer in his lecture entitled "The 'Non-Religious Interpretation of Biblical Concepts,'" which was published in 1955.[81]

As the editors of the *Dietrich Bonhoeffer Werke* edition of *Ethics* write in their afterword, Ebeling interpreted Bonhoeffer's texts in terms of the law-gospel relation, despite the fact that this framework was not central to Bonhoeffer's concerns. And while most responses to Ebeling's interpretation were critical, "virtually every essay and book written in German during the next decade dealing with Bonhoeffer's prison theology cited it."[82] Thus it is not surprising that Ricoeur would pick up on Ebeling's hermeneutical key; as Ricoeur notes in his lecture on Bonhoeffer, he had given a lecture on Ebeling the same weekend.[83] Nevertheless, this essay continues to hold interest, not only because it surveys key issues in Bonhoeffer's prison writings, but also because it documents Ricoeur's engagement with Bonhoeffer during a time (the mid-late 1960s) when Ricoeur himself was undertaking his groundbreaking work on atheism, the hermeneutics of suspicion, and the critique of religion.[84]

Kevin Hart then concludes part 3 by questioning Bonhoeffer's idea of religionless Christianity. After interrogating some possible interpretations of this theme, Hart suggests that Bonhoeffer's retrieval of the notion of an "arcane discipline" is central, and crucial to understanding his conception of the interactions between Christianity, religion, philosophy, and the world. This leads toward a reading of Bonhoeffer within the framework of the theology of religions because, as Hart observes, "unlike Bonhoeffer, we find ourselves in a world that we share with persons for whom the world is differently enchanted, not only those for whom it has become disenchanted."[85] This is a challenge that any appropriation of Bonhoeffer's thought on religion must face.

In part 4, Brian Gregor and John Panteleimon Manoussakis discuss the importance of the Moment (*Kairos*) and the Eschaton in Bonhoeffer's thinking about selfhood and human being. Gregor begins with the model of selfhood that arises from Bonhoeffer's early model of "Christian Social Philosophy" in *Sanctorum Communio*. Through a series of encounters with Heidegger, Levinas, and, most importantly, Ricoeur, Gregor then shows how the picture of selfhood that appears in *Ethics* marks an overcoming of certain limitations in Bonhoeffer's earliest thought. Manoussakis then closes the volume with an essay on Bonhoeffer's eschatology, which he approaches through the ultimate-penultimate relationship. In order to think through Bonhoeffer's eschatology—particularly given the emphasis on eschatology in contemporary philosophical discourse—Manoussakis makes creative use of Kant's account of the teleology in the third *Critique*, followed by a phenomenological description of imagination and anticipation.

The essays in this volume represent a variety of positions, engaging and employing Bonhoeffer's thought in a variety of ways. Thus there is no general consensus regarding what Bonhoeffer's meaning is or what we ought to take from his texts. Nor do these essays encompass his thought in its entirety. Instead, they are just a beginning. Our hope is that they will provoke greater philosophical interest in Bonhoeffer and his resources for future thinking about ultimate and penultimate things.

Notes

1. Eberhard Bethge, *Dietrich Bonhoeffer: A Biography*, rev. ed., rev. and ed. Victoria Barnett (Minneapolis: Fortress Press, 2000), 47.

2. Ibid., 37.

3. Ibid., 44.

4. Ibid., 53–56.

5. Ibid., 55.

6. Ibid., 56.

7. Ibid., 73. These sources are evident in Bonhoeffer's dissertation *Sanctorum Communio* as well as in his habilitation thesis *Act and Being*—which also engages the *Daseinanalytik* of Martin Heidegger.

8. Bethge, *Dietrich Bonhoeffer*, 161. For Bonhoeffer's reflections on pragmatism, see DBW 10, 268–71.

9. Bethge, *Dietrich Bonhoeffer*, 161, 168.

10. See ibid., 212, for a list of Bonhoeffer's lectures and seminars.

11. Ibid., 944.

12. In the DBW edition of *Sanctorum Communio,* "A" denotes the dissertation version of the text, some of which was not published in the book version.

13. For more detailed discussion of Bonhoeffer's interpretation and critique of Heidegger, see Jens Zimmermann's essay in this volume. Also see Brian Gregor, "Formal Indication, Philosophy, and Theology: Bonhoeffer's Critique of Heidegger," *Faith and Theology* 24, no. 4 (April 2007): 185–202; and Charles Marsh, "Bonhoeffer on Heidegger and Togetherness," *Modern Theology* 8, no. 3 (July 1992): 263–83.

14. Translation slightly altered. Cf. DBW 1, 39.

15. Fred Lawrence, "Gadamer, the Hermeneutic Revolution, and Theology," in *The Cambridge Companion to Gadamer,* ed. Robert J. Dostal (Cambridge: Cambridge University Press, 2002). Merold Westphal makes the same point in an interview in the *Journal of Philosophy and Scripture* 1, no. 4 (Fall 2006): 26–27.

16. Adriaan Theodoor Peperzak, *Philosophy between Faith and Theology: Addresses to Catholic Intellectuals* (Notre Dame, Ind.: University of Notre Dame Press, 2005), 149.

17. See ch. 3 of Marsh's *Reclaiming Dietrich Bonhoeffer: The Promise of His Theology* (Cambridge: Oxford University Press, 1994).

18. Bonhoeffer's discussion of Christ and "good people" in *Ethics* (E 339–51) pertains directly to this matter.

19. See E 146–70.

20. We have modified the extant translation by capitalizing "Word," because the context refers to the ultimate Word of Christ himself, as well as to his written and his preached word, which always point to and are carried by the presence of the Word Christ.

21. If we are going to speak about Continental philosophy or, more broadly, Continental thought, we should be clear what this term designates—particularly because it would be something of a foreign expression for Bonhoeffer, as well as many other thinkers from Continental Europe. As Merold Westphal has observed, the term is rarely used there. Instead, it typically appears in English scholarship regarding a particular style of philosophizing that often stands in distinction to the dominant forms of Anglo-American philosophy, primarily analytic philosophy or pragmatism. As Westphal writes, the term designates first, "thinkers, texts, and traditions from the European continent, especially France and Germany, from German idealism to the present," and second, "the work of Anglophone thinkers primarily engaged in the critical analysis and creative development of those thinkers, texts, and traditions." Merold Westphal, "Continental Philosophy of Religion," in *The Oxford Handbook of*

Philosophy of Religion, ed. William J. Wainwright (Oxford: Oxford University Press, 2005), 472.

22. Friedrich Nietzsche, *The Antichrist,* #10, *The Portable Nietzsche,* ed. and trans. Walter Kaufmann (New York: Viking Penguin, 1968, 1982), 576.

23. William Desmond, "Religion and the Poverty of Philosophy," in *Is There a Sabbath for Thought? Between Religion and Philosophy* (New York: Fordham University Press, 2005), 124–25.

24. Heidegger's own definition and critique of onto-theology is often more subtle than one would expect, given the way the term "onto-theology" is so often tossed around indiscriminately. One of the most helpful discussions of Heidegger's position appears in Merold Westphal's *Transcendence and Self-Transcendence: On God and the Soul* (Bloomington: Indiana University Press, 2004), 15–40.

25. Cf. John D. Caputo, "Introduction: Who Comes after the God of Metaphysics?" in *The Religious,* ed. John D. Caputo (Oxford: Blackwell, 2002), 1–19.

26. "Ein Bewusstsein von dem, was fehlt: Über Glauben und Wissen und den Defaitismus der modernen Vernunft," *Neue Zürcher Zeitung* 10, February 2007, online at http://www.nzz.ch/2007/02/10/li/articleEVB7X.html.

27. Ibid.

28. See Heidegger's lecture "Phenomenology and Theology," in *Pathmarks,* ed. William McNeill (Cambridge: Cambridge University Press, 1998).

29. Dominique Janicaud et al., *Phenomenology and the Theological Turn: The French Debate* (New York: Fordham University Press, 2000). Also see Dominique Janicaud, *Phenomenology "Wide Open": After the French Debate,* Perspectives in Continental Philosophy (New York: Fordham University Press, 2005).

30. Janicaud, *Phenomenology and the Theological Turn,* 42–43.

31. Ibid., 27.

32. Ibid., 37–49.

33. Ibid., 50.

34. Ibid., 98.

35. Janicaud writes, for example, that in Levinas experience dictates the appearance of phenomena and comments, "But in virtue of what experience? Evidently something metaphysical. This circularity is perhaps hermeneutical, but certainly not phenomenological" (*Phenomenology and the Theological Turn,* 27).

36. Paul Ricoeur, "Phenomenology and Hermeneutics," in *From Text to Action,* trans. Kathleen Blamey and John B. Thompson (London: Athlone Press, 1991), 31. See in the same volume Ricoeur's essay "On Interpretation," and in the present volume, Paul Janz's essay on the limits of phenomenology.

37. Ricoeur, "Experience and Language in Religious Discourse," in *Phenomenology and the Theological Turn,* 127.

38. Ibid., 128–30.

39. Ibid., 132.

40. Richard Kearney, "Against Omnipotence: God beyond Power," in *Debates in Continental Philosophy: Conversations with Contemporary Thinkers* (New York: Fordham University Press, 2004), 232.

41. Richard Kearney, *The God Who May Be: A Hermeneutics of Religion* (Bloomington: Indiana University Press, 2001), 1.

42. See Kearney's essay "Enabling God," in *After God: Richard Kearney and the Religious Turn in Continental Philosophy,* ed. John Panteleimon Manoussakis (New

York: Fordham University Press, 2006).

43. For the critical discussion of Kearney's work on religion, see Manoussakis, *After God*.

44. This is Kearney's own admission, since he candidly disavows any "claims to theological competence, exegetical expertise, or confessional orthodoxy," "Enabling God," 41.

45. Here it would be worth discussing Bonhoeffer's rejection of "possibility" as a theological category, but given the different conceptions of possibility involved this would require an essay of its own.

46. Contrast this with Kearney's version of the "already—not yet" of the Kingdom as "both (a) already there as a *historical possibility* and (b) not yet there as historically realized Kingdom 'come on earth'" ("Enabling God," 43, emphasis added).

47. For instance, see the following comments in Manoussakis's *After God:* Jeff Bloechl notes that "Kearney's Christology . . . does not need Jesus to have actually died in order to fulfill its role within his eschatology" (135). Kevin Hart notes that the Trinity only appears as the "perfect community," with no attention given to inter-Trinitarian relations in the event of the cross—i.e., "the divinity's dereliction at the torture and execution of the Son" (220). And David Tracy notes that Kearney's "eschatology does not seem to include Cross or Apocaplypse" (354).

48. See Marion's *God without Being: Hors-Texte,* trans. Thomas A. Carlson (Chicago: University of Chicago Press, 1991). See Kearney, *The God Who May Be,* 7, 8. Kearney also criticizes Marion for privileging the theology of the church—specifically, the bishop—in the interpretation of the text. See their dialogue "Hermeneutics of Revelation," in Manoussakis, *After God,* 324. In the same dialogue, Kearney also criticizes Marion's claim that the *saturated phenomenon*—a central theme in Marion's phenomenology—"requires a *pure phenomenology of the pure event.*" There Kearney insists that all phenomenological description is hermeneutical in nature (319).

49. This point appears, among other places, in Derrida's essay "Hostipitality" in *Acts of Religion,* ed. Gil Anidjar (New York: Routledge, 2002), 362.

50. See "The Messianic" in Caputo's *The Prayers and Tears of Jacques Derrida: Religion without Religion* (Bloomington: Indiana University Press, 1997), 117–59. For a critical discussion of Derrida in this regard, consult Jamie Smith's essay "Determined Violence: Derrida's Structural Religion," *Journal of Religion* 78, no. 2 (April 1998): 197–212.

51. John D. Caputo, *The Weakness of God: A Theology of the Event* (Bloomington: Indiana University Press), 115.

52. Ibid.

53. Gianni Vattimo, *Belief* (Stanford, Calif.: Stanford University Press, 1999), 35–36. A related passage: "This [Vattimo's weak ontology] approach emphasizes that the weakening of Being is one possible meaning—if not the absolute meaning—of the Christian message, through the radical reading of incarnation as *kenosis.* This message speaks of a God who incarnates himself, lowers himself, and confuses all the powers of this world" (Gianni Vattimo, *After Christianity,* Italian Academy Lectures [New York: Columbia University Press, 2002], 80).

54. Vattimo, *Belief,* 48.

55. Richard Rorty, Gianni Vattimo, and Santiago Zabala, *The Future of Religion* (New York: Columbia University Press, 2005), 51.

56. John Milbank, Catherine Pickstock, and Graham Ward, *Radical Orthodoxy:*

A New Theology (London: Routledge, 1999), 1. Also see Phillip Blond's "Introduction: Theology before Philosophy," in *Post-Secular Philosophy: Between Philosophy and Theology,* ed. Phillip Blond (London: Routledge, 1998).

57. James K. A. Smith, *Introducing Radical Orthodoxy: Mapping a Post-Secular Theology* (Grand Rapids, Mich.: Baker Academic, 2004), 141.

58. Ibid.

59. Milbank, Pickstock, and Ward, *Radical Orthodoxy,* 2.

60. Ibid., 3.

61. For Pickstock's discussion of this point, see her book *After Writing: On the Liturgical Consummation of Philosophy,* Challenges in Contemporary Theology (Oxford: Blackwell, 1998).

62. Laurence Paul Hemming, ed., *Radical Orthodoxy: A Catholic Enquiry* (Burlington, Vt.: Ashgate, 2000), 83.

63. Moreover, one of the most common objections to RO is their proclivity for misreading thinkers in order to fit their narrative. For a start, see Wayne J. Hankey and Douglas Hedley, eds., *Deconstructing Radical Orthodoxy: Postmodern Theology, Rhetoric, and Truth* (Burlington, Vt.: Ashgate, 2005).

64. John Milbank, *Being Reconciled: Ontology and Pardon,* Radical Orthodoxy Series (London: Routledge, 2003), 118–19.

65. John Milbank, *Theology and Social Theory: Beyond Secular Reason* (Cambridge, Mass.: Blackwell, 1993), 23.

66. There is much more to be said regarding Milbank's criticisms of Bonhoeffer on this count. In his recent book on Henri de Lubac's *nouvelle théologie,* Milbank notes that there are parallel conclusions in de Lubac's *Surnaturel* and Bonhoeffer's *Letters and Papers from Prison:* "For both theologians grace must be sought in the ordinary; the majestic and the pious have now had their dubious day. On the other hand, Bonhoeffer's Lutheranism leads him to exalt a dialectical identity between the presence and absence of God. Thus he finally celebrates exactly what the *Surnaturel* refuses: an autonomous secularity grounded in a univocal ontology, *etsi Deus non daretur.*" *The Suspended Middle: Henri de Lubac and the Debate Concerning the Supernatural* (Grand Rapids, Mich.: Eerdmans, 2005), 65. The strength of Bonhoeffer's ultimate/penultimate distinction, however, is precisely its ability to affirm the ordinary while avoiding "autonomous secularity" on the one hand and theological triumphalism on the other. Milbank makes similar charges elsewhere: See *Theology and Social Theory,* 207–208, 229. Also see "The Last of the Last: Theology in the Church," in *Conflicting Allegiances: The Church-Based University in a Liberal Democratic Society,* ed. Michael L. Budde and John Wright (Grand Rapids, Mich.: Brazos Press, 2004), 243.

67. Hent de Vries, *Philosophy and the Turn to Religion* (Baltimore: Johns Hopkins University Press, 1999); *Minimal Theologies: Critique of Secular Reason in Adorno and Levinas,* trans. Geoffrey Hale (Baltimore: Johns Hopkins University Press, 2005).

68. Merold Westphal, *Overcoming Onto-theology: Toward a Postmodern Christian Faith* (New York: Fordham University Press, 2001); *Transcendence and Self-Transcendence.*

69. The allusion here is the theme of *Mündigkeit* in Kant's essay "What Is Enlightenment?" in *Perpetual Peace and Other Essays,* trans. Ted Humphrey (Indianapolis: Hackett, 1983), 41.

70. Each in their own ways, such theologians as Thomas J. J. Altizer, William Hamilton, John A. T. Robinson, Gabriel Vahanian, and John van Buren took some

of Bonhoeffer's provocative statements in the prison letters as points of departure for their own varieties of atheistic, post-Christian, or secular theology. See Thomas J. J. Altizer and William Hamilton, *Radical Theology and the Death of God* (Indianapolis: Bobbs-Merrill, 1966). Also see John A. T. Robinson's *Honest to God* (Philadelphia: Westminster Press, 1963). Note, however, that despite the journalistic tendency to group such theologians together under the heading of "the death of God theologians," they did not represent a unified movement with a consensus on what their respective theologies meant. See the article "Christian Atheism: The 'God is Dead' Movement," *Time*, 22 October 1965, 62. Nor did these theologians offer a unified reading of Bonhoeffer. As Hamilton himself acknowledges, Bonhoeffer's own intent regarding the meaning of "religionless Christianity" remains a mystery; Hamilton's own thought attempts to work out this possibility independent of what Bonhoeffer himself thought (see *Radical Theology and the Death of God*, 39). For a brief introduction to this matter, see Craig L. Nessan's essay "The American Reception: Introduction to Bonhoeffer's *Christ the Center*," in *Who Is Christ for Us?* (Minneapolis, Minn.: Fortress Press, 2002), 20–30. Also see ch. 2 in Stephen R. Haynes, *The Bonhoeffer Phenomenon: Portraits of a Protestant Saint* (Minneapolis, Minn.: Fortress Press, 2004).

71. One of the boldest misreadings comes from Altizer, who sees Bonhoeffer as advocating a radically kenotic Christology, in which God empties himself entirely of divinity in the Incarnation. Gone is the time when "the Church could know Christ as the cosmic Lord, as the mediator between time and Eternity, as both fully man and fully God" ("Word and History," in *Radical Theology and the Death of God*, 135). According to Altizer, the death of God is a historical event that occurred with the complete emptying of the transcendence of God into the immanence of human existence. See Altizer's *The Gospel of Christian Atheism* (Philadelphia: Westminster Press, 1966), 62–69. What Bonhoeffer teaches us, Altizer proposes, is "that the presence of Christ can be known only in the body of a broken and suffering humanity, for the Jesus whom we know is wholly detached from the divine attributes of his traditional image" ("Word and History," 135). Despite a certain rhetorical similarity, Altizer's celebration of the hypostatic union rent asunder is a far cry from the Christology that we have been discussing thus far in this introduction.

72. Bonhoeffer chose the term "mandates" rather than "orders of creation," to distinguish his sense of a divine reality from the Nazi theologians who justified the regime's politics as conforming to God's created order. See E 68–69; 388–408.

73. As Jean-Luc Marion puts it so well, Heidegger's "Being offers in advance the screen on which any 'God' that would be constituted would be projected and would appear—since, by definition, to be constituted signifies to be constituted as a being." Marion asks hence with Barth, "How is it that . . . what determines the one—manifestedness of beings according to the openness of Being—must necessarily determine revelation as well?" (*God without Being*, 70).

74. Haynes, *The Bonhoeffer Phenomenon*, 2.

75. One recent volume that takes this approach is Peter Frick's edited collection, *Bonhoeffer's Intellectual Formation* (Tübingen: Mohr Siebeck Verlag, 2008).

76. Perhaps the most significant predecessor to this project is Charles Marsh's book *Reclaiming Dietrich Bonhoeffer: The Promise of His Thought* (cited above). Marsh plunges deeper into Bonhoeffer's potential philosophical contribution than most Bonhoeffer scholars, who tend to focus (understandably) on his theological significance and attend to philosophy only insofar as it is a matter of influence. Also see Wayne

Whitson Floyd Jr. and Marsh's edited collection, *Theology and the Practice of Responsibility: Essays on Dietrich Bonhoeffer* (Valley Forge, Pa.: Trinity Press International, 1994). This volume includes a number of essays that read Bonhoeffer with a philosophical eye. Floyd also deserves mention here. See his book, which derives from his dissertation, entitled *Bonhoeffer's Dialectic of Otherness: On Reading Bonhoeffer and Adorno* (Lanham, Md.: University Press of America, 1988).

77. Whereas Tietz's reading of *Act and Being* sees Bonhoeffer as ultimately criticizing Kant's philosophy, Janz maintains that Bonhoeffer sees Kant as an epistemological guide for preserving the balance between act and being.

78. See, for instance, LPP 280–82, 285, 380–82.

79. See LPP 280–82, 286.

80. "Bibliography of Paul Ricoeur: A Primary and Secondary Systematic Bibliography," comp. Frans D. Vansina and Paul Ricoeur, in *The Philosophy of Paul Ricoeur,* The Library of Living Philosophers, vol. 22, ed. Lewis Edwin Hahn (Chicago: Open Court, 1995), 660.

81. Gerhard Ebeling, *Word and Faith,* trans. James W. Leitch (Philadelphia: Fortress Press, 1963), 98–161.

82. "Afterword," E 435.

83. Cf. p. 2 of *Les Cahiers du Centre Protestant l'Ouest,* no. 7 (November 1966), which notes that Ricoeur's lecture on Bonhoeffer was preceded that weekend by his lectures on Bultmann and Ebeling, which were published in subsequent issues (nos. 8 and 9, respectively).

84. For instance, see Ricoeur's essays "The Critique of Religion" and "The Language of Faith" in *The Philosophy of Paul Ricoeur: An Anthology of His Work,* ed. Charles E. Reagan and David Stewart (Boston: Beacon Press, 1978). Also cf. "Guilt, Ethics, and Religion" and "Religion, Atheism, and Faith" in *The Conflict of Interpretations: Essays in Hermeneutics,* ed. Don Ihde (Evanston, Ill.: Northwestern University Press, 1974). Ricoeur also cites his reflections on Bonhoeffer (along with Bultmann, Ebeling, and Moltmann) as important in shaping his reflections on the diverse linguistic forms in biblical faith and theology. See Ricoeur's "Intellectual Autobiography" in *The Philosophy of Paul Ricoeur,* ed. Hahn, 25.

85. See chapter 8 of this volume.

PART ONE

Bonhoeffer on the Limits of Philosophy

ONE

Bonhoeffer on the Uses and Limits of Philosophy

CHRISTIANE TIETZ

Since Bonhoeffer often uses philosophers as interlocutors,[1] the question of how he himself values philosophical thinking is of certain interest. In his earlier writings in particular, Bonhoeffer is in explicit dialogue with philosophy; but his later writings also indicate a philosophical background.[2] In the following, I want to unfold Bonhoeffer's judgment regarding philosophy. For that I will, in the first four sections, present Bonhoeffer's opinion about philosophy as revealed in his earlier works. Since human reason is the means of philosophical thinking, Bonhoeffer's assessment of philosophy includes a judgment of the capacity of reason and thinking as well. In the fifth and final section, I will then turn to his comments on thinking and reason in the later writings.

Thinking as a Closed Circle

In his postdoctoral thesis *Act and Being,* Bonhoeffer discusses several philosophical conceptions of epistemology.[3] The leading question for that discussion is whether these philosophical concepts are of any "use for theology" (AB 76). This means that Bonhoeffer is interested not in the general usefulness of certain philosophical concepts, but in analyzing them from a theological perspective. His judgment about philosophy is therefore a *theological* one.

Bonhoeffer first describes *Kant's* transcendental philosophy. Kant understands thinking as referring "to something transcendent which, however, is not at its disposal" (AB 34). Thinking relates to something beyond thinking that it sees as unavailable.[4] This unavailable something is the "thing-in-itself" and the "transcendental apperception" of the "I think" (AB 35). God (remaining non-objective) in this philosophy is understood as "the basis of possibility for Dasein and thinking" (AB 44). Because of this fundamental and ongoing relatedness of thinking to the transcendent, Kant's philosophy understands human existence as "not in itself self-subsistent but precisely 'in reference to'" (AB 38).

In Bonhoeffer's view, transcendentalism has one big problem: on the one hand thinking presupposes the thinking I, but on the other hand it is unable to recognize it (because the I is understood as beyond thinking). Thus, "this something transcendent cannot prove itself to be genuinely transcendent" (AB 49). Therefore, it cannot be a *given* limit to thinking. Bonhoeffer asks rhetorically: "If it can never be objectively knowable, how can reason fix its limits over against something unknown?" (AB 45). The answer is this: thinking has to set up its limits by itself.[5] It does so by determining the I as transcendent. So the transcendent "remains the self-chosen limit by reason of itself, by which reason once again legitimates itself as that which put the boundaries in place" (AB 45).[6] But since the thinking *itself* sets this limit, it actually has no limits and right away brings itself into force.

Bonhoeffer acknowledges, however, that Kant nevertheless emphasizes the I as the limit of thinking.[7] He conceives of the "thinking I" as the "limit-point of philosophy" (AB 39). So Kant at least acknowledges the necessity of a limit of thinking.

Bonhoeffer notes that while Kant works from the limit of the "thinking I," he formulates another category—idealism, which functions differently. It takes the thinking I as the "*point of departure . . . of philosophy*" (AB 39). It argues for the "creative power of the I" and for a world that "comes about 'through me'" (AB 43f.). Here the ongoing relatedness of thinking to the transcendent, which is typical for transcendentalism, is given up. Instead, it is replaced by a movement of the spirit "in upon itself" in which the human spirit "has, in principle, come to rest" (AB 41). For such a spirit something transcendent is no longer necessary for true self-knowledge. The I can now find its essence by reflecting upon itself. Thus, in this philosophical concept "philosophy means posing the question about the human being and providing the answer in one and the same act. The human being understands himself because he philosophizes."[8] Here God is located in the act of self-knowing: "God is . . . in the execution of that philosophizing" (AB 50). When the I comes to itself, it is in God.

Bonhoeffer, however, judges this to be an illusion. Coming to oneself leads to "the experience of utmost loneliness in its tormenting desolation and sterility" (AB 42), not the fullness and richness of God. As expressed by the phrase "*ratio in se ipsam incurva*" (reason turned in upon itself),[9] the nature of idealistic thinking is an imprisonment in itself (AB 39). It ignores the reality of something existing beyond our thinking, to which we relate. In the end, idealism "forgets that we ourselves exist" (AB 39).

This structure of reason as turned in upon itself is even true for Kant's transcendentalism because in Kant reason itself sets the boundaries. Here too "reason remains by itself, understands itself not 'in reference to' that which transcends it, but 'in reference to' itself" (AB 45). Although reason limits itself and seems to be modest in doing so, it actually is the all-determining force because it sets the limits itself. Therefore even in transcendentalism reason stays with itself. Here too it is "imprisoned in itself, it sees only itself, even when it sees another, even when it wants to see God" (AB 45).

However, there is still a difference between idealism and transcendentalism. While idealism makes the I into the creator of the world, transcendentalism does not. In this transcendentalism preserves the crucial boundary between the creator and the I (*die entscheidende Schöpfergrenze*).[10] But—and this is important for our question about the limits of philosophy—Bonhoeffer adds: It preserves this boundary only "in principle, that is, to the extent to which this is at all possible in philosophy" (AB 44). At a later point we will see what this means.

What about *ontological* conceptions of philosophy? Bonhoeffer counts as "ontological" those models of philosophy that start with the "primacy of being over against consciousness" (AB 59), that is, models that do start not with the primacy of thinking but with the given reality.[11] The given όv ("being") here seems to be a real limit to thinking; it "resists the claim of the logos" (AB 60), which was the dominating signature of transcendentalism and idealism. Ontological thinking gives up the creative power of thinking and wants to think only by viewing receptively.[12]

Genuine ontology, which defines itself by acknowledging the primacy of being, consequently has to be a critical venture insofar as it is aware of the fact that it is not able to really reach being, to view being, through thinking. For whenever it is thinking being, being (*Sein*) becomes *Seiendes*—something that exists. But *Sein* is not *Seiendes;* it transcends it (AB 60). Thus, in ontology "thinking must again and again be 'suspended' [*aufgehoben*] in being" (AB 60) and must express its inability to reach being as such.

But there is also a kind of *systematic ontology* that does not include this self-critique. Because it wants to build a system, it has to view pure being as such, and through this it draws pure being into its system. In building a system it loses the original ontological acknowledgment of the primacy of being: "the result is the system of pure immanence" (AB 67).

Edmund Husserl's phenomenology, in Bonhoeffer's eyes, is systematic ontology.[13] Husserl's concept of the perception of essence "seems to imply that over against the beholding subject there stands an independent, self-contained being"—which is "transcendental realism." But at the same time the transcendent being is dependent on current consciousness: "consciousness is the constituent of all that is." Thus, in the end Husserl's philosophy "rests on the belief in the possibility of grasping intellectually, out of pure consciousness, the absolute as something given . . . The human logos has overcome the ὄν"—which is identical with the idealistic concept (AB 63–64).

In Bonhoeffer's eyes, *Max Scheler* wants to be a realist and to rid Husserl's philosophy of every idealistic nuance.[14] He is convinced of a reality that transcends consciousness. Scheler finds this reality in values, which he understands as "predicates of being" that are "connected with . . . a being logically independent of consciousness" (AB 65). Values are prior to consciousness. For Scheler, this is especially true of God.

Human beings relate to these values by feeling them. Here Bonhoeffer sees a problem. Scheler himself argues that—as Bonhoeffer puts it—"in this 'feeling of values' the beholding I is capable of taking into itself the whole world, the fullness of life, the good and the very deity." This means that "the I bears within itself that which enables it to behold the highest value, to understand God and itself." Through this feeling, reality is "delivered into the hands of the person" and "accessible to the I from itself" (AB 66). Thus the human being is able to reach the transcendent by himself, through viewing and drawing the transcendent into himself.[15] But when being is opened to viewing, it becomes *Seiendes*. This is why Scheler's philosophy is systematic and not genuine ontology. It wants to construct a system,[16] but in a system there is no room for the transcendent, especially not for God. A system is possible only if one negates the possibility of a being that thinking cannot grasp.

In Bonhoeffer's eyes, only *Martin Heidegger's* philosophy is an ontology without a system. It is genuine ontology. Since Heidegger understands thinking as a determination of the being (*Seinsbestimmtheit*) of Dasein, "[t]hought does not . . . produce its world for itself. Rather, it finds itself, as Dasein, in the world." This means that Dasein "already 'is' in every instance what it understands and determines itself to be" (AB 70). Thinking is not creative; it only discloses the being of Dasein. At the same time, being is found only in the understanding of being.[17] In summary, this means that "being has priority over thought, and yet being equals Dasein, equals understanding of being"

(AB 71). But the intended priority of being over thought collapses because of Heidegger's basic thesis "that Dasein in temporality already possesses in every instance an understanding of being" (AB 72). Because the human being as Dasein has the understanding of being at his disposal, we again end with an "idealistic system" (AB 106) in which being is taken over by thinking.[18]

In the end, Heidegger's concept of being is characterized by *Geschlossenheit* (being enclosed) and therefore fails to achieve real transcendence. No real transcendence is conceived. The assumption that Dasein can understand itself leads to a world contained in Dasein.[19] This *Geschlossenheit* necessarily excludes the idea of revelation, which makes Heidegger's philosophy "a consciously atheistic philosophy of finitude" (AB 72). The main ideas of Heidegger's thinking are therefore in Bonhoeffer's eyes nothing other than expressions of the sinful *incurvatio in se ipsum*: everydayness is the decision for solitude, conscience is "a final perseverance of the I in itself," and even death helps the I to find itself.[20] In summary, one can say that the main fault of Heidegger's concept is that the human being, as Dasein, possesses its own possibility of understanding itself, which leads to a closed system of the I and the world. As long as human existence is conceived as having those possibilities, there remains no room for revelation.[21]

The Uselessness of Philosophy

When Bonhoeffer questions these philosophical positions and their use for theology, he does not see this as a narrow, restricted question. Of course, his first concern is whether these positions are of any "help in the understanding of the concept of revelation" (AB 76). But since Bonhoeffer argues that revelation changes everything[22]—our concept of God as well as our self-understanding and our understanding of the world—the question of whether philosophical concepts are of any use for theology in fact means: Are these philosophical concepts of any use for understanding God, ourselves, and the world? Are they of any use for understanding reality?

The fundamental problem of all philosophical concepts is that they can only limit the human being by thinking. But as we have seen this is always "a self-drawn boundary, that is, a boundary the human person essentially has already crossed, a boundary that the person must already have stood beyond in the first place in order to draw it" (DBW 10, 368). From this follows that "there are for reason essentially no boundaries, for even the boundaries are thought away until they are no longer genuine boundaries" (AB 45). Or, as

Bonhoeffer states in a paper given at Union Theological Seminary: "Thinking as such is boundless" (DBW 10, 445).

Paradoxically, this limitlessness of philosophy is the fundamental limit of philosophy. For it leads to "a system confined in the I, a system in which the I understands itself through itself and can place itself into the truth," so that "the I understands itself from itself within a closed system" (AB 76). As we have seen, this is true not only for idealism and systematic ontology, which both aim at developing a system; it is also true for transcendentalism and genuine ontology. As shown, transcendentalism wants to leave space for the transcendent, but because the transcendent cannot prove itself to be transcendent and therefore cannot be experienced as transcendent, reason needs to set the limits by itself. This is why a human being in transcendentalism finally understands himself out of his own reason. The same is true for genuine ontology, which tries to "conceive of being as the a priori of thought" (AB 76); but in conceding to the I an understanding of being, genuine ontology finally gives up all being that transcends thinking, and once again the I understands itself from itself.

Bonhoeffer is convinced that not only the philosophies discussed but every philosophy has to end with such a system, in which the I understands itself from itself. For setting up a system and establishing this self-relatedness is the very character of thinking itself: "thinking is in itself a closed circle, with the ego as the center" (DBW 10, 424). Thinking always draws "all reality into its circle" (DBW 10, 445).

Why is this the case? Because thinking means taking hold of that which is thought: "Through the act of knowing, the known is put at the disposition of the I." It can then be "classified within the system of knowledge. As something known, it 'is' only in this system" (AB 94). Because a real, consistent system needs to be a closed one (otherwise things beyond the open border would again and again disturb the structure of the system), it is the "aim of cognition . . . to close this system" (AB 94).[23] Accordingly, thinking cannot permit something transcendent to the system, especially no transcendent God and no concept of revelation.[24] This means that thinking is unable to recognize God. And because philosophy is unable to recognize God, to whom the human being is fundamentally related, the philosophizing being is also unable to recognize itself.

By drawing reality into its circle, the I has at last "become lord of the world" (AB 94).[25] But this power is a deceptive one. For when reality is drawn into the circle of reason it is a kingship without a kingdom. As reason is turned in upon itself, the power of reason is actually reason imprisoned in itself. Bonhoeffer sees this imprisonment as an expression of the "corruption of the mind" (DBW 10, 425). Human reason has the same structure as the human being as such, namely the *cor curvum in se* (as Bonhoeffer argues with a Lutheran phrase), the heart turned in on itself.[26] Reason repeats what man after the fall generally does: "Man 'in' and 'after' the fall refers everything to himself, puts himself in the center of the world, does violence to reality, makes himself God, and God and the other man his creatures" (DBW 10, 425). That his knowing begins and ends with himself is simply in accordance with this structure.[27] Every "[g]odless thought . . . remains self-enclosed" (AB 89).

The self-enclosure of reason is so fundamental that on the one hand reason cannot even reserve or leave a space for revelation. "*Per se,* a philosophy can concede no room for revelation unless it knows revelation and confesses itself to be Christian philosophy in full recognition that the place it wanted to usurp *is* already occupied by another—namely, by Christ" (AB 76–78). The self-enclosure of reason is so fundamental that on the other hand reason cannot recognize its self-enclosure. For recognizing it would mean to recognize truth to some extent.[28] But then sin would not be an existential category shaping a human being's whole existence. "For it would mean that human beings could place themselves into the truth, that they could somehow withdraw to a deeper being of their own, apart from their being sinners, their 'not being in the truth'" (AB 136).

So one can conclude: that philosophical thinking understands itself out of itself "really means, however, that it basically does not understand itself. Indeed it does not understand itself until this I has been encountered and overwhelmed in its existence by an other" (AB 45). Because of the fundamental and complete self-enclosure of the human being and his reason, truth has to be given him from the outside: "only those who have been placed into the truth can understand themselves in truth" (AB 81). This takes place when human beings are encountered by revelation and begin to believe—when they become Christians.

Christian Thinking

How do things stand with Christian knowing and thought? Is it also an *incurvatio in se ipsum,* or is it somehow sanctified?

To answer those questions one first of all has to acknowledge the general inability of reason to recognize God. Thinking is *always,* even as the thinking of a Christian, a closed circle with the ego as center. The relation to

God is possible only through an act "which makes me transcend the limits of myself, which carries me out of the circle of my selfhood in order to ac-knowledge the transcendent God" (DBW 10, 431). This act is faith.

Faith is a certain kind of recognition that does not seize hold of the other. It accepts the other as a limit.[29] Bonhoeffer understands it as a relation to God as well as a relation to the other human being. Faith acknowledges the other as a person. And a person "resists any inclusion into a transcen-dental I, or any non-objectification; it stands as person over against human beings as persons." Because of its freedom, a person "never falls into the power of the knowing I" (AB 126).

How then can a person be known? A person can be known only by opening him- or herself to me, by revealing him- or herself in love.[30] Some-body who is there only for him- or herself cannot be recognized at all. But when the other reveals him- or herself as being there for me, I become free from myself, from being self-enclosed. My faith corresponds to this because it "acknowledges the freedom of the self-giving person" (AB 126). This ac-knowledgment is possible only because one is touched by the revealed love of the other who is there for me.

As directed towards the other, faith is an *actus directus*.[31] "Faith looks not on itself, but on Christ alone" (AB 133). But faith can become aware of itself in an *actus reflexus,* in which "consciousness has the power to become its own object of attention" (AB 28).

Theology is one special form of such an *actus reflexus.* It reflects on credulity.[32] In this it is "a construction . . . a posteriori" and "the attempt to set forth what is already possessed in the act of faith" (DBW 10, 426). But theology is not living faith. It is "doctrine," "system, autonomous self-understanding" (AB 135). As thinking "it is not excepted from the preten-sion and boundlessness of all thinking" (DBW 10, 426). Even theological thinking turns revelation into something that exists, and thereby misses revelation—unless Christ himself is present and destroys or acknowledges the theological thought. This takes place in preaching.[33]

Whereas "thought remains within itself, in sin as in grace" (AB 89),[34] and wants to build a system,[35] the willingness to be judged by Christ through preaching characterizes the fundamental difference between theological and philosophical thinking. This "holding fast . . . to the word" is the "humil-ity" of theological thinking. Reason here is brought to obedience: "Here, not in its method of thinking, but rather in the obedience of thinking, the scholarly discipline of theology does differ fundamentally from everything profane" (AB 131).

From this follows that theological thinking has to be a church discipline: "Thinking, including theological thinking, will always be 'systematic' by nature and can, therefore, never grasp the living person of Christ into itself. Yet there is obedient and disobedient thinking. . . . It is obedient when it does not detach itself from the church, which alone can 'upset' it as 'systematic' thinking, and in which alone thinking has meaning" (AB 132).

While humble theological thinking has no certain method, it does, however, have a certain presupposition: the fact of revelation.[36] It starts with the reality of God: "Theological thought goes from God to reality, not from reality to God" (AB 89).[37] In starting with this presupposition theology acknowledges that the reality of God cannot be reached by thinking itself, but must be given to thinking from the outside.

How does theology get to this premise? Only through faith: "The basis of all theology is the fact of faith" (DBW 10, 425). Only faith acknowledges God as reality beyond our thinking. Theology is not the existential act of faith. But faith is necessary for the theologian to become humble and obedient to the judging Christ.[38] Philosophical thinking, of course, would not accept this premise of the reality of God.[39] As we have seen, philosophical thinking pulls everything given into its circle. Nevertheless, philosophical thinking is useful for theology.

The Usefulness of Philosophy

Although philosophy has the fundamental deficits named above, it also can be of certain use for theology because of its thorough analysis of the different elements of thinking. "[G]enuine transcendental philosophy and genuine ontology have thoroughly grasped and thought through the philosophical problem of act and being." The philosophical structures of transcendentalism and of ontology, of "in reference to" and of a being beyond the thinking act and of the "'suspension' [*Aufgehobensein*] of the act in being" (AB 79), correspond to certain Christian insights.

Transcendentalism's "in reference to"—its concept of "act"—is in accordance with the Christian idea of revelation as that which comes contingently from the outside.[40] Furthermore, the concept of act is useful for the description of human existence as always in reference to revelation.[41] Finally, the concept of act is a useful means to describe the Christian idea of faith. Faith is an act of "exclusively directing oneself to God" (SC 202). It is an act that accepts the claim of revelation as something that is not at its disposal. Faith does not try to deduce the claim of revelation from anything, nor does it try to see revelation only in relative terms. Rather, it is submission to the truth claim of revelation. All these aspects are reasons why a thoroughly analyzed act-concept is useful for theology.

At the same time the *ontological* assumption of being beyond the thinking act is useful in theological perspective because revelation and the new human existence caused by revelation have to be understood as having a reality beyond the act of faith, a being beyond act.[42] Also helpful for theological thinking is the ontological insight that being transcends what exists and can never be managed by thinking but is at the same time "open to demonstration, namely in that which itself exists" (AB 106). This corresponds to the ontological structure of revelation, which is of such kind that it is a being that can be demonstrated in what exists, but is not identical with it. This is because revelation takes place in the category of personhood—in the person of Christ and the Christian community of persons, that is, the church.[43] As the person of Christ and the community of persons qualified by Christ stand against the cognizing subject but resist being drawn in its circle,[44] revelation encountered through persons is open to demonstration in that which exists, but is not brought under the control of thinking. This insight corresponds to the ontological approach.

The ontological figure of "suspension of the act in being" is finally repeated in the fact that the act of faith is an expression of being part of the Christian community: "Faith has, as its presupposition, being in the church. Faith invariably discovers itself already in the church" (AB 117). These are the reasons why a thoroughly analyzed being-concept is useful for theology.

Because of these parallels, the philosophical structures of act and being are "basically amenable to a theological interpretation" (AB 79). This does not mean that philosophy keeps an open space for revelation. It is absolutely unable to do so. But the structures of the transcendental and ontological approach can be used[45] to describe revelation and the reality qualified by revelation. But to do that one has to start with revelation and to have revelation as premise. And the "concept of revelation itself will restore an entirely new form to those questions" of act- and being-structures (AB 79). Thus the use of philosophical concepts with the premise of revelation leads to "an epistemology of its own" (AB 31). Therefore theological epistemology is fundamentally different from philosophical epistemology.

In the end, only in the Christian concept of revelation is a true act-concept of "in reference to" realized, because only revelation proves itself to be really transcendent. In philosophical concepts of act, as we could see, the transcendent was unable to prove itself to be transcendent—which is why reason had to set up the limits of transcendence. The same is true for the concept of being: only in the Christian concept of revelation is a true concept of being realized, because only revelation discloses itself to human beings. In philosophical concepts of being the given being has to be pulled into the thinking I to be understood.

Against that background of his early judgment on philosophy, it is interesting to consider whether Bonhoeffer's opinion of philosophy changed in his later writing. The last part of this article deals briefly, at least, with this question.

Reason Included in God

In his later writings, Bonhoeffer is still convinced that the process of thinking is affected by the fall: in the origin knowing meant knowing God and only God.[46] Since the fall and the lost unity with the origin, self-reflection became important, as "the never-ending attempt of human beings to overcome their disunion with themselves through thought." After the fall self-knowledge has become the central point of all knowledge: "The original comprehending of God, human beings, and things has now become a sacrilegious grasping of God, human beings, and things. Now everything is pulled into the process of disunion. Knowing now means establishing the relation to oneself, recognizing oneself in everything and everything in oneself" (E 308).[47] So it is obvious that in his later writings Bonhoeffer sees the same problems of reason's self-relatedness as he does in his earlier writing. Again, he judges reason as being unable to recognize God.[48]

But at the same time he sees reason much more positively, because the starting point of his theological insights is not the effects of the fall with their self-relatedness, nor the fundamental disunity with God, other human beings, and things. The starting point of theological insights is the "rediscovered unity, the reconciliation" (E 309). This is the case because Bonhoeffer's concept of reality has fundamentally changed in his later writings. Whereas reality in his earlier writings is either being in Christ or being in Adam,[49] in his later writings reality is defined by the fact that "*[i]n Jesus Christ the reality of God has entered into the reality of this world*" (E 54).[50] This means that one finds "the reality of the world always already borne, accepted, and reconciled in the reality of God" (E 55). Since the coming of Christ, the worldly has to be "seen in the movement of the world's both having been accepted and becoming accepted by God in Christ." This is even true for reason as worldly thinking: reason is "included in God from the beginning" (E 59).[51] This has a twofold consequence.

First, the liberation of reason through the Enlightenment can be understood as something positive. Liberated *ratio* brings "truthfulness, light, and clarity" into society.[52] From then on "[i]ntellectual honesty in all things"—even in questions of faith—has belonged "to the essential moral requirements of Western humanity" (E 115).[53] Since then we know that we have to use reason in an honest and clean way. To go back behind this insight would mean a "salto mortale back into the Middle Ages" (LPP 360).

Nevertheless, "intellectual honesty does not have the last word on things" (E 115).[54] Every concept of reality that ignores Jesus Christ is actually an abstraction.[55] So we still have a certain skepticism about the capacity of reason. But at the same time Bonhoeffer concedes to reason some relevance for recognizing the world. Bonhoeffer sees the epistemological relevance of reason especially in the dimension of "the natural." The "natural" is that part of the fallen creation "which, after the fall, is directed toward the coming of Jesus Christ" (E 173). It is characterized by a relative freedom that is used rightly. (Misused relative freedom characterizes the unnatural.)[56] The natural is not related to Christ through itself, it is related to Christ only through Christ; only Christ becoming human makes the natural become "the penultimate that is directed toward the ultimate" (E 174).

Reason is part of the natural. It is also the means to recognize the natural, that is, it helps to recognize how human lives can be directed toward the coming of Christ. This directedness is not identical with faith, not even a preliminary stage, but it is a "relative openness" for Christ.[57] That reason can recognize the natural does not mean that it has some divine character. Reason is "fallen reason." It focuses on "what is given in the fallen world" and recognizes in it "the universal" (E 175).[58] This means that it recognizes how life can be preserved in general.[59] In this function reason has an importance that Bonhoeffer's earlier writings did not grant. However, the proper function of reason is still dictated by the worldview of faith. It is Bonhoeffer's theological approach to reality that defines the role of reason. Only because it is included in God through Christ does it have its relative value.

Notes

1. Cf. Peter Frick, ed., *Bonhoeffer's Intellectual Formation* (Tübingen: Mohr Siebeck, 2008), on how various philosophers influenced Bonhoeffer's thought.

2. Cf. Ralf Wüstenberg's article in the present volume.

3. For further details cf. my dissertation *Bonhoeffers Kritik der verkrümmten Vernunft. Eine erkenntnistheoretische Untersuchung* (Tübingen: Mohr Siebeck, 1999), 21.

4. Cf. Bonhoeffer's description of Kant's philosophy in DBW 10, 444: "Thinking is an act which [n]ever involves transcendence, but refers to it. The transcendence itself does not enter thinking." (The correction is due to the context).

5. Cf. DBW 10, 445: "So Kant's critical philosophy presents itself as the attempt of man to set himself the limits."

6. Kant's "attempt to limit reason by reason presupposes that reason must have already passed beyond the limits before it sets them" (DBW 10, 445).

7. Cf. DBW 10, 358.

8. DBW 10, 359 (translation from the forthcoming translation in DBWE 10, translated by Douglas Stott, edited by Clifford Green). Bonhoeffer says that this is an illusion because the reality of our concrete life is different: we are "placed in a contingent here-and-there," as "people who are questioning, thinking," who "have to find their way in the midst of it, and have to relate every given situation to themselves" and who have to "decide 'in reference to it'" (AB 42–43).

9. Cf. AB 41. Bonhoeffer pretends to have found this phrase in Luther's Lectures on Romans (cf. AB 41, n.11). But Luther's text has: "*Ratio est, quia natura nostra . . . tam profunda est in se ipsam incurva, ut non solum optima dona Dei sibi inflectat ipsisque fruatur . . . , immo et ipso Deo utatur ad illa consequenda.*"—"The reason for this is that our nature . . . is so turned in on itself beyond measure that not only does it twist God's best gifts to its own purposes and seek self-enjoyment . . . but even uses God for those purposes." That is: Luther speaks about the human nature as being "*in se ipsam incurve,*" not about reason (*ratio*), as Bonhoeffer's quote suggests.

10. Cf. AB 44 and DBW 2, 37.

11. Cf. AB 60: "ontology leaves being fully independent of thinking and accords being priority over thinking."

12. Cf. AB 60–61.

13. Cf. AB 67.

14. Cf. AB 64.

15. Cf. DBW 10, 361.

16. Cf. AB 67.

17. Cf. AB 71.

18. Cf. DBW 11, 214 (my translation): in Heidegger the given is taken up into the understanding Dasein; its character as "given" is robbed.

19. Cf. AB 72. Cf. DBW 10, 365: Heidegger wants to understand the human being as "the human being existing in the world." But because the human being is able to knowingly take upon himself the aspects of this existence in the world, they are no longer boundaries but integrated into his Dasein. Thus, the person finally "remains alone, understanding himself from himself; being in the world has no meaning for one's authentic self-understanding. Ultimately the person himself answers the question about the human being."

20. Cf. AB 147–49 with n15.

21. Cf. AB 76.

22. Cf. AB 78n89.

23. Cf. DBW 10, 444: "At the basis of all thinking lies the necessity of a system.

Thinking is essentially systematic thinking, because it rests upon itself, it is the last ground and criterion of itself. System means interpretation of the whole through the one, which is its ground and its center, the thinking ego."

24. Cf. AB 72–73.

25. Cf. DBW 10, 424: "Thinking does violence to reality, pulling it into the circle of the ego, taking away from it i[t]s original 'objectivity.' Thinking always means system and the system excludes the reality. Therefore, it has to call itself the ultimate reality, and in this system the thinking ego rules."

26. Cf. AB 46.

27. Cf. AB 137.

28. Cf. AB 80.

29. Cf. SC 54.

30. Cf. SC 56.

31. Cf. AB 28 and DBW 12, 185.

32. "Every act of faith is credulous insofar as it is an event embedded in the psyche . . . and accessible to reflection" (AB 154). Bonhoeffer gives as examples (ibid.): enthusiasm, experience, piety, feeling, praying, searching for God, hope. Theology reflects not on faith itself (faith as *actus directus* is broken through reflection) but on credulity.

33. Cf. AB 131.

34. Bonhoeffer sees the reason for this structure of thought in grace not in some sinfulness of thought but in the character of thinking determined by creation and eschata, "in which thought no longer needs to disrupt itself because it is in reality, placed by God eternally into the truth, because it sees" (ibid.). Then *philosophia christiana*, Christian philosophy, will be possible (cf. DBW 11, 215).

35. Cf. AB 130–31: "It seems [!] that . . . theological thinking is in principle indistinguishable from profane thinking. Dogmatic knowledge is positive knowledge reflecting on entities and is, therefore, to be understood as fundamentally systematic."

36. Cf. AB 82.

37. Cf. DBW 10, 424: "Christian thinking has to be conscious of its particular premise, that is, of the premise of the reality of God, before and beyond all thinking."

38. Cf. SC 127: "faith is not a possible method by which to gain academic knowledge; rather, by acknowledging the claim of revelation, faith is the given prerequisite for positive theological knowledge."

39. Cf. DBW 10, 423–24.

40. Cf. AB 82: "Revelation . . . is a contingent event that is to be affirmed or denied only in its positivity—that is to say, received as reality; it cannot be extracted from speculations about human existence as such. Revelation is an event that has its basis in the freedom of God."

41. Cf. AB 82 ("be it as affected by, be it as not affected by revelation" [translation altered]).

42. If God's revelation and the Christian existence would exist only in that act of faith, then they would have no continuity. But God binds himself to human beings (cf. AB 112). And self-understanding is possible only out of continuity (cf. ibid., 46, together with DBW 10, 358).

43. Cf. AB 122: "The being-of-revelation is 'person,' hovering in the tension between the objective and nonobjective, the revealed person of God and the personal community that is founded on God's person."

44. Cf. AB 114–16.

45. Cf. DBW 11, 215.

46. Cf. E 300: "Living in the origin, human beings know nothing but God alone. They know other human beings, things, and themselves only in the unity of their knowledge of God."

47. In accordance with this disunion every ethic, even philosophical ones, aims at the knowledge of good and evil. Human beings are now oriented toward their *own* possibilities of being either good or evil. Christian ethics wants to supersede this knowledge because it understands the possibility of knowing about being good and evil as "a falling away from the origin" (E 300).

48. Cf. E 184.

49. Cf. AB 122: Dasein is either totally in Christ or totally in Adam.

50. This has consequences for the relation between revelation and the rational: because God has entered the reality of the world in Christ the revelation can be had only "in the rational"—even if it is not identical with it (cf. E 59).

51. "Beginning" does not mean before the existence of Christ, but before faith happens. In this sense of inclusion in God from Christ on, one can say that reason has its origin in Jesus Christ and that he is the center and power of reason, under whose protection reason only can live (cf. E 341).

52. Liberated reason discovered the correspondence between the laws of thought and the laws of nature and led to the rise of technology. It has helped to discover eternal human rights. But it also contributed to Western godlessness. Cf. E 116–33. Cf. also LPP 359.

53. Reason belongs to the "goods and convictions of a noble humanity" (E 80).

54. Reason, for example, is overtaxed with the current situation. People led by reason are not able to see the abyss of evil or the abyss of holiness. They overestimate the power of reason and become "[b]itterly disappointed that the world is so unreasonable" (E 78). Cf. LPP 298.

55. Cf. E 48 and 54. Cf. E 249: "Ever since Jesus Christ said of himself, 'I am the life' . . . , no Christian thinking or indeed philosophical reflection can any longer ignore this claim and the reality it contains. . . . The saying of Jesus binds every thought about life to his own person."

56. Cf. E 173.

57. Cf. E 174.

58. On the limits of this recognition of the universal, see E 373–74.

59. Cf. E 174 and 176. Bonhoeffer names several of those "universal" insights. One is for example the *"suum cuique"* as "the highest possible recognition of reason, which corresponds to reality and, within natural life, discerns the right that God . . . gives to the individual" (ibid., 184).

TWO

Bonhoeffer, This-Worldliness, and the Limits of Phenomenology

PAUL D. JANZ

The profound influence that contemporary phenomenology after Edmund Husserl has come to exert on current theological thought and self-understanding would be difficult to overestimate. This influence, moreover, is seen not only in cross-disciplinary exchanges between theology and philosophy or the social sciences, but often also extends right to the heart of Christian doctrine itself, where phenomenological methods can be employed in a number of ways (whether tacitly or openly) for purposes of both coherence and depth. Now, there is unquestionably a certain richness that the phenomenological tradition has on many levels been able to bring to theology, perhaps especially in its provision of the indispensable contexts out of which present-day hermeneutics has been able to take root and grow. Or as Paul Ricoeur puts it, "phenomenology remains the unsurpassable presupposition of hermeneutics."[1] Yet as Ricoeur himself then quickly goes on to add (in an essay that turns out to be a rather severe hermeneutical critique of phenomenology), there are also several implicit errors, with serious epistemological and ethical consequences, that can occur in phenomenology wherever it ceases to be sufficiently "self-critical" in certain ways. I want to follow Ricoeur's lead by employing Bonhoeffer, and by extension also Kant, in order to bring not a hermeneutical but a certain kind of theological critique to phenomenology, or to expose certain inherent limitations of phenomenology for theological purposes. But as a preparation and contextualization for that, let me begin with a brief exposition of Ricoeur's critique of phenomenology before proceeding to the Bonhoeffer-Kant discussion, and then from there on to a concluding exchange between Bonhoeffer and Levinas.

Ricoeur and the Limits of Phenomenology

To come straight to the point, Ricoeur's own major disagreement with Husserlian phenomenology is that it is most essentially and foundationally an "idealism," by which he means an entirely self-sustaining kind of conceptualism or cognitivism. Yet even so, Ricoeur's disagreement as such is not so much that the Husserlian enterprise wants to project itself as something "pure," that is, as a discipline of "*pure* phenomenology." In other words, it is not so much that phenomenology undertakes to be a science that, as Levinas puts it, confines itself strictly to the analysis of "notions in the horizon of their appearing" within consciousness, or as he puts it even more succinctly, as a science of "intentional analysis."[2] Ricoeur's objection is rather that *as* a discipline that restricts itself to mental domains in this way, it thereby also wants to present itself as something "ultimately foundational" for all scientific enquiry per se,[3] offering itself as the quintessential *science of all sciences,* or as what Ricoeur calls the "ideal of scientificity."[4]

We cannot at present discuss in any great depth the specifics of Ricoeur's critique itself, which is intricate and at times difficult, and I limit myself here to five summary points. First, it is vital to note that for Ricoeur it will be *hermeneutics* that will come back to critique the very Husserlian phenomenology within which it finds its own "unsurpassable presupposition," in order to correct and guard against what Ricoeur sees as the overreachingly foundational tendencies implicit in phenomenology. Second, the *way* that hermeneutics will undertake this is not by introducing some new or extraneous method, but rather by subjecting the pure phenomenological enterprise more "radically" to its *own* "intentionally analytical" criteria and modes of questioning. Or in Ricoeur's exact words, "hermeneutics seeks precisely to *radicalize* the Husserlian thesis"[5] in order thereby to limit it. And what he means by this statement is something really quite straightforward, which brings us to the third point. He means simply that in hermeneutics this very "ideal of scientificity" itself, which in phenomenology has become foundational, must *itself* be brought back under the critical eye of "intentional analysis." And when this is done then, fourthly, something crucial must inevitably emerge. When the ideal of scientificity is itself brought more rigorously by hermeneutics under the critical eye of intentional analysis, a certain *non*-phenomenological and indeed non-phenomenologizable limit emerges. To put it more exactly in Ricoeur's words, under the hermeneutical critique an "*ontological* condition of the understanding" emerges for phenomenological reflection, an ontological condition that is encountered in the ineluctable recognition that "he who questions shares in the very thing about which he questions."[6] Ricoeur designates this fundamental limit as "the ontological condition of belonging."[7]

What Ricoeur means exactly by this "ontological condition of belonging" leads us to the fifth summary point, which for the purposes of this essay is the really crucial one. For what Ricoeur accomplishes here is as ingenious as it is subtle, and it has seldom been given the attention it deserves. Let me explain this in a somewhat roundabout way. Many of the most prominent criticisms of phenomenology, at least within Anglo-American discussions, are frequently undertaken from some standpoint or other of "philosophical realism," which is to say some form or other of what is often called an "externalist" or "mind-independent" view of reality. The essence of such realist or externalist critiques can be illuminated helpfully and analogously in reference to the current so-called realism/antirealism debates occurring within these discussions. While Husserlian phenomenology is in certain important respects different from antirealism, the two are in one essential way close relatives, in that both are focused on what is often called a "mind-dependent" or "internalist" view of reality, or of what can be said about the way the world is. In other words, both are as such oriented against the "realist" view, which by contrast begins from what it takes to be certain ineluctable assumptions about the status of reality independently of mental interpretation, or independently of conceptual schemes, and thus "externally" to the mind. And this "mind-independent" reality is seen by realist proponents as being able to declare its authority as such in one of two basic ways. It can be defended either straightforwardly on the basis of the commonsense physical or empirical embodiment of the human questioner per se, an embodiment that is not the product of the mind, but that is the actual physical (causal) ground and source of all mental activity. Or it can be defended more subtly and sophisticatedly through metaphysical defenses of "objectivity."[8]

But while such realist critiques may carry a certain weight within the realism/antirealism debates themselves, they remain with a few exceptions essentially ineffective against phenomenology. The reason for this is that phenomenology, which has *defined* itself as a discipline concerned purely with what appears *within* consciousness, has through its definitive mechanism of the *epoché* already "bracketed out" any authority that such commonsense assumptions (or also metaphysically externalist assumptions) could possibly claim to contain. We cannot get into the further debates about the philosophical "legitimacy" of the *epoché* as such. (Certain realist arguments, for example, will object to the *epoché* as permitting phenomenology to win its own argument merely by default or through a definitional technicality. But in phenomenology's defense, these critiques can often misunderstand the basic character of the *epoché*, which is not an outright denial of empirical physical reality. It rather denotes a complete withholding of judgment—of either assent or dissent—over the "external" commonsense world, for the simple reason that this can have no bearing on a science that has confined itself by definition to what appears within consciousness.) At any rate, we must set those discussions aside here. The important and essential point to be made for present purposes is simply that realist critiques of phenomenology are mounted from within exactly the domain that phenomenology brackets out, and accordingly they can at bottom be of no real philosophical consequence to it.

But this brings us to the really vital consideration of Ricoeur's critique of phenomenology, which is entirely different from any such realist critiques. For, far from taking an "externalist" or "mind-independent" standpoint, and indeed, far from rejecting the phenomenological method as *excessively* "internalist," Ricoeur's hermeneutical critique actually applies the internalist method of "intentional analysis" with *greater rigor* than Husserl or any of his followers do. And this brings us back to the crux of the fifth summary point as stated initially above. The crucial point is that the *epoché* itself—that is, the very "bracketing" mechanism by which the "ideal of scientificity" is achieved—this *epoché* is *itself* in Ricoeur effectively brought back to *within* the phenomenological "horizon," as an element that must itself be scrutinized with full hermeneutical rigor under the intentionally analytical critique.

And it is here finally that two basic results emerge, which will be found implicitly always to underlie Ricoeur's whole broader project. The first has already been mentioned. Under the hermeneutical critique, a fundamentally non-bracketable "ontological condition of the understanding" comes into view, albeit not now as an "externalist" or "realist" starting point, but rather as an ineluctable result of the phenomenological method itself, when exercised in its greatest hermeneutical rigor. This first result then yields a second and perhaps even more unexpected consequence, which is as follows. In its radicalization of the intentionally analytical method, hermeneutics for Ricoeur points phenomenological reflection back *to the very sensible-causal world it brackets out.* In other words, even though hermeneutics, as a pure discipline of interpretation, remains by definition within textual domains, nevertheless in its properly rigorous mode, as Ricoeur sees it, it will in an array of implicit ways always be illatively and ontologically (i.e., no longer merely phenomenologically) *referential* back to the real world. Or, as Ricoeur states this exactly, the rigorously hermeneutical task is necessary "if phenomenology is not to be understood as the necessity of losing the world, the body and nature, thereby enclosing itself within an acosmic realm."[9]

In sum, there is a crucial twofold result with regard to the Ricoeurian hermeneutical enterprise to which all of this has been leading as a segue into Dietrich Bonhoeffer. To state this in the simplest of terms, Ricoeur remains both (a) "critical" and, (b) even as a hermeneut, essentially "this-worldly" in a way that any of the phenomenologies in the Husserlian mode have ceased to be. And it must be added that the "phenomenologies in the Husserlian mode" will include approaches like those of Levinas or Marion. For even though, as we shall see, these will be found to resist Husserl in important ways (from within Husserl), nevertheless the underlying point is that they will for their own purposes find it no less necessary to retain the "pure" status of phenomenology as a foundationally guiding orientation than did Husserl.

But now there is one further observation, a third thing that must be added to this twofold result. It concerns a certain fundamental alignment that is always implicit in Ricoeur and that lingers beneath the surface of all of this. The point is that in this essential twofold orientation ("critical" and "this-worldly") Ricoeur remains by his own admission *at bottom* essentially Kantian in outlook. The basic indebtedness and orientation of Ricoeur's overall project to Kant is clearly evident in different ways throughout much of his work. But he gives us one of the most succinct expressions of this when elsewhere he describes his own enterprise as coming to development most basically within the framework of a "post-Hegelian Kantianism."[10] Indeed, Ricoeur goes as far as to suggest that "it is this exchange and this permutation" between Kant and Hegel "which still structures philosophical discourse today."[11]

But the characterization of his basic view as most essentially a "post-Hegelian Kantianism" and not conversely a "post-Kantian Hegelianism" is important. For although Ricoeur does indeed see Kant as having been in some sense "vanquished" by Hegel, nevertheless in the end, as Ricoeur summarizes, it is always "Kant [who] remains. What is more he surpasses Hegel [or, one might add, any of the phenomenologies that follow "idealistically" in Hegel's wake] from a certain point of view."[12] And the reason that for Ricoeur it is always in the end Kant who "remains," and Kant who "surpasses" (albeit an altered Kant, now being re-read through and in the light of Hegel), is that the fundamental nature of the "Kantian challenge," as we shall explain further below, is such that it continues inexorably to resurface and to exert its uniquely "critical" and "this-worldly" force even, or indeed especially, in any of its "vanquishings."

Bonhoeffer and Barth

Let me now draw all of this into the central focus of the essay by saying that Dietrich Bonhoeffer's thought can also be seen as playing out fundamentally in a certain kind of Kantian exchange, albeit now not an exchange between Kant and Hegel, but an exchange between Kant and Karl Barth. And while Bonhoeffer's uncompromisingly "incarnational" project is in fundamental respects very different from Ricoeur's uncompromisingly "hermeneutical" enterprise, nevertheless the basic "critical" and "this-worldly" disposition, in both thinkers oriented fundamentally to Kant, is importantly the same. (A vital caveat must be added here, however, which is to say that Bonhoeffer's orientation to Kant is really always only secondary to his more fundamental orientation to Luther. Wherever he does align himself with Kant—and even this alignment is limited to Kantian epistemology and largely dismissive of Kant's moral philosophy—he does so with more basic theological and incarnational commitments to Luther in mind.) But having acknowledged this, let me commence by discussing more fully Bonhoeffer's unique placement between Barth and Kant, first with reference to the former, and then to the latter, before proceeding from there to a particular phenomenological application in Levinas.

Eberhard Bethge, Bonhoeffer's biographer and closest confidant, speaks of Bonhoeffer as having early on encountered a "new master" in Karl Barth, who was at that time expounding a radically different kind of theology than that with which Bonhoeffer had become familiar. To comprehend properly what it was exactly that had so captured the young Bonhoeffer about the Barthian project, it is necessary to review briefly what will be familiar territory for many readers. Bonhoeffer's own theological education (no less than Barth's before him) had placed him within what came to be known as the "liberal" theological tradition of the nineteenth century in the vein of Strauss, Baur, Ritschl, and from there on to Hermann and Harnack, the last of whom was Bonhoeffer's own teacher in Berlin. All of these proceeded in one way or another from the spirit of German idealism in the vein of Hegel. And they remained essentially idealistic in disposition, as Bonhoeffer himself explicitly states,[13] even when they claimed to align themselves more basically with Kant or Schleiermacher than with Hegel. Idealism, for Bonhoeffer (agreeing here with the early Barth), had presented Christian theology with what he called the "wrong metaphysical premises," especially for a proper theological orientation to its defining subject matter, that is, incarnational revelation. And the primary error of idealism as such, for Bonhoeffer, was that it located what it saw to be *true* or "authentic" human nature most essentially within the realm of "spirit," that is, self-conscious mind, in a way that devalued and demoted the authority of the real world of sensible human embodiment in empirical history into which God had become incarnate in Jesus Christ. What followed from this for theology was something vital, something that Karl Rahner had already described similarly in a different kind of discussion.

The nineteenth-century theological adoption of the idealistic definition of human nature quintessentially as "spirit," or *Geist,* had made, in Rahner's words, not only "human orientation toward God" but also human "ordination to God" an intrinsic and fundamental aspect of what it *means to be* human. Or more fully, this essentially spirit-defined human orientation and ordination to God, it was claimed, "makes human beings [most basically] what they experience themselves to be."[14] Now Bonhoeffer, as Bethge explains, had always been somewhat dissatisfied with this view, especially insofar as it rooted theology indispensably in anthropology, in a way that seemed to make it impossible for theology to speak entirely and originally in its own right and on its own terms, that is, genuinely and fundamentally as *theo*-logy. And it was his discovery of Barth's early "dialectical" theology that, following Kierkegaard, spoke not of an "intrinsic human *orientedness*" to God, but radically to the contrary of an "infinite qualitative *distinction*" between humanity and God, or between this world and the next, that provided Bonhoeffer with a way of addressing this dissatisfaction. As Bethge puts it, Barth "made the religious experience that Bonhoeffer had long sought with youthful enthusiasm, the religious experience that had caused him such difficulties, seem a matter of no importance. The certainty for which he strove [as he now saw through Barth] was anchored, not in man, but in the majesty of God, with the result that it was not a theme in itself apart from God."[15]

Nevertheless, from the very beginning, even in his first alignments to Barth's earliest "dialectical" writings before the *Church Dogmatics* (primarily in Barth's *Epistle to the Romans* and *Das Wort Gottes und die Theologie*), Bonhoeffer found room to be critical of Barth. The earliest criticisms came with regard to what Bonhoeffer already then saw as the tendency in Barth to construe the "infinite qualitative distinction" between God and the world as something that drew theological attention *away from* the world rather than *back into* the real world of sensible embodiment in space and time.[16] For, as Bonhoeffer would continually emphasize in contrast to Barth, it is precisely the infinite qualitative distinction itself that has entered *into* the world in a human body in the incarnation of Jesus Christ; and therefore theology must always remain fundamentally "this-worldly," which is to say "incarnational" in its basic orientations. These earliest reservations then became even more accentuated in what Bonhoeffer perceived in Barth's subsequent writings in the *Church Dogmatics* to be a further "regression" from the initial promise of the Barthian project,[17] especially as this had for Bonhoeffer been expressed so forcefully in Barth's *Epistle to the Romans*.

One of the most effective ways of explaining the essential character of what Bonhoeffer perceived as "regressive" in the *Church Dogmatics* is in connection to what Bonhoeffer would later come to advocate as the need for a "non-religious interpretation" of revelation. Let me clarify this. As Bonhoeffer himself would later say (in his prison writings), he had seen Barth's early work as providing precisely an important opening for engaging the task of non-religious interpretation, and indeed as having begun it, but then as not having carried it through to completion, and in fact in the *Church Dogmatics* as having effectively abandoned it.[18] But in order to understand this properly, it is crucial to recognize the real import of "non-religious interpretation" in this connection. A "non-religious" orientation to revelation is always precisely and never anything less than what Bonhoeffer calls a "this-worldly" (i.e., incarnational) orientation to revelation. Or as Bonhoeffer himself states this explicitly, any *religious* interpretation is, by its very denotation *as* "religious," essentially an interpretation whereby theology seeks either to create "a room for religion ... *against* the world" or even to create a *separate* "room for religion *in* the world."[19] To the contrary, a genuinely *non*-religious interpretation allows for no such "alterity to" or "separation from" the world—that is, from the "secular," the "profane," or the "natural"—at all.[20] Instead, it focuses fundamentally nowhere else than *on* and *into* the real world of human embodiment in space and time. And the "real world" here, moreover, is to be understood not in any idealized or eschatologically purified sense of a perfected *imago dei*. It is rather to be understood as precisely, and nothing less than, the present fallen and sinful state of the world into which Jesus Christ became incarnate "in the likeness of sinful flesh" (Rom 8:3).

It is against this uncompromisingly incarnational, that is, this-worldly, backdrop that some of Bonhoeffer's most controversial statements not only are given their full theological weight (i.e., not merely a "rhetorical" weight), but also are shown to be not as over-radical or revisionist as they are often taken to be. Consider for example Bonhoeffer's well-known statements that because "in Jesus Christ the reality of God has entered into the reality of this world," therefore now "the sacred is to be found *only* in the profane," "what is Christian is to be found *only* in the worldly," and the "supernatural" is to be found *only* in the natural (E 59). Far from being over-radical or revisionist, any and all such statements are really for Bonhoeffer only an amplification of the consequences of what the incarnation of God in a real human body in Jesus Christ continues to demand even today.

Bonhoeffer's increasing unease with Barth's "dogmatical" writings is therefore always essentially focused on what he sees as a growing abandonment in Barth of the indispensably incarnational and thus this-worldly character of revelation. And indeed, when we come to the first volume of his *Church Dogmatics*, we find that Barth has already completely and unequivocally made exactly the move that Bonhoeffer resisted, by reconfiguring revelation itself as a divine communication occurring essentially and entirely within *mental* domains, in abstraction from the world of real embodied life. Barth's own words on this could not be clearer: "the encounter of God and man takes place primarily, pre-eminently and characteristically in this sphere of *ratio*"; "it is the divine reason communicating with human reason"; "revelation in itself and as such . . . is talk, speech."[21]

Now it is precisely this relegation of revelation to the status of an essentially cognitive communication or mental "event" that is also the source of Bonhoeffer's later criticism that Barth's theology engages in a "positivism of revelation." And it is also in this positivistic criticism that we come finally to the real culmination of the "regression" from the critical rigor of his earlier work that Barth's dogmatics increasingly represented for Bonhoeffer. For as a "positivistic" discipline—that is, one that simply "posits" its subject matter (revelation) merely as a "presupposition" already within a conceptual or ideal system of ordering (i.e., within doctrine)—Barthian theology regresses back to precisely the spirit of idealism that it had initially railed against and sought to overcome. But what is even more alarming about this—as Bonhoeffer now states with force—is that the subsumption of revelation positivistically or merely presuppositionally within a doctrinal system amounts to nothing less than a "mutilation" of its inalienably incarnational (i.e., this-worldly) character "—that Jesus Christ has come in the flesh!" (DBW 8, 416).

Bonhoeffer and Kant

This now brings us to the other side of the basic exchange within which Bonhoeffer's overall project takes shape. For wherever Bonhoeffer does resist Barth (even though, as Bethge says, he always "criticized as an ally"), he characteristically and invariably turns to Immanuel Kant to retrieve what, in his Lutheran commitments, he saw as the necessary "critical" or self-limiting disposition required for a genuinely this-worldly orientation to revelation in its indispensably incarnational character. In fact, in Kant the "critical" and "this-worldly" dispositions of philosophy are inalienably intertwined. Let me explain this briefly.

Kant describes his own "critical philosophy"—and the "Copernican revolution" which it wanted to inaugurate through an inversion of "all previous philosophy"—as most essentially an *empirical realism*.[22] Kant's "empirical realism" was meant originally to be set apart from and contrasted with the "metaphysical realism" that had preceded him in continental rationalism. But Kant himself later also sets his critical project equally against any of the "metaphysical idealisms" that followed him, for example, in Fichte (and also Hegel), which he saw as engaging in the errors of "dogmatism" to an even greater degree than its rationalistic predecessors. (Dogmatism for Kant means basically a natural propensity of discursive reason to overstep its own proper bounds and to claim a kind of lordship or possessiveness within areas where it cannot legitimately—i.e., rationally—demonstrate any proper jurisdiction. Dogmatism in Kant is thus at bottom always a form of irrationalism). It is true that Kant describes his "empirical realism" as *also* a "transcendental idealism."[23] But these terms, as Kant explicitly stipulates, are meant to be virtually equivalent or logical corollaries of one another. And a proper recognition of their equivalence is indispensable for an adequate understanding of the uniquely "critical" nature of Kantian philosophy as laid out foundationally in the *Critique of Pure Reason*. The basic logic of the equivalence between the two terms is quite straightforward. It means simply that when reason tries to "transcend" sensibly embodied or empirical reality with a view to locating a putative supra-sensible reality or "realm," it finds that this sensibly "transcendent" domain is populated solely by *ideas* or concepts of the mind, and thus is not a *real* "realm" at all but merely an "ideal" one. Or in other words, when we try through an exercise of reason to *transcend* the real empirical world in pursuit of an entirely non-empirical (i.e., purely "noumenal") "realm," we find that we arrive at a destination which is composed solely of *ideas*. Hence "transcendental idealism" is shown to be a corollary of "empirical realism."

But it is important to add that this equivalence has for several reasons largely been lost sight of in English-language exchanges over the past century,[24] an oversight that has often led to a fundamental misapprehension of the Kantian critical project in one of two ways. Kant is in these exchanges often seen falsely either (a) as the *culmination* of the rationalist metaphysics that preceded him (e.g., Descartes, Leibniz, Malebranche, Spinoza, Wolff) or (b) as the *progenitor* of the metaphysical idealism that followed (e.g., Fichte, Hegel).

These false English-language depictions are entirely uncharacteristic of the perception of Kant in either German or French circles, as we have already seen in Ricoeur and as we shall see further below in the discussion with Levinas.

At any rate, that Bonhoeffer does not make the error of collapsing Kant into either rationalism or idealism, but attends to Kant in the same correct and critical way that Ricoeur and Levinas do, is clearly borne out in his statement that "Kant did not want to be called an idealist or a dogmatist [i.e., metaphysical realist]; he considers both positions untenable."[25] Indeed, Bonhoeffer goes as far as to state unequivocally his view that there "is *only one* philosophy" that has found it possible to escape *both* the errors of "idealism [which] sees God as eternal subject" *and* the errors of metaphysical "realism [which sees God's] reality as transcendent object."[26] And this "one philosophy" he then goes on to identify explicitly as "Kantian philosophy."[27] Bonhoeffer's own work bears out this central Kantian orientation consistently from *Act and Being* onward; and this so much so that Bonhoeffer finds himself willing to consider the question of whether Kant should not be considered "from the outset as *the* epistemologist of Protestantism" par excellence (AB 34).[28] This of course is not to say that Bonhoeffer saw Kantian philosophy by itself as somehow actually being able to achieve what Barth had abandoned. Indeed, in Bonhoeffer's estimation, the Kantian project, as a non-theological one, was in the end forced by its own critical principles into embracing a kind of "deism" (DBW 8, 532). Nevertheless, it is to Kant that Bonhoeffer invariably turns for providing the necessary and appropriate "critical" dispositions required for theology's indispensably this-worldly (incarnational) focus.

The underlying and summary result of all of this, therefore, is to say the following. It is Kant's this-worldly characterization of his philosophy as most essentially an "*empirical* realism" that at bottom gives his enterprise what both Bonhoeffer and Ricoeur recognize as its uniquely "critical" edge. Or more exactly, it is precisely *this* world—in which we find ourselves *causally* susceptible and conditioned as *sensibly embodied* beings—that for Kant provides *the* most fundamental "critical limit" for discursive reason. We will discuss further below (in the section on Levinas) the more exact reasons for why it is that empirical reality must constitute such a limit for reason. But it is sufficient for now simply to re-emphasize that empirical reality constitutes a limit to which for Kant all epistemological and metaphysical enterprises must at bottom be oriented. Indeed, Kant goes as far as to say that even in its most speculatively abstract reaches, discursive reason can find utterly no point of *real* orientation unless, even here, it is always "directed back to its empirical use."[29] Hegel by contrast would later claim to the contrary that sensible empirical reality is capable only of offering up what he calls the "the poorest kind of truth,"[30] and even more than this, that the causally dynamic, spatio-temporally sentient "world" may not be spoken of as properly "real" in any case, until only after it has come to an appropriately sophisticated "determination" *as* a "world" by the *mind*.

Kant, again, saw any such unilateral claims of what Hegel called the "lordship" of reason over sensible embodiment as involving an illegitimate and irrationally over-reaching activity of reason, which he called "dogmatism." And his rejection of the dogmatism that he saw as implicit in any such forms of idealism is stated with especial force in a particular exchange with Fichte. In his *Wissenschaftslehre,* Fichte had gone on to offer what he suggested was a "completion" of the Kantian critical project *within* a system of idealism. But Kant himself rejects this in the strongest of terms and with an unusually virulent polemical flourish. He dismisses the *Wissenschaftslehre* as presenting "a totally indefensible system" and ridicules its "attempt to cull a real object out of logic as a vain effort and therefore a thing that no one has ever done." He thus rejects any claim by "the Fichtean philosophy to be a genuine critical philosophy" (it is for Kant in fact an extreme example of "dogmatism"), and goes on to "renounce any connection with that philosophy."[31] Against any such idealistic "dogmatisms," as we have seen, Kant repeatedly claims that it is only in its *empirical* orientation, or in its this-worldly orientation, that reason is able to become genuinely "critical" or self-limiting, which is to say, oriented to the sensibly embodied limits within which it always actually finds itself operative.

It begins to become clear, therefore, how Kant could have become such an important methodological source for Bonhoeffer. For Kantian philosophy limits any claims by reason to be able to assert ultimate jurisdiction over sensibly embodied reality, and shows to the contrary that thinking must always self-critically "leave room" for the empirical reality that challenges and confronts thinking on its own causal terms. And it is precisely in its basic critical and this-worldly comportment as such that Bonhoeffer finds Kantian philosophy to be uniquely predisposed to point a way also for theology to "make room" for God's self-revelation in the world as a genuinely incarnational or this-worldly revelation.[32]

But having established this, and in order to press the incarnational emphasis in Bonhoeffer even further and in a somewhat different way, I want now to engage in a comparative exchange with contemporary phenomenology, which exerts such a strong influence on theology today, in order to point out a certain basic incompatibility between what phenomenology can offer and what theology requires. I will approach this, however, not by going directly to Husserl, who would be much too easy a target (especially in light of the opening volley by Ricoeur). I want instead to look at the thought of Emmanuel Levinas, who inhabits phenomenology in a much more problematic and resistant way.

Bonhoeffer and Levinas

Part of the enigma of Levinas is that he finds it necessary to operate entirely from within the consciousness-enclosed confines of the Husserlian phenomenological project of "intentional analysis" (i.e., the conceptual analysis of phenomena purely *within* consciousness), even while constantly resisting this confinement, or even while constantly struggling against it.[33] We shall see below why it is that Levinas finds it necessary to confine himself to the analysis of phenomena purely *within* consciousness for his project of *"exteriority,"* paradoxical as this may initially appear. But for the present it is quite vital to recognize that wherever Levinas *is* resistant to Husserl (from within Husserl), this criticism (in addition to Jewish influences) invariably springs again from a basically Kantian, which is to say an eminently "critical," orientation to first philosophy. In fact there are few phenomenological thinkers who have understood and inhabited the genuinely critical spirit of Kant's first *Critique* with greater insight and resolve than Levinas.[34] One might accordingly describe Levinas overall, on the one hand, as sufficiently Husserlian to adopt the constrictions of intentional analysis as an unavoidable necessity for his philosophical project of "exteriority" or alterity, but on the other hand, as also sufficiently Kantian at heart so that he always labors under this necessity as a kind of affliction rather than an outright advantage.

But while Levinas thus aligns his basic critical orientation to Kant, he also seeks to be "critical" beyond Kant in a certain way (even though as we shall see, it is questionable whether he really succeeds in surpassing Kant "critically," and arguably in the end in fact falls short of him, at least in one important way). At any rate, Levinas is "critical" *with* Kant insofar as, like Kant, he sets his own basic project in *Totality and Infinity* in direct opposition to what, with Kant, he likewise rejects as "dogmatism" (or what Kant also calls "proud ontology"). These central commitments and alignments are laid out especially carefully early on in *Totality and Infinity* (and reiterated again in *Otherwise Than Being*),[35] where Levinas is at pains to connect his basic project of "exteriority" to a certain distinction between two fundamentally different ways of approaching what he calls "first philosophy," or to two basic different dispositions in developing a theory of "being."

For Levinas, the historically vastly predominating exercise of first philosophy—which he rejects—is concerned primarily with "the comprehension of beings."[36] Levinas calls this approach "ontology." The two most basic characteristics of an ontology are that it "reduces the other to the same" and that it thereby "promotes freedom."[37] While this term "the same" has several functions in Levinas, in the present context it denotes most straightforwardly simply the perduring "I," or as Levinas calls it, "the I that is identical in its very alterations."[38] And the way that the "reduction of the other to the same" occurs most exactly within this "ontological" disposition is that by adopting it I orient myself to the other in such a way that I "receive nothing in the other but what is already in me."[39] The philosophies of Hegel and Fichte, and also Heidegger, are thus in different ways for Levinas the quintessential forms of ontology, but also those of Plato, Leibniz, and Spinoza. At any rate, it is quite clear that *this* kind of first philosophy, which assimilates the other into the same, is unable to accommodate a project of genuine "exteriority" or alterity as Levinas wants to expound this.

But Levinas now speaks of a second basic way of engaging first philosophy, which in its primary disposition at the very least does not close off an openness to exteriority or alterity in the way that the ontological disposition does intrinsically. And this is a first philosophy that Levinas himself calls "critical." A "critical" philosophy is one that, as Levinas describes it, orients itself to the question of "being," not first as a comprehensive ontology, but rather first by retreating one step and calling into question (or "critiquing") this very propensity of reason to want a "comprehension of beings" or a comprehensive account of being in the first place. Thus, when Levinas says that "Western philosophy has most often been an ontology,"[40] and wants to distance himself from it as such, he is essentially echoing the position of Kant, who begins his *Critique of Pure Reason* by attacking what he sees as a long and pervasive history of what he also calls "dogmatism" within philosophy. In Kant's view, the initial disposition of philosophy must not be "dogmatic"; it must rather be "critical." That is, it must, *before* proceeding *out of* itself, begin from an "antecedent critique *of its own capacity*,"[41] in order to determine its own proper limits or integrity with regard to the reality of human embodiment in space and time within which it has its ground and source.

The initial point therefore is that both Kant and Levinas are similarly "critical" in their shared concern to set *limits* against the propensities of representational thinking to claim a kind of "lordship" or jurisdictional ownership over everything that enters into its field of apprehension. Kant, again, does this by showing that *sensible* reality confronts the intellect with a causally dynamic authority on its *own* terms, such that philosophy sacrifices its *own* integrity (i.e., becomes irrational) whenever it seeks "dogmatically" to claim a kind of ownership or full jurisdiction over what can be given to it receptively only through the senses via sensible intuition.

Nevertheless, as deep as Levinas's respect is for the Kantian critical project per se, it is still insufficient in his view really to be able to stop dogmatism in its tracks. For as the subsequent idealisms of Hegel and Fichte had shown, Kant's own critical principles could be used (even if in the end by again fully abandoning them) to yield even greater and more tautologically self-assured dogmatisms than those of the continental rationalism (and Platonism, etc.) that had initially been the main objects of Kant's polemic. The reason for this—as Levinas appears to think—is that dogmatism will *always* find ways of rearing its head whenever there still exists what Levinas calls a "*common frontier*"[42] between the thinking I ("the same") and any "other" it encounters. Or in other words, whenever intentional consciousness sees such a "common frontier," it will *inevitably* reduce the encounter between the same and the other to a possessively ontological relation of a "totality," which is again to say a relation in which I "receive nothing in the other but what is already in me."[43]

It is on this specific front, in other words, that for Levinas the Kantian "critical" project does not go far enough to accommodate a project of genuine exteriority or alterity. For the point is, of course, that Kant indeed leaves *precisely* such a "common frontier" open and available to representational consciousness, in his emphasis on the primacy of the empirical or sensible world, and this not only as a reality of *shared* bodily human experience, but also as the reality to which all discursive philosophy must at bottom be oriented. Or to state the contrast more fully, the very same sensible resistance with which the empirically *embodied* "other" in Kant stands over against the representational intellect as a *critical limit* to it: this very same sensible reality provides for Levinas precisely the most basic and final *common frontier* between the same and the other, in virtue of which the representational intellect will again and again ignore the "Kantian challenge" and "reduce this other to the same" anyway. What is therefore required for Levinas is a "critical project" that is able to *remove any and every "common frontier"* between "the same" (the perduring I) and "the other" (the not-I). For any common frontier between the same and the other will always be seen by representational consciousness as the possibility of an ontology, or a totalizing relation, and as such also, in Levinas's words, "the permanent possibility of war."[44] It is in this light then that it becomes fully clear why Levinas in the end thinks he must abandon the Kantian critical project and locate himself more fundamentally instead within the Husserlian project of a *pure* phenomenology, or within what Ricoeur calls "the ideal of scientificity." For the phenomenological project, as we have seen, has already, through its definitive mechanism of the *epoché, by definition* dispensed with or "bracketed out" any possible relevance that such a common sensible frontier could have for *pure* phenomenological reflection.

However, it is also exactly at this juncture that the epistemological incompatibility of a genuinely incarnational theology and phenomenology—even in its resistant Levinasian mode—begins to emerge. And I stress here that the critique of Levinas that I am about to put forward is aimed entirely at epistemological or methodological problems, and is by no means as such meant to diminish the immense value and power of the basic ethical focus of his work, for both philosophical and theological discussions. The intention here, in other words, is not to disparage the important insights and corrections that Levinas achieves from within the phenomenological constraints he adopts (even while constantly pushing at and challenging them). It is rather only to say something about the limitations of phenomenology itself, even in its most "critical" modes, with respect to providing an appropriate methodology for any theology that wishes to remain as unapologetically incarnational as do Bonhoeffer and Luther, and thereby also to bring a certain theological critique to bear on phenomenology per se.

With this proviso in mind then, let me continue by saying that it is precisely in removing or "bracketing" this final "common frontier" of sensible embodiment itself that, rather than surpassing Kant to a more intractable critical limit, Levinas will be found actually to regress from him in a certain way, not dissimilarly to Bonhoeffer's critique that the Barthian "dogmatics" had become "regressive." Indeed, what emerges in this removal or bracketing-out of the authority of sensible embodiment is an odd and somewhat ironic agreement between Levinas and the very Hegelian idealism that bears the brunt of his polemic (although Heidegger is equally a target), inasmuch as both Hegel and Levinas want to undercut the authority of sensibly embodied reality, although for different reasons. On the one side, Hegel undermines sensible authority because, especially in its Kantian expression, sensible reality *stands in the way* of idealism's own ultimate project *toward* conceptual *resolution* (or a "comprehensive ontology") into absolute freedom. On the other side, Levinas diminishes sensible reality because (again in its Kantian expression) its resistance is deemed *insufficient* to provide a limit of adequate force and finality to be able to *staunch* the relentless advance of dogmatism (or a "comprehensive ontology") toward absolute freedom at the expense of justice. Paradoxically as such, it is for Levinas only by retreating back to *within* the primacy of the mental (no less than Hegel had done, albeit through Husserl now without the same "totalizing" claims) that the last and most basic "common frontier" (i.e., sensible embodiment) can be overcome: the last "common frontier," that is, by which a relation of totality could be claimed "ontologically." This regression by Levinas into a kind of idealism reaches its clearest and in some ways most perplexing exemplification in his description of the "face-to-face" relation, in which alone the properly ethical orientation to genuine "exteriority" can for Levinas be reached. What I mean exactly by the "regressiveness" of this face-to-face relation in Levinas can be made especially clear through an analysis of his unique treatment of the particular kind of "proximity" that the face-to-face relation expresses or demands. So let us look at this more closely.

"Proximity" in the Levinasian Face-to-Face Relation

Under normal circumstances, one would expect a "face-to-face" relation to be one whose reality and authority is constituted straightforwardly and most basically in the actual, sensible embodiment of the real enfleshed other standing before me in real *empirical* proximity in space and time. But Levinas's "face-to-face" can never be meant in this way, as we have already clearly seen, at least not fundamentally for philosophical reflection. For any allowance of such an empirical or sentiently causal proximity as an authority for philosophical reflection would precisely be an allowance of a proximity involving a "common frontier," by which the other standing physically before me could again be encountered possessively. Far from this, therefore, what Levinas sees as the *genuine* proximity in the face-to-face relation must come to expression again as a purely *phenomenological* "proximity," which is to say a "proximity" coming to definition already *within* phenomenal consciousness. Although this account can be highly intricate in its later stages,[45] it can for present purposes be laid out in basic terms as follows. The proper and genuine "proximity" of the face-to-face relation for philosophical reflection, that is, the proximity of "me" to the stranger before me, can never, for reasons just addressed, be a proximity of real sensible embodiment, never a proximity of real *sentient pressure* on retina and flesh, of real breath, real odor, real stature. The *true* measure of "proximity," which is to say the genuine "distance" of the stranger before me as "other," is always for Levinas only "the proximity *achieved by the idea of infinity*."[46] And it is in this view of proximity, as it is achieved in the idea of infinity, that we come to what for Levinas is the true threshold moment for apprehending "a relation whose terms do not form a totality."[47]

To explain this, consider first that what Levinas always has in mind when he speaks of a relation "mediated by infinity" (as opposed to a possessive relation of totality) is a relation rooted specifically in what he calls a certain "Cartesian" idea of infinity. Let us look at this briefly. On the Cartesian formula (as Levinas reads it), all focuses of reflective interest, whether "things, mathematical or moral notions" are "presented to us by their ideas and are distinct from them. But the idea of infinity is exceptional in that its *ideatum* [i.e., its referent] surpasses its idea."[48] The essential point here is that "we could conceivably have accounted for all [other] ideas" by ourselves, but not that of infinity; for infinity is the one "idea whose *ideatum* overflows the capacity of thought," and as such it is "infinitely removed from its idea, that is, exterior, because it is infinite."[49] What does Levinas mean exactly when he says that the "referent" or *ideatum* of infinity infinitely surpasses my own idea of it? Most simply he means that because I can never actually *think* or mentally represent "infinity" to myself referentially, even *in* my idea of it (since any such mental representation would *eo ipso* be a "determinate" one and hence something finite): therefore I can claim no possessive jurisdiction over this "referent" at all. For the "signification" of the referent itself (or the *ideatum*), of which I have the idea, surpasses anything that can be thought. And this is why for Levinas the idea of infinity alone is now able further to open up my vision in a way that allows the true, transcendent exteriority of the other to be welcomed and encountered entirely on its *own* terms.

On the basis of the foregoing preliminaries then, let me summarize the essential character of Levinasian "proximity" in the face-to-face relation as follows. There may indeed be a real embodied other standing before me in the face of the stranger. But the only way to apprehend the stranger, in the genuine exteriority and "distance" that the stranger qua *stranger* demands, is to bracket out any common sensible proximity by which I could still claim any totalizing possession over this stranger or this other. The proximity of the stranger must rather be mediated through my own idea of infinity, over which I cannot claim any possession, for the "referent" of infinity infinitely surpasses my very idea of it. Yet even more than this, it is crucial to note further that this mediation of the other through my idea of infinity is not something I decide to do on my own. It is rather the stranger, the other, that impels me to take recourse to this idea, or "calls out" this disposition from within me, in order to welcome the stranger in the genuine exteriority that the stranger qua stranger demands.

But we must now state clearly the really vital result of all of this for the present purposes of comparing what an incarnational or this-worldly theology demands to what phenomenology can provide. For the point is that even in Levinas, who arguably more than anyone else resists the phenomenological confinements within which he finds himself compelled to work, even here the "this-worldliness" demanded by incarnational revelation as Bonhoeffer expresses it, following Luther, has become an impossible source of genuine orientation for human reflection. For through the relegation of face-to-face proximity to what is essentially an intentional attitude within phenomenality as this is mediated through the idea of infinity, Levinas has effectively ensured that "the exteriority of the other is [essentially] a *metaphysical principle*."[50]

To be sure, there are occasions where Levinas himself speaks of the face-to-face meeting in "incarnational" terms.[51] But he always makes it quite clear that the term "incarnational," as he uses it, is not to be understood in its more usual sense as involving embodiment in real sensible human flesh. It is rather again always a fundamentally *phenomenological* "incarnation" that is intended. And this means most essentially, as Levinas makes quite clear, the "incarnation" of *thought* into *speech*.[52] We cannot address these Levinasian "incarnational" discussions further here except to say that Levinas's more general avoidance of empirical reality *as an authority for philosophical reflection* is only accentuated in them.

The lengths to which Levinas is willing to go in blocking out the authority for philosophy of the real empirical world of sensible human embodiment as exerting a *causal* pressure whose authority can work prior to and independently of mental determination, is made especially clear later on in *Totality and Infinity*, where a deep mistrust, suspicion, and even fear of the causal empiricality of *physical* life becomes evident. More fully, for Levinas, when empirical or sensibly causal reality is seen apart from the dignity and clarity that mentally determining intentionality (phenomenality) bestows on it, it is then but a "mocking intention," an "equivocation" and an "apparition"; and "it is as though in this silent and indecisive apparition a lie were perpetrated."[53] This determinatively silent, "lying" world of causal physicality in turn, which has not yet risen to the dignity conferred on it through the intentional "determination" of it by the mind, "is a world that comes to us from the Other, be he an evil genius. Its equivocation is insinuated in a mockery." Its "silence is not a simple absence of speech." Rather "speech lies in the depths of [this] silence like a laughter perfidiously held back. It is the inverse of language: the interlocutor has given a sign, but has declined every interpretation; this is the silence that terrifies."[54]

Now to be sure, writing as he is against the historical backdrop of the Jewish horrors of the 1930s and '40s, Levinas has his own very good reasons for this fear of empirically causal reality *as an authority for philosophical reflection,* or as a proper epistemologically orienting source for either philosophy or revelation. For the "common frontier," which, for him, any granting of a shared causal world of human embodiment would involve, is always an opening for an "ontological" orientation to the other, which, in its intrinsically possessive propensity, is always "the permanent possibility of war."[55] What is sought instead is what Levinas calls an "eschatological vision," a relation from which every common frontier has been removed through the idea of infinity, and which can thus guarantee "the certitude of peace."[56]

Bonhoeffer and the Limits of Phenomenology

But the eschatological certitude of peace comes at a cost. For in the first place it is an entirely utopian or idealized certitude of peace. To live in the real world of space and time, which Levinas himself must do as an embodied thinking (phenomenologizing) human being, *just is,* tragically, to live with the permanent possibility of war. And it is here that the most crucial differences between Bonhoeffer's account of a genuinely incarnational revelation on the one hand, and any of the mechanisms that phenomenology finds itself able to provide on the other, come most clearly into view. For it is precisely into *this* world, this *real* "fallen" world of the permanent possibility of war, and not into some idealized "world" guaranteeing the certitude of peace, that for Bonhoeffer Jesus Christ comes as God's self-revelation in a real human body in space and time. This is the hard and uncompromising meaning of many of the early passages in Bonhoeffer's *Ethics.*

> Ecce homo—behold God become human, the unfathomable mystery of the love of God for the world. God loves human beings. God loves the world. Not an ideal human but human beings as they are, not an ideal world, but the real world. What we find repulsive in their opposition to God, what we shrink back from with pain and hostility, namely, real human beings, the real world, this is for God the *ground* of unfathomable love (E 84).

But Bonhoeffer does not stop here. He continues on to say that it is "not enough to say that God embraces human beings." For even "this affirmation rests on an infinitely deeper one": namely, "that God, in the conception and birth of Jesus Christ, has taken on humanity *bodily* . . . by entering as a human being into human life, by taking on and bearing bodily the nature, essence, guilt and suffering of human beings. . . . God does not seek the most perfect human being with whom to be united, but takes on human nature as it is" (E 84–85).

But the contrast between Levinas's eschatological certitude of peace and Bonhoeffer's incarnational this-worldliness becomes even starker. Reflecting directly now the time in which he wrote, Bonhoeffer goes on to state that this "message of God's becoming human attacks the heart of an era when [either] contempt for humanity or idolization of humanity is the height of all wisdom, among bad people as well as good" (E 85). He explains this further by adding that even "good people . . . who see through all this, who withdraw in disgust from people and leave them to themselves, and who would rather tend to their own gardens than debase themselves in public life, fall prey to the same temptation as do bad people." And while such a "righteous" contempt may in some ways be laudable, or while in Bonhoeffer's words it may originate in "more noble, more upright" intentions, nevertheless, when "faced by God's becoming human, this contempt will stand the test no better than that of the tyrant. The despiser of humanity despises what God has loved, despises the very form of God become human. . . . Only because God became human is it possible to know and not despise real human beings" (E 87).

Now let me be quite clear that in citing these passages in contrast to Levinas, I am emphatically *not* trying to make the ludicrous suggestion that Levinas should be grouped among the "despisers" of humanity. He is quite clearly anything *but* this, and is indeed a formidable intellectual example of just the opposite, an example from which Christian theology can gain important corrections and insight in other ways. I am only attempting through Bonhoeffer to sharpen, in a way that Levinas does not, the basic incompatibility of any *foundational* project of pure phenomenology (as even Ricoeur criticizes this), including Levinas's, for the incarnational difficulties with which Christian theology in Bonhoeffer's view finds itself confronted. And in fact nothing in this essay has yet offered anything in the way of a response or a "*solution*" to these difficulties as presented here. It has merely explored in certain ways the nature of the *problem* that theological thinking confronts in the biblical stipulation that God reveals himself incarnationally in the *real* world, which *as* the real world is inevitably the world of the permanent possibility of war. For the essential point here is that it is neither in the "likeness" of an idealized or utopian eschatological perfection nor in the "likeness" of an idealized pre-lapsarian utopian perfection, but rather nothing less than "in the likeness of sinful flesh" (Rom 8:3), that Jesus Christ comes into the world as God's incarnate self-revelation. And to this the further stipulation has been added, following Bonhoeffer, that God's self-revelation as such must *even today* be no less incarnational, no less this-worldly, than it was exactly, and nothing less than this, in the days of Jesus' mortal flesh.

The task of showing how to address theologically what Bonhoeffer maintains must even today be the *ongoing* incarnational (embodied) character of revelation remains an open one therefore. And Bonhoeffer himself will go on to respond to this in a certain way, or at least to offer the beginnings of such a response later on in his *Ethics*. What the foregoing discussions have sought to do, in addition to stressing the necessary this-worldly and thus critical focus of theology as Bonhoeffer sees it, is only to throw into question the adequacy, or even the propriety, of foundationally phenomenological projects to be able to address the incarnational challenge of theology, or indeed even to visualize it.

Notes

1. Paul Ricoeur, *Hermeneutics and the Human Sciences*, ed. and trans. John B. Thompson (Cambridge: Cambridge University Press, 1981), 101.

2. Emmanuel Levinas, *Otherwise Than Being, or Beyond Essence*, trans. Alphonso Lingis (Pittsburgh: Duquesne University Press, 1981), 183.

3. Ricoeur, *Hermeneutics and the Human Sciences*, 109.

4. Ibid., 102.

5. Ibid., 106.

6. Ibid., 107.

7. Ibid., 106.

8. Thomas Nagel's *The View from Nowhere* (New York: Oxford University Press, 1986) is a prominent example.

9. Ricoeur, *Hermeneutics and the Human Sciences*, 105.

10. Paul Ricoeur, "Freedom in the Light of Hope" (1968), reprinted in *Essays on Biblical Interpretation*, ed. Lewis S. Mudge (Philadelphia: Fortress Press, 1980), 155–82, 166.

11. Ricoeur, "Freedom in the Light of Hope," 166.

12. Ibid., 168.

13. See "The Theology of Crisis and Its Attitude to Philosophy and Science" in DBW 10 (*Barcelona, Berlin, Amerika*), 442.

14. Karl Rahner, "Nature and Grace," in *Theological Investigations* 4 (London: Darton, Longman, and Todd, 1966), 170.

15. Eberhard Bethge, *Dietrich Bonhoeffer: Theologian, Christian, Contemporary*, trans. Eric Mosbacher (London: Collins, 1970), 52.

16. Ibid., 53.

17. Ibid., 54.

18. DBW 8, 480–81; see also 415–16; and Bethge, *Dietrich Bonhoeffer,* 52–54.

19. DBW 8, 480, emphasis added.

20. And it might be added that a non-religious interpretation, precisely *as* non-religious (i.e., *as* this-worldly), is for Bonhoeffer the only genuinely *theological* interpretation. See, e.g., DBW 8, 414 where Bonhoeffer explicitly makes "non-religious interpretation" and *genuinely* "theological interpretation" equivalent.

21. Karl Barth, *Church Dogmatics* I.1 (Edinburgh: T&T Clark, 1975), 132, 135 (hereafter CD).

22. See, e.g., Kant, *Critique of Pure Reason* (Cambridge: Cambridge University Press, 1998), A28/B44, B308 (hereafter CPR); *Prolegomena to Any Future Metaphysics* (Cambridge: Cambridge University Press, 1997), 45.

23. CPR A370–72, A28/B44, B308.

24. This can in large part be blamed as much on Norman Kemp Smith's deeply flawed translation of the *Critique of Pure Reason,* as it can on the massive influence that Peter Strawson's highly polemical book *The Bounds of Sense* has exerted on two whole generations of Kantian scholarship in the English language. See my discussion of this in *God the Mind's Desire: Reference, Reason and Christian Thinking* (Cambridge: Cambridge University Press, 2004), 129–34.

25. "The Theology of Crisis and Its Attitude to Philosophy and Science," in DBW 10, 442.

26. Ibid.

27. Ibid.

28. English translation altered slightly.

29. CPR A672–73/B700–701.

30. G. W. F. Hegel, *Phenomenology of Mind* (Oxford: Clarendon, 1977), 55.

31. Kant, "Open Letter on Fichte's *Wissenschaftslehre,* August 7, 1799," in *Kant: Philosophical Correspondence 1759–99,* ed. Arnulf Zweig (Chicago: University of Chicago Press, 1967), 253–54.

32. "The Christian Idea of God" in DBW 10, 426, 427.

33. See e.g., Levinas, *Totality and Infinity* (Pittsburgh: Duquesne University Press, 1969), 28–29, 44–45; *Otherwise Than Being,* 183, where Levinas clearly declares the basic "faithfulness" of his project to the main Husserlian orientation of confining itself to "intentional analysis."

34. See e.g., *Totality and Infinity,* 42–48; *Otherwise Than Being,* 129.

35. See e.g., *Otherwise Than Being,* 129.

36. *Totality and Infinity,* 42.

37. Ibid., 42.

38. Ibid., 36.

39. Ibid., 43.

40. Ibid.

41. CPR Bxxxvi.

42. *Totality and Infinity,* 39.

43. Ibid., 43.

44. Ibid., 21.

45. See especially chapter 3, "Sensibility and Proximity" in *Otherwise Than Being,* 61–97.

46. *Totality and Infinity,* 50, emphasis added; see also "Sensibility and Proximity" in *Otherwise Than Being,* 61–97.

47. *Totality and Infinity,* 39.

48. Ibid., 49.

49. Ibid., 49.

50. Leora Batnitzky, *Leo Strauss and Emmanuel Levinas, Philosophy and the Politics of Revelation* (Cambridge: Cambridge University Press, 2006), 89, original emphasis. Batnitzky's excellent book argues likemindedly about the inherent limitations of Levinasian philosophy with regard to Jewish revelation as law.

51. See, e.g., *Totality and Infinity,* 204–205

52. See, e.g., *Totality and Infinity,* 204: "To regard language as an attitude of the mind does not amount to disincarnating it, but precisely to account for its incarnate essence." See also *Totality and Infinity,* 40, 51–52, 201–18.

53. *Totality and Infinity,* 90.

54. Ibid., 90–91.

55. Ibid., 21.

56. Ibid., 22.

PART TWO

Bonhoeffer vis-à-vis
Nietzsche and Heidegger

THREE

Aristocratic Christendom: On Bonhoeffer and Nietzsche

FRITS DE LANGE

"Christianity has sided with all that is weak and base, with all failures; it has made an ideal of whatever *contradicts* the instinct of the strong life to preserve itself," Friedrich Nietzsche wrote in *The Antichrist,* the book he composed in 1888 at the boundaries of insanity.[1] It was not the first time that he tangled with Christian faith, but here he did it more aggressively than ever before.

In Nietzsche's eyes, the two thousand years of Christian culture represents the biggest moral injury ever committed in the history of humankind. Its history can be read as the paradoxical success story of the unsuccessful human being. It is the story of the cultural hegemony of the weak and powerless, who religiously exalted and exploited the fear of living to the extent that they were eventually able to consider it their strength. In its preaching of the God of pity and the virtue of charity, Christianity patented the pathetic, crowned the failure.

Life hereafter, Nietzsche wrote, is a fantasy, a castle in the sky, constructed by people who are incapable of making their own earthly home inhabitable. The Christian ethic of serving the neighbor and obeying God is the servile interiorization of a spineless morality. "Christianity is the rebellion of everything that crawls on the ground against that which has *height*: the evangel of the 'lowly' *makes* low,"[2] Nietzsche states. Away, then, with consciousness, away with the notion of sin, away with "spiritual life," away with God! And long live the body, long live the senses; long live freedom, long live . . . the loss of all foundations. From now on, let us exploit the heights and depths of life, and no longer anxiously dream them away. Therefore, avoid the safe havens of metaphysics, the dusty attics of Christian theology. Whereas nineteenth-century German idealists still considered Christianity as the apotheosis of civilization and culture, Nietzsche, the son of a pastor, knew better: Christianity is the summit of decadence, the embodiment of an instinctive hatred of reality: "Life itself is to my mind the instinct for growth, for durability, for an accumulation of forces, for *power*: where the will to power is lacking there is decline."[3]

Theology can react in two ways to this message, according to the young Nietzsche-amateur and theologian Dietrich Bonhoeffer in a lecture on the history of systematic theology in the twentieth century during Winter semester of 1931/1932. Either one can shrug one's shoulders and ignore Nietzsche and say that he did not understand anything of Christian faith, or one can be apprenticed to him (DBW 11, 187). When we look at the whole of Bonhoeffer's theology, we can conclude that he himself chose the latter.

A Distaste for Weakness

That Dietrich Bonhoeffer found his natural conversation partner in Nietzsche is not entirely surprising. In the Berlin academic milieu of the twenties in which Bonhoeffer was raised, the reading of Nietzsche was as current as that of Goethe and Kant. But there is more: Bonhoeffer's personality was so to speak built on Nietzsche's philosophy. Bonhoeffer shared with Nietzsche a natural distaste for weakness, and showed little patience with complainers and moaners. Bonhoeffer developed this attitude during a childhood and adolescence within the very demanding pedagogical milieu of the Bonhoeffer family. The Bonhoeffers were educated as people with "backbone," who should keep their *Haltung* in stormy weather too.

In April 1943, Bonhoeffer was imprisoned because of his resistance activities. From the beginning, the death sentence, which Bonhoeffer finally received on April 9, 1945, was hanging over his head and remained constantly in his mind. In his letters from prison, Bonhoeffer makes reference to the heavy pressure under which he is living. One might expect him to get disoriented under such extreme conditions, living now at the other end of the social spectrum. But his upbringing betrays itself even more in prison than at home. During air strikes, Bonhoeffer loses his temper with people who—literally—are wetting their pants from fear. He simply despises them. In such a moment, he, the pastor, is incapable of uttering a simple consoling Christian word or saying a short prayer. "In ten minutes it will be over again," is all he can say (LPP 199). In his letters to Eberhard Bethge, he mentions his "tyrannical nature," with which he sometimes criticizes and bluffs fellow prisoners (DBW 10, 188, 214).[4]

Though he would not have liked to be called a bruiser, one can safely say that in Dietrich Bonhoeffer we have a strong personality, a powerful man, who shared—by nature and by nurture—Nietzsche's dislike of spineless and half-hearted life.

Bonhoeffer was raised in an atmosphere of almost instinctive distaste of petit-bourgeois narrow-mindedness. In his family, the word *bürgerlich* represented a responsible lifestyle with grandeur, and not the small-minded scrupulosity of a clerk existence commonly associated with it. The members of the family were all intended for leading positions in German society. The children were raised with the values "freedom" and "responsibility"; "humility" and "obedience" were not ranked high in the virtue catalogue of the Bonhoeffers. Thus, when Dietrich declared that he wanted to study theology and become a pastor, instead of a lawyer or a natural scientist (like his brothers) or a psychiatrist (like his father), he received little support among his own kin. "Does he want to bury himself and his talents in that stuffy institution?" "Bad air! Bad air!" his brothers could have exclaimed, borrowing Nietzsche's words.

In the Weimar period, the Bonhoeffers made a clear choice for democracy. Though convinced democrats in politics, culturally they never were. They turned up their noses at mediocrity, the taste of the masses. In this circle, "elite" was not a dirty word, but an honorific. And the more the "mob" took possession of power in the thirties in Germany (was the Nazi movement not above all pushed forward by the resentment of the lower middle classes?), the more a "sense of quality" became manifest in Bonhoeffer and his family.

Nietzsche and the End of Metaphysics

What does the theology of someone who feels so close to Nietzsche look like? It must lead to some kind of "aristocratic Christianity." This very term occurs in Bonhoeffer's letters from prison, on the back of a letter of Bethge from June 3, 1944 (LPP 318). Especially during the last period of his life, which he spent in prison, Bonhoeffer tries to develop a theology that integrates the heart of Nietzsche's critique of religion—a Christianity that might respond to the call of Zarathustra: "I beseech you, my brothers, *remain faithful to the earth,* and do not believe those who speak to you of otherworldly hopes!"[5] A dignified faith, which does not try to force its way through the back door of human weakness, but knocks properly at the front door and stays courteous, even when it might not be shown in.

In the eyes of Nietzsche, Christian faith escapes earthly reality by constructing a duplicate world, where one can comfortably withdraw for a while when life is getting too rough. Religion, Nietzsche says, cannot handle this one world, and must therefore add a second one—a double, "real," but invisible world, transcendent and divine. It complements the world we experience: the visible one, but—as is clear now—only really in appearance. Though it is palpably near, it cannot be the true world. Truth and illusion, the metaphysical and the physical world—from Plato until Kant the one and only world is, according to this religious mechanism, divided in shadow and substance.

In his parable of the madman, Nietzsche executes the death blow to this dualist construction, which apparently formed the "natural niche" for almost twenty centuries of Christian theism:

> Have you not heard of that madman who lit a lantern in the bright morning hours, ran to the market place, and cried incessantly: "I seek God! I seek God!"—As many of those who did not believe in God were standing around just then, he provoked much laughter. Has he got lost? asked one. Did he lose his way like a child? asked another. Or is he hiding? Is he afraid of us? Has he gone on a voyage? emigrated?—Thus they yelled and laughed.
>
> The madman jumped into their midst and pierced them with his eyes. "Whither is God?" he cried; "I will tell you. *We have killed him*—you and I. All of us are his murderers. But how did we do this? How could we drink up the sea? Who gave us the sponge to wipe away the entire horizon? What were we doing when we unchained this earth from its sun? Whither is it moving now? Whither are we moving? Away from all suns? Are we not plunging continually? Backward, sideward, forward, in all directions? Is there still any up or down? Are we not straying as through an infinite nothing? Do we not feel the breath of empty space? Has it not become colder? Is not night continually closing in on us?"[6]

There is only one world, and that's ours. Whoever says goodbye to metaphysical dualism wipes out the horizon that separates This Side and the Other. Then religion suddenly appears to be an illusion, and God to be dead. Why? Who is responsible for that event? Well, Nietzsche argues, we did that all by ourselves. We killed God, because, eventually and finally, we became honest with ourselves. We did it by admitting that up till now we were fabricators of gods, metaphysical machines who lacked the courage to face clearly the human condition, the reality of death and finitude, of unrealizable desires, of loneliness, and therefore compensated for the earthly human shortage with a divine credit in heaven. Because we cannot hold out in this world, we become dreamers and builders of castles in the air. We create for ourselves a "spiritual life," promise ourselves a life hereafter, and bathe ourselves in the warm, imaginary sun of the grace of a God, or of an eternal Truth, or of an unshakable foundational Being.

To the one who once has passed beyond this dualism, the notions of truth and illusion, substance and shadow, have lost all meaning. There is just life, will to power, body, pain, death. That truth is not pleasant. Who has the courage to say unconditionally "yes" to that naked life? "I am still waiting for a philosophical *physician* in the exceptional sense of that word—one who has to pursue the problem of the total health of a people, time, race or of humanity—to muster the courage to push my suspicion to its limits and to risk the proposition: what was at stake in all philosophizing hitherto was not at all 'truth' but something else—let us say, health, future, growth, power, life."[7] Nietzsche himself, constantly goaded by his bad health, liked to take on this role as the great physician of Western culture.

Faithful to the Earth

A few decades later, Dietrich Bonhoeffer, son of a physician, felt himself called to purge Christian faith in the spirit of Nietzsche and make it healthier. He grew up in the twenties, when the German intelligentsia had already exchanged its nineteenth-century idealism for a philosophy of life, a hymn on the irrationality of the lived life, which proceeds and transcends reflection. Not the reasonable steadiness of the wise old man, but the spontaneity of the playing child—for Nietzsche the image of his "*Übermensch*"—is the model in which the cultural elite mirrored itself in those years.

In 1928, as a vicar in Barcelona, Bonhoeffer preaches with an unbiased, youthful rhetoric, preaching in this spirit, about the earth as our mother and God as our Father. "Only those who are faithful to their mother, may lay themselves down eventually in the arms of the Father," he states in a lecture for his parish recorded in "Basic Questions of Christian Ethics" (DBW 10, 345). In that context, he refers to the Greek saga of the giant Antaeus, the son of Poseidon and mother earth, Gaia. Antaeus was said to be invincible, because every time he touched his mother, he received new force. Heracles, however, discovered Antaeus's secret and conquered him by lifting him up from the earth.

To a Christianity unfaithful to the earth, Bonhoeffer proclaims, the same will happen. It will weaken and die. Nietzsche considered Christian morality as nothing but a servile duty-ethic, a slavish legalism that follows blindly the divine commands. The young Bonhoeffer, however, pictured the Christian rather as a Nietzschean hero, who creates his own Tables of Law in

his God-given freedom. "The human being who loves is the most revolutionary human being on earth. He is the subversion of all values, the dynamite
of human society, the most dangerous human being," he writes in a sermon
in 1932 (Sermon on John 8:32, July 24, 1932—DBW 11, 461).

One can say: Here Nietzsche is so mixed in with Luther that the anti-
Christian venom of the former is so diluted that it has lost all its force. What
do we have here? A reckless flirt with philosophy, a theological juvenile sin? But
the more ripened Bonhoeffer continues to share Nietzsche's distaste of an un-
worldly Christianity, even radicalizes it. If the Christian message concerning
the God who, in Jesus Christ, becomes human, really means something, then
the Christian perspective will be exactly the opposite from the "religious" one:
not away from the earth toward heaven, but the other way around. The metaphysical "God" is a religious wish construction that sanctions escape from this
world, but the God in whom Jesus Christ did put his trust does not estrange
us from life, but—Jesus himself proves it—sharpens our eyes for the contours
of reality. In his *Ethics*, Bonhoeffer paints Christian faith as a perspective on
life in which the extremes of anger and love, death and life, suffering and joy,
crucifixion and resurrection are plumbed to the bottom, kept together, and
lived through in a dynamic, contradictory unity.[8] The God of Jesus does not
sanction the narrow-minded fear for life, but, on the contrary, unmasks and
dismantles it. In the eyes of Bonhoeffer, Christian faith finally has but one
content: Jesus Christ. Being a Christian does not imply the adherence to a
metaphysical belief-system; it only means that one puts all one's cards on Jesus,
and sides with his God. This is a comprehensive life practice, not a partial and
inward religious act.

A Religion Leaving Religion Behind

In the virulent attack on Christianity that Nietzsche undertakes in his *The
Antichrist*, Christians get it hot. But the tone attenuates when the One whom
they follow, Jesus, comes up. For he too was a "free spirit," and belonged to
the kind of people Nietzsche liked so much. When Jesus and his followers are
compared to one another, the whole of Christianity appears to be one big misunderstanding: "[I]n truth, there was only *one* Christian, and he died on the
cross. . . . [O]nly Christian *practice*, a life such as he *lived* who died on the cross,
is Christian. . . . Such a life is still possible today . . . genuine, original Christianity will be possible at all times. . . . Not a faith, but a doing; above all, a *not* doing
of many things, another state of *being*."[9] But Christianity betrayed the cause

of Jesus. "What has been called 'evangel' [*Evangelium*, good message] from that moment was actually the opposite of that which *he* had lived: '*ill* tidings,' a *dysangel*."[10] The whole theology of Nietzsche—if one may call it that—is entirely wrapped up in an analysis of the Christian betrayal of Jesus' life practice. One can say that Bonhoeffer's critical theology, though in a more constructive manner, has the same content. Reduced to its kernel, it actually consists of two things: a Christology (a vision of Jesus) on the one hand and a critique of religion (a coming to terms with a derailed Christendom) on the other. Christians following the path of Jesus, Bonhoeffer states in a lecture in 1933, do not have a world in reserve at their disposal. They cannot live as—and Bonhoeffer uses a term coined by Nietzsche—"*Hinterweltler*," residents of a duplicate world, as is so common in religion (DBW 12, 264–78).[11] Already at this early point in his development, Bonhoeffer becomes aware that Christian faith actually represents a paradox, a kind of impossible possibility. Not as the history of decadence and decay, as Nietzsche would say, but as a religion that, in the doctrine of the incarnation, carries its own impossibility in itself. It is a religion, so to say, that in its proclamation of the Word become flesh turns the premise of religion (a God enthroned in heaven) upside down. So it is a religion that leaves behind the land of religion ("*une religion de la sortie de la religion*").[12]

In his general critique of religion, Nietzsche—the philosopher with the hammer—hits the Christian nail right on the head. Christian religion has been practicing the denial of this-worldly life, an escape from earthly responsibilities. But Nietzsche has a second grievance against Christian faith, concerning Christianity's morality of charity and pity. Here, in its ethics, Christianity really shows itself a unique religion. The losers in life, the "*Schlecht-hinweg-gekommenen*," succeeded in making a virtue of necessity within Christianity, by sanctioning and glorifying their own incapability. So, we don't measure up to life? We don't need to; God takes care of the weak. Do we despise ourselves? Good! In the command of neighbor love, we can escape the burden of being someone on our own. Are we enjoying our bodies? Fortunately, we have a bad consciousness. Are we dying? No fear! God offers us an immortal soul. Humble service to the neighbor, servile obedience to God—that is what Christian morality is in its kernel. A morality for cowards, afraid of life.

Who Is Lazarus?

The aristocratic theologian Dietrich Bonhoeffer does not recognize himself at all in this picture of Christian ethics. Obviously he has much difficulty in identifying himself with the pathetic person, who wallows and fosters self-pity in himself. In Christian sermons on the rich man and the poor Lazarus, the hearers are usually allowed to identify themselves with the suffering Lazarus, who ends up in the bosom of Abraham (Lk 16:19–31). In his sermon on this parable, held in Berlin in 1932, Bonhoeffer refuses that common rhetorical strategy (DBW 11, 426–35). Instead he identifies his addressees with the rich man: "How should a gospel be our concern that is addressed to the weak, the common, the poor and the sick? We are men, healthy and strong, we despise the masses of Lazarus, we despise this gospel of the poor. It spoils our pride, our race, our power" (DBW 11, 430–31). Only at the end of the sermon does he allow the question: "You think you are Lazarus yourself?" The question receives an unexpected answer: "Who is Lazarus? Always the other, the crucified Christ who comes to you in a thousand despicable figures" (DBW 11, 434).

It is a hard gospel that Bonhoeffer preaches here, no comfortable oasis for a weakened spirit. Yes, eventually, ultimately, when everything has been done and said, then the rich man perhaps, as a "last possibility," is a Lazarus as well (DBW 11, 434). But grace is an ultimate word and has to remain so. "You should not speak the ultimate word before the penultimate. We live in the penultimate and believe the ultimate, don't we?" Bonhoeffer wrote ten years later in prison, after he had extensively analyzed the relationship between the ultimate and penultimate shortly before in his *Ethics* (LPP 157; cf. DBW 6, 137–62).

While Nietzsche's own ethic requires an extreme creativity from individuals in order to realize their authenticity, Bonhoeffer also makes high demands upon free, strong human beings—not, however, for their own self-realization, but for the other, the weak and poor Lazarus. In his sermon, Bonhoeffer exploits an idiom that reminds us of Levinas's severe ethics of responsibility. So does this reintroduce the familiar Christian glorification of weakness, after all? It depends on what you understand by weakness. There are at least two different meanings of the same word. Weakness can be understood as a synonym of culpable incapability, proceeding from spiritual laziness and lack of courage. In that case, people take the role of victim because it fits them well. This weakness Bonhoeffer, together with Nietzsche, holds as contemptible. But there is also a weakness for which people cannot be held responsible. It simply happens to them, when they are struck by fate. By bad luck, they happen to be right at the spot where evil and misfortune hits them, without having been able to build up resources to cope with it. They are the real victims. In order to develop a real relationship with these sufferers much Nietzschean courage, power, and health will be needed, even more than is necessary for one's own self-realization. For these weak live in the dark, and normally, "those in darkness one does not see" ("*die im Dunklen sieht man nicht,*" Bertold Brecht).[13] You have to put a lot of energy into looking them closely in the eyes. "Who is Lazarus? You know it yourself: the poor, the people who, outwardly and inwardly, cannot cope with life; often stupid, often insolent, often intrusive, often godless, yet infinitely needy, and conscious of that fact or not, suffering human being" (DBW 11, 434). You really have to be confronted with one of them to understand their suffering, to listen to their call, and to forget about your repugnance (DBW 11, 431).

As the artist of life, Nietzsche may be highly demanding; but as the preacher of Jesus' gospel, Bonhoeffer seems to demand even more. In the Christian perspective, developed in Bonhoeffer's sermon on the strong and the weak, the strong should look upward to the weak and not down on them. For the weak is Christ, our crucified Lord. This view also represents a "revolution of all values" (*Umwertung aller Werte*), but one that is diametrically opposed to the one Nietzsche stood for. Nietzsche only felt disgust, not respect, for the weak. However, one should add: Bonhoeffer's emphasis on the weakness of the Other and the responsibility of the self is also at right angles to the sort of Christianity that pretends to "glorify in weakness" (2 Cor 12:9), but only to cover its laziness and indolence.

The Fullness of Life

In Bonhoeffer's letters from prison the Nietzschean elements in Bonhoeffer's thinking become even more manifest. "The sense of quality doesn't let itself be killed, it just gets stronger year by year," he writes to Eberhard Bethge from his cell (cf. LPP 271). This applies not only to his personality, but to his theology as well. His distaste for metaphysical speculation and his critique of the division of reality into two spheres, already expressed and analyzed in his *Ethics,* are being ratcheted up now, together with a growing resistance against a Christianity that unfolds as an apology for human weakness. The aristocrat Bonhoeffer now finds himself right at a spot where evil and misfortune hits him heavily. He, a born leader, perceives the world now from the opposite side, from "the perspective of the outcast, the suspects, the maltreated, the powerless, the oppressed, the reviled—in short from the perspective of those who suffer" (LPP 17; TF 486). But once in that position, Bonhoeffer refuses to let this "view from below" "become the partisan possession of those who are eternally dissatisfied" (LPP 17; TF 486).

Confronted with the possibility of death near at hand, Bonhoeffer develops a theology of life, which celebrates health and strength.[14] In these letters we read, for example, that while lying in the arms of a woman, it is distasteful to long for heaven (letter of December 12, 1943). We also read that the world has come of age and "people as they are now simply cannot be religious any more." We should speak of God "not on the boundaries but at the center, not in weaknesses but in strength; and therefore not in death and guilt but in man's life and good" (LPP 282; TF 501, 503). A Christian apologetics that wants to attack this *Mündigkeit* is senseless, not Christian, and—not aristocratic (*unvornehm*) (LPP 324–29; cf. 343–46). We read that the weakness of people (their stupidity, *Dummheit*) is a greater danger than their wickedness, and that Christ makes human beings not only "good" but strong as well (LPP 391–92). Still in the same letters we read that God should not be used as a stop-gap, a *Lückenbüsser*. Christian "soul grubbing" of modern spiritual care, trying to trace out a contaminated spot of sin in simple and innocent happiness, is a kind of religious blackmail (LPP 343–46). Christian faith is not a religion of salvation, and the hereafter for the immortal soul is not a Christian doctrine. Resurrection means: the divine affirmation of earthly life, which we may exploit for the full hundred percent (LPP 374–75). We read that Jesus was not a pitiful dropout, unfit for life and thus ending at the cross, but "'the one for others!,' and *therefore* the Crucified" (LPP 380–83). The questions at the boundaries of life should be left unanswered, and grief and suffering uninterpreted (LPP 203).

These are fragments of a theology in which some central Nietzschean intuitions are tentatively integrated. Bonhoeffer, perhaps a little too confidently, called it a "non religious interpretation" of Christian faith. When we want to think further in his track, where do we end up? With a vitalistic "muscular Christendom," which is blind when life enters its periods of night? I don't think so. This is why Bonhoeffer emphasized so heavily the *fullness* of life, and embraced in his theology all its dimensions: the yes and the no, the suffering and the joy, the cross and the resurrection altogether. I do think, however, that we might end up with a theology that, because of its demanding and critical character, at least leads to a radical fitness program for Christianity. For, once the escape into a dualistic "metaphysics" has been rejected, Christian faith no longer fills the role of a religious belief-system, in which the basic life questions are answered once and for all. It keeps them alive, to be sure, but from that moment on its strength lies elsewhere—in its dedication to the fullness of life, as once embodied in and by Jesus.

Notes

1. Friedrich Nietzsche, *The Antichrist,* in *The Portable Nietzsche,* ed. and trans. Walter Kaufmann (New York: Viking Penguin, 1982), section 5, 571.

2. Ibid., section 43, 620.

3. Ibid., section 5, 572.

4. Cf. Bonhoeffer's letters from November 18 and 28, 1943.

5. Friedrich Nietzsche, *Thus Spoke Zarathustra,* prologue, in *The Portable Nietzsche,* 125.

6. Friedrich Nietzsche, *The Gay Science,* trans. Walter Kaufmann (New York: Vintage Books, 1974), 181.

7. Ibid., 35.

8. Cf. especially the chapter on "History and the Good," DBW 6, 250f.

9. Nietzsche, *The Antichrist,* section 39, 612–13.

10. Ibid., 612.

11. Cf. John D. Godsey, "Thy Kingdom Come," in *Preface to Bonhoeffer: The Man and Two of His Shorter Writings* (Philadelphia: Fortress Press, 1965), 27–47.

12. Marcel Gauchet, *Le désenchantement du monde: Une histoire politique de la religion* (Paris: Gallimard, 1985), 133.

13. From the refrain of Brecht's song *Mackie Messer,* in *Die Dreigroschenoper* (*The Threepenny Opera*).

14. Cf. Ralf K. Wüstenberg, *A Theology of Life: Dietrich Bonhoeffer's Religionless Christianity,* trans. Doug Stott (Grand Rapids, Mich.: William B. Eerdmans, 1998).

FOUR

"Who Stands Fast?" Do Philosophers Make Good *Résistants*?

JEAN GREISCH

1942: Antigone in Germany (Martin Heidegger)

In the summer semester of 1942, the philosopher Martin Heidegger gave a course at the University of Freiburg-im-Breisgau on Hölderlin's *The Ister*. The lectures, following the thought of Hölderlin's *Stromdichtung*, aimed at an initiation into the fundamental truth of history, according to which one discovers the essence of what is one's own only by venturing through the unfamiliar and laying oneself open to it. The entire second half of the course is devoted to an interpretation, developed over almost one hundred pages, of the Greek interpretation of man which is recorded in the first chorus of Sophocles's *Antigone*. Here Heidegger takes up again the substance of the interpretation that he had already sketched in his 1935 course, "Introduction to Metaphysics."

As soon as one compares the texts, two differences become obvious.

The first novelty of the later text is to be found in its numerous allusions to the contemporary political situation. When Heidegger mentions "the spatio-temporal expansion of world domination and that of the movement of settlement [*Siedlungsbewegung*] in service to it,"[1] he evidently has Hitler's *Siedlungspolitik* in mind—an association all the more impossible for Heidegger to ignore insofar as he is interested in the Danube, which, as opposed to the Rhine, heads for the lands of the East. Other allusions are even more explicit; they sometimes take on an appearance of outright demagoguery and are quite in tune with the themes of the propaganda of the period. Thus Heidegger declares: "We now know that the Anglo-Saxon world of Americanism is determined to destroy Europe, that is, the homeland [*Heimat*]— to destroy, in other words, the beginning of the West. . . . America's entry into this global war is not its entry into history; rather, it is already the ultimate American act—an act of American ahistoricality and of its auto-devastation."[2] Drumming the lesson in, Heidegger will go so far as to assert that "Bolshevism is merely a derivative form of Americanism"—the excesses of which are all the more pernicious as they present themselves "under the form of the democratic bourgeoisie blended with Christianity."[3]

The second novelty, which is of greater interest to us, is that Heidegger now focuses on the figure of Antigone, whom he had totally neglected in the first interpretation of 1935.

In both courses, Sophocles appears as the chief witness to the Greek understanding of man. Heidegger attempts to show this in his commentary, which focuses on the following three passages:

> Manifold is the unsettling,[4] yet nothing more unsettling than man bestirs itself, rising up beyond him. (v. 332)
>
> *pantoporos aporos ep'ouden erchetai:* Having everywhere experiences underway, inexpert, with no exit, he comes to nothing. (v. 360)
>
> That he may thus, in his knowledge, take part in the laws of his city and the justice of the gods to which he has vowed faithfulness! *He will then rise high* in his city, whereas he *expels himself* from the city the day he allows crime to defile him in his rashness. (vv. 367–71)

Verse 370, which I have just quoted in an English rendering of Paul Mazon's French translation,[5] has as its center of gravity the expression *hypsipolis apolis*, which Heidegger translates as "*Hochüberragend die Stätte, verlustig der Stätte*"—in English, this is "Towering over the site, cast out from the site."[6]

Heidegger carefully avoids translating *polis* by "city" or "state," which would put one on the track of the "political" definition of the human being which we owe to Aristotle: "Man is by nature a political being," a *politikon zōon* (*Politics* I.9, 1253a3). For Heidegger the city is first and foremost the place where a certain history is decided, the protagonists of which are kings, priests, poets, and thinkers. All of them are "violent," but each in his own way. Their violence is necessary in order to establish the city as a site of living-together. No one is capable of establishing such a site except one who "towers over" it (*hypsipolis*)—which, paradoxically, makes him a stranger to the city (*apolis*).

One can of course imagine another reading in which the phrase *hypsipolis apolis* would apply directly to the fate of Antigone, whose *hybris* elevates her above the city and its values, culminating in her "excommunication" from it. On this reading, the chorus's final warning is aimed directly at Antigone and those who would be tempted to identify themselves with her. Antigone, in Sophocles's tragedy, is no admirable saint, but a terrifying being, just as Creon is.

According to Heidegger, the expression *hypsipolis apolis* merely clarifies the meaning of the fundamental determination of the "unsettlingness" (*to deinon*) and of the "aporicity" (*pantoporos aporos*) of Dasein's being-in-the-world. His interpretation culminates in the thesis according to which man is a "fault" (*Bresche*) in Being because he is condemned to "fail"—that is, to break up. Later, Heidegger will even speak of a *Zwischen-Fall* ("in-cident").[7] Man is an in-cident in the history of Being. Such would be, if Heidegger is to be believed, the profound truth which lurks behind the tragic warning against *hybris*, presumption, and the overestimation of oneself. Even if we should want to, we cannot escape the immoderation which characterizes our deepest being.[8]

The numerous philological objections which one could raise against the Heideggerian interpretation of these verses seem to me of less importance than the fact that Heidegger says nothing about the figure of Antigone—what one could call "the Antigone incident"—which is the true theme of the tragedy. Can one ignore or obscure the fact that the expression *hypsipolis apolis* relates directly to her heroic act? But for Heidegger, the tragedy merely shows that she who is closest to the domestic hearth and to its values best illustrates what is unsettling in the human being. His resolutely ontological interpretation of the chorus obscures the fact that violence and aporicity manifest themselves nowhere better than in the "tragic action."[9]

In a certain way, Heidegger breaks this silence in the new interpretation of Sophocles's tragedy which he develops in the second part of his course on Hölderlin's *The Ister*.[10]

What is unsettling in man expresses itself in the fact that, regarding his relationship to the *polis*, he must reckon with the possibility of a "sojourn of conflict" in it. This *Gegenwendigkeit* is not merely a consequence of the unsettlingness of Dasein, but instead constitutes its very essence: "It is because he must allow the unfolding in its historical being of the unsettling, which in its extreme contrariety manifests and simultaneously veils itself within the *polis*, that man is the most unsettling of beings."[11]

This interpretation maintains, however, the ontological orientation of the 1935 reading,[12] and, indeed, takes it to an extreme, to the point where Heidegger asserts that the "character of man's sojourn is founded in the fact that Being in general has opened itself to man, and that it is this Open which, in its opening, immerses man within itself and so destines him to be at a site."[13] Contrary to what he had done in 1935, however, Heidegger now accords an important place to the question as to whether the verse which speaks of the expulsion from hearth and home equally concerns the fate of Antigone.[14] To him, Antigone's proper being seems to be expressed in the phrase *pathein to deinon,* which he paraphrases as *"ins eigene Wesen aufzunehmen das Unheimliche, das jetzt und hier erscheint"*[15] ("to receive in one's own being the unsettling that manifests itself here and now"). In a polemical reaction against all Christian and moralizing interpretations, he insists: "Antigone is within the unsettled in a way which surpasses every other form of unsettledness. She towers over the site of all beings—and not only after the manner of Creon, who in his own way also looms over it. But Antigone takes herself wholly from the site. She is utterly unsettled."[16]

For Heidegger, this amounts to making out of Antigone the true "keeper of Being." This is shown by the astonishing interpretation which he gives of the verse which mentions the expulsion from hearth and home. If, as Heidegger postulates, man is the most unsettling of beings, can Antigone be even more unsettling than all other humans? Heidegger resolves the question with a conceptual *coup de théâtre:* "That which is unsettled in its most intimate being, that, in other words, which is most remote from everything familiar, at the same time" shelters "within itself that belonging-to-the-familiar which is most intimate to it."[17] The expatriate, the exile, those who have been chased from hearth and home—such would be the true keepers and shepherds of the familiar. In proclaiming this, has Heidegger in mind the great number of his fellow citizens who, during the ten years which have passed since Hitler's regime seized power, were forced into emigration or exile—such as his former students Hannah Arendt and Hans Jonas, or his friend Elisabeth Blochmann?

However this may be, Heidegger nonetheless does not hesitate to overload his long interpretation of the verse that relates to the expulsion from hearth and home with an ontological meaning. According to him, the hearth is "the true site of settledness," "the site of sites, so to speak."[18] The domestic hearth, and the fire which glows unceasingly within it (*Herdfeuer*), is neither a mere metaphor nor an image to illustrate the concept of Being. On the contrary, it occupies a central place in Heidegger's meditation on the unsettlingness of Being. Only a reflection relating to the field of experience which circumscribes the domestic hearth will help us to understand the essential rapport between the unsettling (*das Unheimliche*) and the unsettled (*das Unheimische*). "All knowledge relating to the *deinon,* to the non-familiar," declares Heidegger, "is borne, directed, illuminated, and engaged by the knowledge regarding the hearth."[19] This "knowledge relating to the hearth" (*Wissen vom Herde*) is, in his view, the true knowledge of Being, so much so that "what is unsettled, despite all its unsettledness, dwells in the circumscribing of Being," and, in this respect, does not cease "to stand in relation to settledness."[20]

That which "is most intimately unsettled, and therefore furthest removed from all settledness," retains, according to Heidegger, "the most intimate belonging to settledness."[21] Antigone exhibits both sides of this thesis: she suffers under that which is supremely unsettling (*pathein to deinon*) and she is closest to the domestic hearth, the true "site of settledness."[22] Her intimate "knowledge of the hearth" is manifestly not a science in the sense of *episteme;* it is a "phronetic" wisdom ("*Sinnen und Besinnen*"[23]), which has no other object but Being itself. Such is, in effect, the thesis which the Heideggerian interpretation of Antigone opens onto: "the hearth around which all—man in particular—gather" is none other than Being itself: "Being is the hearth"![24]

At the close of Heidegger's ontological—or better, *ousiological*—interpretation, Antigone has been transformed into a Vestal virgin of some kind, as is shown by the allusions to the Greek goddess Hestia and the Latin goddess Vesta.[25] If the hearth is a word for Being itself, "in whose light and radiance, in whose heat and warmth, all being has bathed and already gathered itself,"[26] then the oblivion of Being is, in truth, an "oblivion of the hearth."[27] Unsettledness, adds Heidegger, can be a way of putting an end to this oblivion, by devoting oneself to Being (*Andenken*)—a "devotion" or piety of questioning which is inseparable from "the belonging to the hearth."[28] Antigone is not at all shut out from hearth and home; on the contrary, her greatness consists in the fact that she takes it upon herself "to settle down" in Being by uncovering "the difference between that settledness which is authentically human and that which is not."[29] This makes her neither a saint nor a martyr, but instead "the poem of supreme and most authentic unsettledness."[30]

1942–43: Are We Still of Any Use? (Dietrich Bonhoeffer)

Let us now leave behind the strange thoughts of the thinker of *Ereignis,* thoughts which evidently first came to light by the home-fire of the Todtnauberg *Hütte* on the slopes of the Stübenwasen. They show how Heidegger tried to achieve in the field of thinking the breakthrough which Hölderlin had made in the field of poetic saying. If Hölderlin was a "prophet" for him, he was, despite the grandeur of his poetry, yet a "small prophet," who kept Heidegger from the risk of becoming himself an active *résistant.*

The scenery and the style of the discourse—though not its problematic— change radically when we read "After Ten Years," the missive which Dietrich

Bonhoeffer, as 1942 passed into 1943, intended to send as a Christmas gift to his all-too-few friends and relatives. Written while Bonhoeffer could already feel the net tightening around the resistance group to which he belonged, the missive was found buried under a heap of tiles and crossbeams after its author was executed in the morning gray of April 9, 1945, in the concentration camp of Flossenbürg.[31]

That the retrospective is about the fateful decade 1933–43 is easily grasped. From the very first page, Bonhoeffer refuses to give his meditation the shape of a nostalgic reflection on time lost. This refusal is itself already an act of intellectual resistance. The time would be "lost" only if "we [had] failed to live a full human life, gain experience, learn, create, enjoy, and suffer." Time truly lost is not the time which has passed, elapsed, and is no more; "it is time that has not been filled up, but left empty" (LPP 3).

Bonhoeffer does not hide from his addressees all that they have lost beyond recall, all that will never be restored to them. It may even be that he already has a vague premonition that some of them will soon lose their most precious possession: life. But he insistently reminds them that they have not lost the time that is theirs. From his perspective—that of a "responsible life," which records "results harvested from the soil of humanity within a communal circle of those who partake of the same spirit, results laid end to end, brought together only by their relevance to a shared experience"—the important thing is not to run after novelties, but rather to reclaim things which "were, in times gone by, known quite well for a long time, but which are given" to their generation "to be tested and learned anew" (LPP 3).[32]

In what can be read just as easily as a "confession" in an almost Augustinian sense of the term, Bonhoeffer cites a primary truth—the truth of a generation which feels to the core of its being that the ground is giving way under its feet. His prison letters unceasingly revolve around this experience, which finds its most touching expression in the great letter of July 16, 1944, in which Bonhoeffer ponders the possibility of a non-religious interpretation of biblical concepts, and of living "before God" in the world, *etsi deus non daretur* (LPP 360).[33] What at first presents itself as a merely personal experience expands into a question concerning the "responsible thinkers of a generation from the moment they were required to confront a crucial turning-point of history" (LPP 4). Such thinkers in times past were likewise required to overcome the alternatives of their present—alternatives which to them appeared "equally intolerable, life-denying, and senseless" (LPP 3).[34]

Viewed against this background, the question "Who stands fast?" displays its existential issues. As he looks around himself, Bonhoeffer discovers everywhere the effects of the great "masquerade of evil,"[35] which, like a hurricane blast, jars all notions of morality loose. The paradox is that evil wears the mask of enlightenment, of humanitarianism, of historical necessity, of social justice. Every single one of these terms is easily converted into a slogan of the Nazi ideology.

Who is capable of tearing off these masks, of making out the hideous leer of evil? Not, for Bonhoeffer, the "reasonable people," who are doubtless full of good intentions but completely misunderstand the realities they are dealing with, who will manage only to patch up a tumble-down structure with a slap of rational mortar. Needful for this task is a different, more penetrating gaze—that of the biblical prophets. Like them, "the Christian who lives from the Bible" will discover that these masquerades "only witness to the unfathomable malice of evil" (LPP 4).[36]

The powerlessness of "reasonable people," who, saddened by the world's irrationality, lapse into resignation—if, that is, they are not ensnared by the seductions of the powerful—is not as tragic as what Bonhoeffer calls "the total collapse of moral fanaticism" (LPP 4). The moral fanatic is a kind of Don Quixote who brandishes the lance of purity at principles opposing his own. Bonhoeffer compares him to the bull in the arena who, seeing only the red cloth which is waved in front of him, does not see (or is blind to) those who wave it. The clash of great principles is a fight already lost; it serves, for those who really pull the strings, merely to play to the gallery.

The third figure in the kind of typology of the unhappy moral consciousness which Bonhoeffer deploys here is that of the man of conscience, whose ears hear its voice only. The conflicts which he must confront are so numerous that they would eventually tear him up, were he not to be "counseled and borne along" by a Voice stronger than that of his own conscience. Just as he does not recognize this Voice, so also does he fail to catch sight of evil's underhanded ruses, which then leave his conscience so anxious and uncertain that he is doomed to a headlong, calamitous flight. Only by lying to himself, so as not to despair, does the man of conscience keep it safe, but at the cost of what Sartre would call a "*mauvaise foi.*" Here Bonhoeffer once more pronounces a verdict without appeal: "a man whose only support is his conscience can never realize that a bad conscience may be stronger and more wholesome than a deluded one" (LPP 4).

The various figures of the unhappy consciousness which we have just touched upon link together in a sort of crescendo, which reaches its climax in the morality of duty. This is the morality regularly invoked by those, such as Eichmann in Jerusalem, who stand accused before tribunals which judge crimes against humanity. With exceptional lucidity, Bonhoeffer denounces such fiendish sophistry: "Here, what is commanded is accepted as what is most certain, and the responsibility for it rests on the commander, not on the person commanded. But no one who confines himself to the limits of duty ever goes so far as to venture, on his sole responsibility, to act in the only way that makes it possible to score a direct hit on evil and defeat it. The man of duty will in the end have to do his duty by the devil too" (LPP 5).

In the face of all of these temptations, Bonhoeffer sides with those who believe in the necessity of action which springs from a freedom most truly one's own. And yet this manner of standing fast and confronting evil only exposes one to every temptation and every kind of fall. In addition, one can also be taken in by an illusion which corrupts actions from within—an illusion that gnaws from within at the actions of those who become accomplices in order to avoid an evil worse still. As tragic wisdom teaches us, however, "the even worse evil, which one would avoid, could very well be the better alternative" (LPP 5).[37]

The last figure of the unhappy consciousness mentioned by Bonhoeffer is that of private virtue, which renounces all public debate. This purely private morality shields its eyes from injustice and condemns itself to a culpable muteness. This is the most subtle form of self-delusion: one keeps one's hands clean and sins by omission. According to Bonhoeffer, the two possible consequences of this attitude—either an unhappy conscience, eaten away by feelings of guilt, or else a supremely hypocritical pharisaism—are equally fatal.

At the conclusion of this pitiless *examen de conscience* dealing with false ways of resolving the question "Who stands fast?," Bonhoeffer ventures his own answer: "Only the man whose final standard is not his reason, his principles, his conscience, his freedom, or his virtue, but who is ready to sacrifice all this when he is called to obedient and responsible action in faith and in exclusive obedience to God—this responsible man, who tries to make his whole life an answer to the question and call of God" (LPP 5).

This answer continues with a dramatic question: "But where are these responsible men?" Thus Bonhoeffer is led to ponder the absence of "civic courage" (*Civilcourage*) in the German people. It is by this virtue—the only virtue which could in some measure illumine the darkness into which the Germans are plunged—that a man makes public avowal of his convictions, paying, if necessary, the ultimate price. According to Bonhoeffer, its absence cannot be explained by some peculiarly German cowardice. The case is too serious for one to be able to rest content with a naive psychology of that people with which Kant's *Anthropology from a Pragmatic Point of*

View concludes[38] (an echo of which one finds in Hegel's *Encyclopedia of the Philosophical Sciences*).

Bonhoeffer's analysis is far more profound. It highlights the affinities, masterfully analyzed by Max Weber, between the notions of mission, profession, and vocation. To devote all of one's strength to a great cause which surpasses us and, through precisely this, not only to attain one's freedom, but to approach God—this is one of the leading motives in German thought "from Luther to the philosophy of German Idealism" (LPP 6).[39] Without failing to recognize the grandeur of this idea, Bonhoeffer catches a whiff in it of a certain misreading of reality, of an inability to grasp the possible ways in which such readiness to surrender oneself and to commit one's life to the mission entrusted to one can be abused: those who serve great causes can become the unwilling instruments of evil. The time has come to understand "the necessity of free and responsible action, though it be contrary to what one has professed and contrary to one's mission" (LPP 6).[40] Not to everyone is it given to cross the threshold where we discover that we serve a purpose precisely in accepting that we are no longer of service! For this to happen, one must avoid the Scylla of a cynicism without scruple and the Charybdis of a self-destructive scrupulousness. What is needed, in brief, is a "faith": "Only now are the Germans beginning to discover the meaning of free responsibility. It depends on a God who demands responsible action in a bold venture of faith, and who promises forgiveness and consolation to the man who becomes a sinner in that venture" (LPP 6).

It is on behalf of this latter sense of reality that Bonhoeffer invites his addressees to reconsider their judgments about moral utilitarianism, asking them if the success of a moral action is really as morally neutral as the theoreticians of ethics and moral philosophy claim it is. So long as the victory of good over evil can be taken for granted, there is never a need to pose this question: good *will* prevail "in the long run." One could express the postulate underlying the ethical optimism so widespread during the Enlightenment by amending Hölderlin's celebrated line: "*Lang ist die Zeit, / Es ereignet sich aber / das Wahre*" by: "*Lang ist die Zeit, / Es ereignet sich aber / das Gute.*"

Yet what is to be done in an age when this robust optimism has given way before the discovery that evil endures more than good? It is then that the necessity of reflecting on the ethical problem of success imposes itself. A declaration that the end justifies the means, an apology for opportunism, which is tantamount to the capitulation of the moral conscience, will evidently not do. The real question is that of our responsibility for future generations. What sort of world will we leave to them? A world that is bearable or a world that is unbearable? A world more humane or more inhumane? These future generations are, in point of fact, the young. Bonhoeffer credits them with a very good nose for the matters which he has in mind when he insists that moral action finds a fruitful rapport with historical events, and when setting himself against all theatrical heroism, he emphasizes that "the ultimate question for a responsible man to ask is not how he is going to extricate himself heroically from the affair, but how the coming generation is to live" (LPP 7). To compare Bonhoeffer's theses with those which Hans Jonas develops in *The Imperative of Responsibility*[41] is surely anachronistic; yet nothing precludes a remarkable convergence of these two thinkers, who are equally sensible of our responsibility to future generations and who were both outstanding *résistants.*

In the same "ethical" vein Bonhoeffer presents a trenchant analysis of the phenomenon of foolishness—in particular, the ideological foolishness which can afflict intellectuals quite as much or perhaps even more than ordinary people. "Foolishness," declares Bonhoeffer, "is an enemy to the good more dangerous than malice. Malice can be protested against. It can be denounced. It can, if necessary, be opposed by force. Malice always carries within it the germ of its own dissolution, inasmuch as it at the very least makes men uneasy. When confronted with foolishness, however, we are helpless" (LPP 8).[42]

What sort of foolishness are we dealing with here? Bonhoeffer straightaway distinguishes it from any sort of intellectual deficiency. Philosophers have been quick to turn their backs on those who lack the capacity to follow the subtlety of their reasonings, and so to retreat into the elitist's consciousness of his own superiority. One can even, like Hegel and Heidegger after him, go so far as to define philosophy as "the inverted world" (*die verkehrte Welt*), objecting to a philosophy which judges only by "plain good sense." But the situation becomes much more complicated in the moment one realizes "that there are men of extraordinary intellectual gifts who are nonetheless foolish, just as there are people slow of wit who are anything but foolish" (LPP 8).[43]

The problem posed by the foolishness, which is due not to a lack of intellect but to intellect badly employed, is not a psychological problem. It is instead a problem that is political, ideological, and sociological—sociological, because certain circumstances produce foolishness in the "most lucid" of minds. Bonhoeffer, who played an active role in the struggles of the Confessing Church, knows exactly what he is talking about when he says, "[I]n certain circumstances, men are *made foolish,* or they let themselves be made foolish" (LPP 8).[44]

The production of foolishness seems to him to be an unavoidable consequence of the exercise of religious or political power. Whatever be the field
under consideration, "the power of some has need of the foolishness of others" (LPP 8).[45] The language of propaganda which swept through Germany
during those years is an emblematic expression of an ideological foolishness
which deprives human beings of their autonomy and urges them to shun the
risk involved in finding their own responses to a situation of crisis. (In later
years, Vaclav Havel will turn his attention to a different aspect of this strategy
of producing foolishness, an aspect which is analogous to the first, but which
Bonhoeffer does not mention: bureaucratic pseudo-rationality.) Bonhoeffer's
manner of describing the phenomenon is somewhat reminiscent of Heidegger's analysis of the "dictatorship of the 'they.'" The acid test of foolishness, the
situation in which it betrays itself, is none other than dialogue: it is here where
he who "has ears to hear" senses that he is dealing not with another person,
with another *oneself*, "but with slogans, catchwords, and the like, which have
taken hold of him" (LPP 9).

The moral of Bonhoeffer's analysis is that we must give up trying by
means of a strategy of argumentation to convince those stricken with ideological foolishness. A healthy mind will be restored not by "instruction,"
but by "liberation" (LPP 9). Bonhoeffer knows very well that such liberation
is often a long time—perhaps too long—in coming. When he states that,
most of the time, it is only once exterior liberation (the death of a tyrant or
the collapse of a totalitarian regime) has taken place that interior liberation
can occur, he proclaims, in a way that is almost prophetic, the sorrowful
process of de-Nazification which Germany would experience after the end
of Hitler's regime.

Bonhoeffer knew that his days were numbered and that he had no time
to waste on, for example, taking soundings of "what people think," as is so
often done nowadays by those politicians who multiply surveys and surround
themselves with spin doctors—the "soft" version of the foolishness which he
denounces. Yet he also knew—and it is this that makes him a *résistant*—that he
himself lived from an interior freedom, from the Pauline *parrhesia* which has
its origin in the experience of liberation. Beyond its New Testament roots, this
freedom derives from the wisdom literature of the Old Testament, for which
the fear of God is the beginning of wisdom (Ps 111:10)—and for Bonhoeffer,
this means that "the only real victory over foolishness is that of a man liberated
inwardly for a life that is responsible in the eyes of God" (LPP 9).[46]

Harsh though it may be, this condemnation of foolishness is not an
expression of some sort of misanthropy. One finds numerous expressions

of such misanthropy in the writings of Heidegger (particularly from 1945), when he denounces the foolishness of the functionaries of the Nazi regime. Misguided by the originary malice of Being, these would-be "guides" (*Führer*) were merely contemptible puppets. But this is a disguised manner of excusing them and of denying the seductive power, which they held for the philosopher for quite a long time—a power to which Hans Blumenberg has recently devoted a penetrating book.[47]

Bonhoeffer's attitude is completely different. In his view, we forget all too easily that "[n]othing that we despise in the other man is entirely absent from ourselves" (LPP 10). Between the misanthrope who knows that men are capable of the worst and the beautiful soul who believes that they are capable of better there is room for a "third man"—"the fallible man,"[48] who, like each one of us, is exposed to temptation. His ethical maxim: "We must learn to regard people less in the light of what they do or omit to do, and more in the light of what they suffer" (LPP 10). It is then that one enters what Pascal terms the "order of charity,"[49] which, for Bonhoeffer, finds its origin in the divine "philanthropy" invoked by Paul in *The Letter to Titus* (3:4).

Grounding philanthropy in this theological foundation does not prevent Bonhoeffer from paying his respects to the ancient virtue of prudence cardinal to the ethics of Aristotle and St. Thomas. Such "practical wisdom" fights foolishness on its own proper ground, but does so within the limits defined by the immutable laws of a common social life. *Hypsipolis apolis:* even if Bonhoeffer should admit that extreme situations may require us to break the law, and even if he should take Antigone's side, he nonetheless resists the temptation of giving a facile treatment of Creon, the guardian of law and order, of "the bastards" ("*salaud*") in the Sartrean sense. Bonhoeffer expresses his own compromise solution—that is, his way of handling the conflict proper to action—in the form of a carefully weighed conviction: "The immanent righteousness of history rewards and punishes only men's deeds, but the eternal righteousness of God tries and judges their hearts" (LPP 11).

This thesis raises us above the Hegelian theme of the cunning of Reason, which, in order to bring about consciousness, turns anything to good account by exploiting those passions which animate "world-historical individuals."[50] Nothing shows this better than the fact that Bonhoeffer's thinking on history is set forth in the form of an abridged *credo*. Not a single one of these articles of faith has lost its relevance, and we can still, in the fashion of the disciples of Epicurus, make use of it as a sort of prayer book which keeps us company in the hours when we are forced to make extreme decisions:

> I believe that God can and will bring good out of everything, even out of the greatest evil. For that purpose he needs men who make the best use of everything. I believe that God will give us all the strength we need to help us in all times of distress. But he never gives it in advance, lest we should rely on ourselves and not on him alone. A faith such as this should allay our fears for the future. I believe that even our mistakes and shortcomings are not in vain, and that it is no harder for God to deal with them than with our supposedly good deeds. I believe that God is no timeless fate, but that he waits for and answers sincere prayers and responsible actions. (LPP 11)

The faith expressed in these lines fully merits its Lutheran name of *fiducia*. It is the expression, as Bonhoeffer emphasizes later in his meditation, of a basic trust stronger than the suspicion and mistrust which poison the times in which he lives. This daring trust needs no further proof than the experience in which it is received as a gift.

Such trust establishes a self-esteem which does not need to go begging for the approval of someone else. It implies a newly found intuition of the quality of things and persons, an intuition which knows how "to keep one's distance"—not so as to retreat into a feeling of one's own superiority, but the better to recognize the uniqueness of each person, who constitutes, as Levinas puts it, a "chosen one." Christian faith ought to fly to the aid of such self-esteem: "When we forget what is due to ourselves and to others, when the feeling for human quality and the ability to keep one's distance cease to exist, chaos is at the door" (LPP 12).[52] The nobility of soul advocated by Bonhoeffer "arises from and exists by sacrifice, courage, and a clear sense of duty to oneself and society, by expecting due regard for itself as a matter of course; and it shows an equally natural regard for others, whether they are of higher or lower degree" (LPP 13).

What one could call an "ethic of distanciation" is at the same time an ethic that has something in common with the ancient virtue of magnanimity. In this matter also, Bonhoeffer proposes, as it were, an alternate reading of the second verse of Hölderlin's hymn, *"Patmos"*: "*Wo aber Gefahr ist, wächst / Das Rettende auch*" ("Yet where the danger lies, / Also grows the one which saves"). The wish to escape danger, to "save one's skin" is, in certain circumstances, a morally excusable attitude. But when the moment of decision, which is not of our own choosing, presses itself upon us, magnanimity merges with "authentic compassion, which arises not from anxiety"[53]—nor from "care" in the Heideggerian sense—"but from the liberating and redeeming love of Christ for all who suffer" (LPP 14). One could speak of an "incarnate magnanimity"—not founded in the experience of our own proper sufferings, but in that of the sufferings of all of the members of the Body of Christ. Bonhoeffer thus meets up with the intuition of another *résistant* (who provided Paul Ricoeur with the title *Oneself as Another*), Georges Bernanos, writing in his *Diary of a Country Priest:* "How easy it is to hate oneself! True grace is to forget. Yet if pride could die in us, the supreme grace would be to love oneself in all simplicity—as one would love any one of those who themselves have suffered and loved in Christ."[54]

This humble love of oneself can be found only after the long and sorrowful labor of an apprenticeship in accepting the sufferings which beget responsible freedom and the burdens of solitude, public disapproval, and bodily affliction. Such is, according to Bonhoeffer, the true image of the Suffering Servant, which is far removed from any plaintive caricature: "Christ suffered as a free man alone, apart and in ignominy, in body and spirit; and since then many Christians have suffered with him" (LPP 14).

To know how to lose one's time so as not to lose one's soul: thus could one summarize the close of Bonhoeffer's meditation, where he revisits his opening theme of the fulfillment that a responsible life grants us. This fulfillment demands a renunciation which brings Bonhoeffer's situation closer to that of the first Christian generations. Their relationship to time is not defined in terms of a lifelong project, which is progressively realized by "letting time do its work." Chronological time gives way before a "kairological" time of decisions that must be made urgently. This feeling of urgency, which could be lived in anxiety, is transformed by Bonhoeffer into a carefree attitude fully in accord with the gospel—the attitude of one who lives each moment of his life as if it were the last, his attention fixed upon future generations.

What makes a good *résistant* is an optimism of a very particular sort, which does not confuse itself with the naive conviction that things will, by improving sooner or later, turn out well in the end. The sort of optimism that Bonhoeffer advocates takes its impulse from and draws upon the reserves of that hope against all hope shared by those who dare to believe that the future is up to them, even if that future will come to light only after their deaths. Such an "optimism" does not fear death because it knows that death is not the worst of evils and that the question, "O Death, where is your victory?" is put in order to be heard.

At this point the two terms which make up the title of Bonhoeffer's posthumous work, *Widerstand und Ergebung,* cease to stand in contradiction. They can do this because the term *Ergebung* is no longer synonymous with passive submission to fate, which blindly crushes us. In *Ergebung,* one must hear "-*geb-*," that is, "gift"—the gift which is not given to all, but only to the "*résistants*," of *yielding ourselves* to the task which falls to us, even if it seems to outstrip our strength. The official French translation of Bonhoeffer's title is *Résistance et soumission*, that is, *Resistance and Submission*. A more accurate rendering would be *Standing Fast and Yielding*.[55] This, at least, is what is suggested by Bonhoeffer's recapitulation, in the last paragraph of his missive, of its opening question: "Who stands fast?"

"Who stands fast?" This, indeed, is the question of a "*résistant*"! Closely intertwined with it is the question, "Are we still of any service?" Bonhoeffer's only reply is negative and indirect. Disqualified from the title of "*résistant*" are the genius, the cynic, the misanthrope, the subtle tactician; the only ones who resist are those humble guardians of the other man's humanity whom the Jewish tradition calls "the just."

"Is There a Measure on Earth?"

I here interrupt this simple re-reading of Bonhoeffer's missive, which has lost none of its relevance and which can at any moment again become a salutary *vade mecum* for those who have to struggle against terror, whatever its source may be.

Although the texts of Heidegger and Bonhoeffer are nearly contemporary, it would be practically meaningless to try to compare them point by point. The two are incommensurable documents of the era, having nothing in common except a certain way of envisaging the relation between man and the city, and the possibility—or rather the necessity—for the one to rise above the other.

One who desires to draw a sharper contrast would have to attend to the manner in which, in the concluding remark of his "*Der Ister*" lecture, Heidegger retrieves the question posed by Hölderlin: *Gibt es auf Erden ein Mass?* ("Is there a measure on Earth?") To this question, taken from "In Lovely Blue," a poem which he describes as "a veritable δεινότατον," Heidegger joins Hölderlin in replying, *Es gibt keines* ("There is none"). In his view, this admission does not lead to disillusioned resignation, because the absence of a measure is a summons for him who has the fortitude for thinking.

Yet Heidegger's reply offers no response at all to Bonhoeffer's crucial question, "Who holds fast?" Like his missive, Bonhoeffer's prison letters suggest an answer which is altogether different from Heidegger's: the measure does indeed exist for those who pay the price to find it. This measure traces out on Earth the great sign of contradiction which is the Cross, the expression of an immeasurable love in whose bosom "standing fast" and "yielding" are no longer two but one.

Translated by Caroline and Joseph Haggarty

Notes

This chapter, "Les philosophes sont-ils des bons résistants?," first appeared in the proceedings of del Convegno Internazionale di Torino-Vercelli February 9–11, 2006, as "I filosofi possono essere dei buoni resistenti?" in *Dietrich Bonhoeffer. Eredità cristiana e modernità*, ed. Ugo Perone and Marco Saveriano (Turin, Italy: Editrice Claudiana, 2006). Thank you to Ugo Perone for permission to publish this translation.

1. Martin Heidegger, *Hölderlins Hymne "Der Ister,"* Gesamtausgabe Bd. 53 (Frankfurt am Main: V. Klostermann, 1984), 60 (hereafter Ga 53). The translators have provided their own renderings of Heidegger's German text throughout this essay. The published English translation—*Hölderlin's Hymn "The Ister"*—is by William McNeill and Julia Davis (Bloomington: Indiana University Press, 1996).

2. Ga 53, 68.

3. Ibid., 86.

4. Translation altered. It is common to translate *das Unheimliche* (in French, *l'inquiétant*) as "the uncanny." This is, for instance, how it appears in Gregory Fried and Richard Polt's recent translation of Heidegger's *Introduction to Metaphysics* (New Haven, Conn.: Yale University Press, 2000), 156. In the present essay, however, the translators have used "the unsettling" throughout, since it better retains the etymological connections between *das Unheimliche, das Unheimische,* and *das Heim,* upon which Heidegger relies and to which Greisch draws the reader's attention.

5. The first two quotations, however, are English renderings of Heidegger's own German translations of Sophocles.

6. Martin Heidegger, *Einleitung in die Metaphysik* (Tübingen: Niemeyer, 1966), 113. In Fried and Polt's translation, the line is rendered "Rising high over the site, losing the site" (157).

7. See *Introduction to Metaphysics*, 174n67.

8. "*Als die Bresche für die Eröffnung des ins Werk gesetzten Seins im Seienden ist das Dasein des geschichtlichen Menschen ein Zwischen-Fall, der Zwischenfall, in dem plötzlich die Gewalten der losgebundenen Übergewalt des Seins aufgehen und ins Werk als Geschichte eingehen*" (Heidegger, *Einleitung in die Metaphysik,* 125). Translation: "As the fault in being for the disclosure of Being-put-to-work, the Dasein of historical man is an '*in-cident*'—the incident in which the forces of the unbound overwhelmingness of Being suddenly arise and enter into that work as history."

9. It is under this title (in the Blamey translation) that Paul Ricoeur puts the interpretation of *Antigone* sketched in his *Oneself as Another* (Chicago: University of Chicago Press, 1992), 241–49.

10. Ga 53, 63–151.

11. Ibid., 107.

12. See Jacques Taminiaux, *Le théâtre des philosophes. La tragédie, l'être, l'action* (Grenoble: Jérôme Millon, 1995).

13. Ga 53, 113.
14. Ibid., 121.
15. Ibid., 127.
16. Ibid., 128–29.
17. Ibid., 129.
18. Ibid., 130.
19. "Wissen, das vom Herde weiss" (ibid., 133).
20. Ibid., 135.
21. Ibid., 19.
22. Ibid., 130.
23. Ibid., 135.
24. Ibid., 136.
25. Ibid., 131.
26. Ibid., 143.
27. Ibid., 144.
28. Ibid., 151.
29. Ibid., 146.
30. Ibid., 151.
31. Volume editors' note: This letter was not, however, written while Bonhoeffer was in prison, since he wrote it during the Christmas of 1942, and was not arrested until April 5, 1943. And as Eberhard Bethge notes, "one copy was kept under the roof-beams of Bonhoeffer's parents' house in Charlottenburg, Marienburger Allee 43" (LPP 17).
32. Translation altered.
33. Bonhoeffer's rendering of this phrase from Grotius is "as if God did not exist."
34. Translation altered.
35. LPP 4.
36. Translation altered.
37. Translation altered.
38. Immanuel Kant, *Anthropology from a Pragmatic Point of View,* trans. and ed. Robert B. Louden (Cambridge: Cambridge University Press, 2006), 219–21.
39. Translation altered.
40. Translation altered.
41. Hans Jonas, *The Imperative of Responsibility: In Search of an Ethics for the Technological Age,* trans. Hans Jonas and David Herr (Chicago: University of Chicago Press, 1984).
42. Translation altered.
43. Translation altered. A good example of this sort of intellectual foolishness can be found in Carl Schmitt's writings during the period of the third Reich. See David Cumin, *Carl Schmitt: Biographie politique et intellectuelle* (Paris: Cerf, 2005), 135–81.
44. Translation altered.
45. Translation altered.
46. Translation altered.
47. Hans Blumenberg, *Die Verführbarkeit des Philosophen* (Frankfurt: Suhrkamp, 2000).
48. Cf. Paul Ricoeur, *The Fallen Man,* rev. trans. Charles A. Kelbley (New York: Fordham University, 1986).

49. *"C'est un mauvais signe de voir une personne produire au-dehors dès l'instant de sa conversion. L'ordre de la charité est de s'enraciner dans le cœur avant que de produire de bonnes œuvres au-dehors."* Blaise Pascal, *Oeuvres Complètes,* éd. Lafuma (Paris: Éditions du Seuil, 1963), 639.

50. See the introduction to Hegel's *The Philosophy of History,* trans. Leo Rauch (Indianapolis: Hackett, 1988), 32–36.

51. Translation altered.

52. Translation altered.

53. LPP 14. Translation altered. What Greisch and Bonhoeffer are discussing here is not sympathy (which is primarily passive) but compassion (which is primarily active). Also, Greisch's *"l'angoisse"* is not fear (*peur*) but anxiety.

54. Georges Bernanos, *The Diary of a Country Priest,* trans. Pamela Morris (New York: Image/Doubleday, 1937), 230.

55. The English translation omits this main title entirely, using only the subtitle, *Letters and Papers from Prison.*

FIVE

Dietrich Bonhoeffer and Martin Heidegger: Two Different Visions of Humanity

JENS ZIMMERMANN

In relating the thought of Dietrich Bonhoeffer and Martin Heidegger, this essay aims to answer two questions: First, what was Heidegger's influence on Dietrich Bonhoeffer's theology? And, second, how does Bonhoeffer's theology address central hermeneutical issues arising in the wake of Heidegger's philosophy? In order to tackle these questions with any degree of success we require an interpretive focus which allows us to gauge Heidegger's influence on Bonhoeffer, and, in turn, to establish Bonhoeffer's contribution to post-Heideggerian philosophical theology. The question of self-understanding, understood broadly as the question of human identity, provides this common denominator. Whether we see ourselves, with Heidegger, as shepherds of Being, or whether we define true humanity, with Bonhoeffer, as being in the Shepherd, that is, as communion with God, makes every difference in our assessment of post-metaphysical conversations about God and humanity.

The Focus on Human Identity in Bonhoeffer and Heidegger

Without question, human identity as determined by the incarnation is the central impulse in Bonhoeffer's Christocentric theology: in the incarnation, God becomes human to represent humanity, to affirm it, to judge it, and to renew it so that henceforth the resurrected Christ defines true humanity as participation in God. This emphasis is found in Bonhoeffer's earliest theological work and persists into his unfinished book on Christian ethics and the *Letters and Papers from Prison*. Already in *Sanctorum Communio*, Bonhoeffer defines the church as the new humanity in Christ, in contrast to a mere social club or religious association.[1] Stressing the ontological participation in the new humanity of Christ, Bonhoeffer identifies the church with "Christ existing as community" (DBW 1, 127), the new humanity drawn into communion with God through Christ,[2] and concludes: "So the new humanity is altogether concentrated in one single historical locus, in Jesus Christ, and only in him is it [humanity] understood as a whole. . . . Now, because in Jesus Christ the entire new humanity is truly established, he represents in his historical life the entire history of humanity" (DBW 1, 91–92).[3]

This definition of the church already reveals many of Bonhoeffer's characteristic themes: his emphasis on historicity, the social self, and the structure of responsibility, even the anticipation of his later concept of Christ as the center of reality and history, make their appearance. Because God's dealings with humanity are summed up in Christ, and Christ exists in the world as the church, "church history is the hidden center of world history." In accordance with Karl Barth's critique of religion, Bonhoeffer does not mean to identify a particular cultural manifestation of Christianity as the correct interpretation of history; rather, he refers to the church's essential being in Christ and its consequent proclamation of the new humanity brought about by God's redemptive work (DBW 1, 142–43).

We find a similar focus on human identity in Bonhoeffer's habilitation *Act and Being*, where Bonhoeffer takes up his earlier conception of "Christ as existing in community," arguing again that Christ reveals himself as the new humanity, the "δευτερος άνθρωπος, as the new human being, or better: as the new humanity itself" (DBW 2, 108–109). In his effort to establish an ontological realism in which the Christian participates in God's transcendence without compromising genuine historicity, Bonhoeffer correlates act and being by defining Christian existence as "that historical human being, who knows himself transposed from the old into the new humanity, who is, what he is through the membership in the new humanity, as that in Christ newly created person," who exists only in his knowledge of Christ and whose reflection is possible only because it is ontologically grounded by his participation in the being of Christ (DBW 2, 117).[4]

Bonhoeffer's Christology lectures in 1933 continue to expound the theological significance of the incarnation for human identity. Christ appears again as the new humanity but more clearly now also as the center of nature, history, *and* the church, a position which will find greater application in the final work, *Ethics*, and an apparent new phase in Bonhoeffer's "prison" theology, the infamous idea of "religionless Christianity."[5]

Bonhoeffer's emphasis on our human identity as being-in-Christ also explains why Bonhoeffer rejects preset ethical principles for a more hermeneutical conception of ethics. For him ethics, we recall, is *Gestaltung*, the formation of Christ, the new human being formed in us, not by striving to become like Jesus, but through the transforming encounter with him. Bonhoeffer's description of this encounter demonstrates how central the theme of a renewed humanity is to his theology. Against any other Nietzschean or Heideggerian visions of what authentic humanity entails, Bonhoeffer asserts that "to be conformed to the one who has become human—that is what being really human means" (DBW 6, 81; E 93–94). The central message of *Ethics* is a call to Christian life in freedom and realistic responsibility to the new humanity in Christ, to find and work out this human identity in participation with the incarnated, crucified, and risen one. Consequently, the church is not merely a religious society but represents this new humanity in embryo;[6] it is the place which calls the world to its true identity: "The church is nothing but a piece of the new humanity, in which Christ has truly taken shape. . . . The church is the new human being who has been incarnated, judged, and brought to new life in Christ" (DBW 6, 84).

Finally, this focus on the incarnation as the source of humanity's and the world's identity also persists in Bonhoeffer's last thoughts, when he contemplates the idea of a this-worldly or religionless Christianity. With this provocative concept, Bonhoeffer more clearly articulates the hermeneutic project of applying the triadic dynamic of the new humanity in Christ (incarnated, judged, resurrected) to the world. For Bonhoeffer, Christ, as the new human being, is the ultimate center of reality from whom the penultimate world derives its worth. Therefore, participating in the new humanity in Christ does not mean escaping the world but, following God's incarnational pattern itself, living in and for it. Consequently, Christianity "is not about the world beyond but all about this world, as it is created, preserved, and renewed. What transcends this world in the gospel wants to be for this world; I don't mean this in the anthropocentric sense of liberal, mystical, pietistic or ethical theologies, but in the biblical sense of incarnation, crucifixion, and resurrection in Christ" (DBW 8, 415). Participation in the new humanity of Christ enables one to be truly human in this life and the life to come. With reference to the contemporary discussion concerning transcendence in Continental philosophy, it is significant that Bonhoeffer regards transcendence as an essential source of our humanity and that he defines this experience of transcendence—as we will see later on—Christologically as a mode of being truly human in service of one's neighbor. Jesus's "being-there-for-others is the experience of transcendence" that determines our true humanity and thus the only authentic way of being Christian (DBW 8, 558).

So far we have established the identity of the human as Bonhoeffer's focus, but is it also Heidegger's? Heidegger himself uses the *Letter on Humanism* to explain the purpose of his philosophy in terms of a new humanism, a new understanding of human identity and purpose that is free from the Platonic metaphysical distortions of earlier humanisms.[7] The motifs of the *Letter* already occur in essence in his 1935 lecture, published as *Introduction to Metaphysics,* in which Heidegger seeks to retrieve from pre-Platonic philosophy the human essence as relation to Being and concludes that "man should be understood, within the question of being, as *the* site which being requires in order to disclose itself."[8] Let us turn for a moment to the crucial passage from Heidegger's *Humanismusbrief,* in which he links the theme of humanism to his central philosophical concern about the question of being (1946–47). Jean Beaufret's question was how Heidegger's focus on ontology to the exclusion of anthropology and his subordination of human being to Being still allow us to speak about humanism.[9] Heidegger claims that the essence of our humanity can be derived not from self-analysis, as classical humanism was wont to do, but from our relation to Being.[10] True to his earlier analysis of language, Heidegger insists that attunement to Being's address leads us to the essence of our humanity:

> But in the claim [of Being] upon man, in the attempt to make man ready for this claim, is there not implied a concern about man? Where else does "care" tend but in the direction of bringing man back to his essence? What else does that I turn betoken but that man (home) become human (humanus)? Thus *humanitas* really does remain the concern of such thinking. For this is humanism: meditating and caring, that man be human and not unhumane, "inhuman," that is, outside his essence. But in what does the humanity of man consist? It lies in his essence.[11]

Heidegger intuits the understandable anxiety which motivates Beaufret's question posed in postwar and post-Holocaust Europe. He answers that to subordinate human being to Being (*Sein*) itself does not deny the basic humanist idea that "man become free for his humanity and find his worth in it."[12] Heidegger defines humanism as "meditating and caring that man be human and not inhumane," a goal whose pursuit hinges on our definition of "freedom" and "the nature of man."[13] Indeed, Heidegger rejects traditional humanisms, not because he dismisses their concern for human dignity, but because they "still do not realize the proper dignity of man. . . . Humanism is opposed [in the thinking of *Being and Time*] because it does not set the *humanitas* high enough."[14]

Heidegger upholds traditional humanism insofar as he accords human being the unique role as the site of transcendence.[15] Thinking, insofar as it traces the eventing of Being (*Sein*), partakes of transcendence because we think something that is greater than ourselves and partake in something beyond our control. This also means, however, that unlike traditional humanism, Heidegger's post-metaphysical subjectivity is not the measure of all things—Being is.[16] Only insofar as he rejects the traditional humanist definition of human beings as rational animals is he anti-humanist. He claims, at least, to pursue a different human vocation: to think Being is to experience true human identity. Subjectivity in this neo-humanism is determined by our relation to Being. Human being as essentially open to Being, as "standing in the lighting of Being," Heidegger calls the "ek-sistence of man."[17] Here lies the "ground of possibility not only of reason, *ratio*, but also that in which the essence of man preserves the source that determines him."[18]

Heidegger explains that fallenness in *Being and Time* referred to man's forgetfulness to understand his identity in relation to Being. Indeed, "what is essential is not Man but Being."[19] This transcendent, open relation to Being is not, Heidegger insists, atheism but, on the contrary, a seeking to establish a proper ontological footing from which any subsequent relationships of man, including that to God, may be ordered. Only "from the truth of Being can the essence of the holy be thought or said what the word 'God' is to signify."[20] Apparently Heidegger believes that adequate thinking about God requires a prior understanding of human identity as dwelling truthfully in Being, as guarding being. This role is not a loss of human dignity, but the true essence of who we are. We are not Masters over existents but the shepherds of Being, a high vocation bestowed on us by Being itself.[21]

Having established that both Bonhoeffer and Heidegger are intensely concerned with the essence of our humanity, with the question of who we are as human beings, we can now move to answer the first proposed question: how much influence did Heidegger have on the development of Bonhoeffer's theology?

The Influence of Heidegger's Philosophy on Bonhoeffer

The degree of Bonhoeffer's familiarity with Heidegger's work and the depth of its influence on the young theologian is difficult to assess. It has become customary in this context to invoke Bonhoeffer's habilitation supervisor Wilhelm Lütgert's typecasting of him as a "Heidegger man,"[22] but other than the documented engagement of Heidegger in *Act and Being*, we have little evidence that Heidegger's influence extended beyond serving as a useful philosophical justification to conjoin human reflection to action and to confirm Bonhoeffer's own incarnational instinct that Christian theology must ever be historically conscious. Both of these tendencies, however, are already present in Bonhoeffer's dissertation *Sanctorum Communio*, wherefore we cannot say with any certainty that Heidegger, unlike Karl Barth, radically changed Bonhoeffer's thinking. We find references to Heidegger in many of Bonhoeffer's works but upon closer inspection all of them, except for two, turn out to be, at best, ancillary rather than central, and they don't go beyond Bonhoeffer's critique of Heidegger's philosophy in *Act and Being* and its summary in his inaugural lecture "The Question Concerning Man."

In this lecture, Bonhoeffer appreciates Heidegger's notion of facticity and the correlation of existence and reflection, but criticizes Heidegger's too positive estimations of *Daseinsstrukturen* (existential structures), of man as a site for truth.[23] In short, *Act and Being* and the inaugural lecture provide the only sustained textual evidence concerning Heidegger's influence on Bonhoeffer's thinking. The following analysis will thus draw mainly from *Act and Being* and use the inaugural lecture as supporting evidence. In keeping with our initial focus, we will try to show that while Bonhoeffer shares with Heidegger the desire to overcome dualistic views of human identity and self-knowledge, he also judges Heidegger's hermeneutic ontology (because of its atheistic contours) ultimately to be of little use for his own theological project. We will first establish what this project was and then proceed to Bonhoeffer's use and criticism of Heidegger in achieving his goal.

BONHOEFFER'S PROJECT

Bonhoeffer's main concern, which connects the habilitation *Act and Being* (AS) with his doctoral dissertation *Sanctorum Communio* (SC), is to articulate Christian existence as an ecclesial mode of human life.[24] This link derives from the abiding theological interest Bonhoeffer established in SC, namely that true, authentic human identity derives from being in Christ and that Christ exists in this world as the church which is "Christ existing as community." Hence the reappearance of this thesis from SC in *Act and Being* that "God reveals himself in the church as Person. The church community is the final revelation of God as 'Christ existing as the church,' prescribed for the last days of the world until the return of Christ" (DBW 2, 108).

The main issue of AS is a problem which continues to inform contemporary debates in philosophical theology, namely how we can have knowledge of God and talk about him objectively without falling either into idolatry by objectifying God on the one hand or into apophatic obscurantism by refusing to say anything definite about him on the other. Bonhoeffer puts the problem this way:

> It is a question of the "objectivity" of the concept of God and an adequate concept of cognition, the issue of determining the relationship between "the being of God," and the mental act which grasps that being. In other words, one has to interpret theologically, what "the being of God in revelation" means and how it is known, how faith as act and revelation of being relate one to another, and, correspondingly, how human beings will be situated in the light of revelation. (DBW 2, 22–23; AB 27–28)

Bonhoeffer begins his philosophical analysis of this act-being problematic with Kant because he regards him as the watershed between either loss of transcendence or loss of immanence. Kant himself, Bonhoeffer argues, recognized that self-reflection implies a threshold or barrier of transcendence, an absolute limit to self-understanding. In self-reflection, thought experiences the aporia that it is impossible to understand oneself in the process of reflection. On the one hand, the desire to understand ourselves is deeply ingrained in human reason as an integral part of our humanity. It is natural for us to think about this already existing self. On the other hand, however, the very attempt to grasp who we are through reason obliterates the limit presented by the objective, empirical givenness of the self whose resistance to probing constitutes precisely the transcendent quality that marks objective knowledge.

Bonhoeffer outlines two possible responses to this aporia. The first option is to acknowledge this self-limitation and hence remain silent before the mystery of otherness or transcendence, of something greater which determines it. The second option is that thought can succumb to the temptation of explaining this threshold of transcendence, and thus effectively abolish it as the threshold to true self-understanding, which always requires transcendent limit.[25] Kant himself, Bonhoeffer believes, followed the first option, which meant that human reason cannot really say anything definitive about either self or God. Postmodern movements of ethical transcendence championed by Levinas, and of deconstruction, as advanced by Derrida, follow this Kantian self-limitation of reason. Although Bonhoeffer was obviously unfamiliar with postmodern philosophy and its religious turn, his notion of "transcendentalism" captures their basic sentiments.

Idealism, and its counterpart materialism, by contrast, follow the opposite route and succumb to the temptation of totalizing explanations. The materialist variant of Marxism, for example, rejects the notion of transcendence altogether. Idealism, on the other hand, severs human reflection from ontology to achieve the possibility of self-understanding based on consciousness alone. Even when idealist philosophy tries with Hegel to reconnect with the historical conditioning of mental activity, it remains rather inhumanly idealist in its attempt at complete self-comprehension. Even Hegel, claims Bonhoeffer, "writes a philosophy of angels but not of human existence (Dasein)" (DBW 2, 36). Even in Hegel, the basic movement of idealism persists to draw the world into the subject and to judge it always ultimately "in relation to myself." Emmanuel Levinas has described this tendency of self-understanding as egology, which makes impossible genuine otherness, either of being as such or of another human being.[26] Karl Barth raised this objection with respect to God and his self-revelation against idealism in all its forms. God must remain other in his substantive, objective (not objectivist) reality, lest the divine too be already implicitly comprehensible, and even his incomprehensibility remain defined by the transcendental categories of the reflective subject.

Yet radical transcendentalism, with its refusal to say anything substantive about either God or the human self, does not fare much better in Bonhoeffer's eyes. On the one hand, the followers of Kant's transcendental barrier to self-understanding are correct in wanting to keep human self-knowledge and knowledge about God resolutely in the structure of "in-relation-to" the transcendent. On the other hand, however, this laudable desire for the transcendent goes too far in its fear of ontology by disallowing *any* objective statements about the nature of transcendence, thereby implying its own *dogmatic* refusal of self-knowledge. In what sounds like a summary of Derrida and the fear of positive theological statements in much current discussion about God after metaphysics, Bonhoeffer explains that in this "transcendentalism," "the concept of God, as the basis of possibility for Dasein and thinking, remains nonobjective. Never can transcendental thinking pronounce 'God is,' for that would be reifying, making finite, dogmatizing. . . . Thus God always remains at the back of human beings, no matter which way human beings may turn" (DBW 2, 38).

Bonhoeffer seeks, instead, a way to turn toward God for self-understanding and identity, while preserving His freedom and otherness, yet without sacrificing substantive content concerning His character. *Act and Being* addresses this problem on the basis of his conclusion reached in his dissertation, SC: for an incarnational Christology, revelation of God requires participation in God as community to establish an ecclesiologically grounded epistemology. Bonhoeffer does not primarily respond to general problems of epistemology but seeks to establish a theologically adequate way of knowing for the Christian faith, thereby offering an implicit evaluation of the relation between philosophy and theology. Bonhoeffer never wavers from his conviction that only theology, as the unfolding of God's self-revelation, albeit with the help of philosophy, provides truly human self-understanding and identity.

At least his academic writings clearly revolve around this focus on identity and self-understanding. When Bonhoeffer sums up his habilitation AS in his inaugural university lecture, the title of this lecture reveals the main thrust of his thinking: "The Question Concerning the Human Being in Contemporary Philosophy and Theology" (DBW 10, 357–78). Bonhoeffer's overall question, which ties his early works together, is a theologically adequate approach to human self-understanding. SC asks what the new humanity in Christ looks like as the church, whereas AS pursues a theological conception of ontology in order to arrive at an ecclesial epistemology in which the objective and subjective poles of God's revelation find equal recognition.

HEIDEGGER AS RESOURCE FOR BONHOEFFER

Once he has identified the philosophical problem of a holistic understanding of human self-knowledge, Bonhoeffer looks particularly to Heidegger's philosophy to help him unite an existential understanding of knowing as participation in reality and the act of reflectively unfolding this being. Yet even here, Bonhoeffer translates Heidegger into prior theological categories. Within his reworking of theological conceptions received from Protestant theology, Bonhoeffer seeks to unite the *actus directus,* that is, faith as participation in Christ, and its reflective understanding in a secondary *actus reflexus,* which constitutes theology and doctrine.[27] In other words, Bonhoeffer seeks to define the self-understanding of the Christian faith through a mode of knowing which welds together the immanence of ontological participation with the transcendence necessary to grant objectivity to this participation and our reflective understanding of it. Philosophically, he tries to steer a middle course between idealism, materialism, and transcendentalism,[28] a middle path determined by the incarnation as that singular event in which transcendence and immanence dwell in unity.

The central question becomes, "How can we know God and speak about God without objectifying him, and how can Christian reflection fully acknowledge the existential, ontological aspect of human knowledge without having to give up definite theological statements about God?" Idealism obliterated otherness by holding that only same can understand same.[29] Transcendentalism, on the other hand, emphasizes difference. To maintain difference with respect to God and others is important, but radical difference abolishes the idea of content and its interpretive limits: how can we know "what" we are thinking and talking about? Pure difference allows no communication, yet God's self-revelation is all about communicating himself to humanity. Moreover, how do we reflect on this self-communication by God without objectifying and distorting it? And if we can't do this, how can we ever say we know God? And if we cannot have access to God's word about reality, how can we have genuine, objective self-knowledge?

Bonhoeffer tackles this problem with the help of Heidegger, but his solution, as we shall see, goes beyond Heidegger by employing the relational categories of ethical transcendence which Levinas has since re-introduced into post-Heideggerian philosophy. Bonhoeffer finds in Heidegger the necessary purgation of any residual idealism from phenomenology and a congenial emphasis on the ontological as that which always precedes and hence transcends us. Cartesian and idealist attempts to get from the isolated mind back into reality are rejected by Heidegger as the presumption to separate reflection from ontological determination. Heidegger manages to hold being and act together: "Being is essentially Dasein; Dasein, however, is mind in its historicity. . . . Dasein understands itself in its existence as mind. Dasein is, however, the existence of man in historicity, in the respective decisions, which have already been made." And so Heidegger succeeds where others have failed:

> From the perspective of the problem of act and being, it would seem that here a genuine coordination of the two has been reached. The priority of being turned out to be the priority of mind-being in which the mind does not annihilate being but "is" and "understands" it. The solution, though reminiscent of Hegel, is fundamentally different from Hegel's theory, in that being is Dasein, "being in the world," existing in temporality. Thus, pure consciousness in Husserl's sense does not dominate; neither does the material a priori in Scheler's sense. Heidegger has succeeded in forcing together act and being in the concept of Dasein. (AB 71; DBW 2, 65)

Heidegger, in other words, comes closest among Bonhoeffer's philosophical interlocutors to realizing the ancient theological insight that being precedes reflection without sacrificing the transcendence of the human spirit. Bonhoeffer appreciates Heidegger's depiction of humanity as temporal-historical. Human understanding exists only as being in time. Self-knowledge has to unfold interpretively within human historicity, culture, and tradition. Heidegger's description of human existence avoids the reification of the human on the one hand or subjectivism on the other. Yet, despite its success in holding thinking and being together, Bonhoeffer deems Heidegger's ontology ultimately unsuitable for a genuinely theological conception of human knowledge.

BONHOEFFER'S CRITICISM OF HEIDEGGER

True enough, in Heidegger's hermeneutic phenomenology, human reflection remains tethered to ontology, firmly grounded in existence. Heidegger avoids either a Cartesian conception of human being as "free floating in timeless space" or the materialist notion of human being as mere object (*Vorhandenes*) (DBW 10, 363). Human being is neither a thing, since it reflects on its own existence, nor merely a disembodied mind, since this reflection takes place within concrete historical situations. Dasein doesn't produce its world but finds itself always already in the world. Both realism and idealism thus attain a certain legitimation in Heidegger (DBW 2, 64).

But, as Charles Marsh already pointed out, Bonhoeffer raises two objections to Heidegger's existential analytic of Dasein, namely the intrinsic potentiality of man to understand himself and Heidegger's failure to provide a theologically viable holistic understanding of the human self.[30]

Bonhoeffer believes that Heidegger's success in overcoming the dualism of act and being is only partial, because his Dasein can heed the call of conscience (later the voice of Being) and tear itself away from inauthentic existence to a more authentic being toward death. By realizing his potential toward authenticity and understanding his life within the hermeneutical circle of being toward death, he

> overcomes its liminal character, does not reach toward the end but toward completion, to the entirety of his Dasein. Human being masters the world, he understands himself out of himself; his being in the world has no real meaning for his actual self-understanding. In the final analysis the question about man is answered once again by man himself.... [Heidegger's] fallenness in the world is eventually merely a passage way to the spirit's finding himself.[31]

In what is probably an unconscious but is nonetheless an ironic reversal of Heidegger's own statement that theology cannot philosophize because it does not take seriously the question why is there something rather than nothing,[32] Bonhoeffer asserts that the basic openness of Heidegger's Dasein toward self-understanding shows that *his* question of human being "possesses no ultimate seriousness" (DBW 10, 366). For all his insight, Heidegger falls short, in other words, of real transcendence, of the exteriority Bonhoeffer deems necessary for genuine self-understanding.

Bonhoeffer's second objection to Heidegger, what Marsh calls the problem of the self's continuity, flows from the first. As Marsh points out, Bonhoeffer finds in Heidegger the same problem as in the early Barth: the self remains split between its reflective insight concerning its authentic identity (the new self of faith in Barth, and the authentic being toward death in Heidegger) and its ongoing identity in daily life. While not at all denying Marsh's analysis, we can better understand the hermeneutical significance of this problem when we employ Bonhoeffer's own description of the self's continuity as holistic existence. Bonhoeffer chooses the terms "*Ganzheit des Daseins*" and "*Einheit des Ich*" (DBW 10, 365; DBW 2, 118). What emerges on this reading is that Bonhoeffer's critique of Heidegger anticipates Levinas's accusation of hermeneutics as remaining still a totality, even if it is an open totality.[33]

We must remind ourselves that self-understanding, who we are as human beings, is a central concern of Bonhoeffer. He undertakes the holistic correlation of *Dasein* and *Wiesein*, of being and knowing, in the service of "a theological doctrine of human self-understanding" (DBW 2, 132). Bonhoeffer understands Heidegger's *Being and Time* as a congenial attempt to understand human existence, as another project of self-knowledge. Yet for Bonhoeffer, true self-knowledge requires two things: real or radical exteriority to guarantee objective knowledge, and a whole in relation to which the part, each individual existence, gains its meaning. Access to this whole from which each individual and his actions gain meaning has to be ontological, and reflection on its content and substantive shape has to balance immanence and transcendence. Self-knowledge arises from our participation in ontological structures—otherwise it would not pertain to our embodied existence. Yet this reflection cannot be reduced to the flux of being if there is to be continuity of identity within history. An additional problem is the kind of transcendence required to establish a truly human self. If we are persons in relation, our identity must be anchored not only by exteriority but by another who knows who I am. As Bonhoeffer had outlined earlier, the real transcendent barrier, and hence the threshold to exteriority, is found in the relational encounter, in social categories of knowing.

However, in the first instance, Bonhoeffer's criticism of Heidegger is a hermeneutical one. The problem is not that Heidegger argues for a hermeneutical circle, but that this circle remains closed to genuine transcendence by remaining in the same self-reliant mode which had already characterized idealist self-understanding. The whole of Heidegger's hermeneutic circle by which he can correlate act and being is humanity's being toward death. Within this trajectory, humanity alone is transcendent or ek-static in its openness to Being. This transcendence places within human reach the possibility of self-understanding *as* being toward death. For Bonhoeffer, Heidegger's analytic of Dasein thus represents yet another Pelagian attempt of the self to understand itself out of itself. In the end, even Heidegger does not have an absolute barrier to human self-understanding and therefore lacks real transcendence. "The phenomenological method," concludes Bonhoeffer, "proceeds within human existence; for they must already bear within themselves the potentialities of perceiving being, or, in this case, knowledge of revelation and 'discover' being in the manner of something existing, since they already know in principle what being is" (AB 107; DBW 2, 103).

It is important to grasp fully Bonhoeffer's criticism of Heidegger, for his challenge is philosophical *as well as* theological, and cannot simply be dismissed by returning to Heidegger's claim that theology is an ontic discipline dependent on philosophical ontology. Bonhoeffer argues that genuine self-understanding as such requires actual exteriority from which the existence of a person is addressed as a whole. Because they too proceed from the familiar and from a preconceived understanding of being, not even the social categories of I and thou can offer this transcendence (DBW 2, 102). Only God who stands above even the other provides the ultimate limit of human understanding. Divine revelation, approaching from utter exteriority, from the one who provides a transcendent and holistic view of ourselves is thus necessary for genuine self-understanding.

That this revelation must occur within ontology, to make any sense to human beings, is the problem of revelation (DBW 2, 102). Revelation requires communication within ontology without losing its otherness; revelation, to remain such, must not become mastered by objectifying human discourse. This, according to Bonhoeffer, is the demand of any real ontology: "Only here *real* ontology comes into its own by determining the 'being in' in such a way that cognition, which already finds itself within being, is ever again relativized before objectified existence, so that it can never be forced to be at its disposal" (DBW 2, 105). Revelation can never mean something that is already in any way at our disposal or it would nullify genuine transcendence, true exteriority, and hence genuine objectivity for human self-understanding: "Whether understood transcendentally or phenomenologically and ontologically, revelation seen this way does not lead to contact with the existence of human beings."

Revelation about who we are has to come from outside to address human existence as a whole, but it must also be able to affect all of human existence, which it can only do as a mode of being (DBW 2, 101–102).

Heidegger's philosophy, however, fails to fulfill these demands. He does in fact posit a hermeneutical whole, namely authentic being toward death. Bonhoeffer argues, however, that grasping this possibility does not confront man with a true limit of his existence but rather gives him access "to its completion, to the unity [*Ganzheit*] of human existence [*des Daseins*]" (DBW 10, 365). One could state here in fairness to Heidegger that he tries to open up this conception with his later departure from hermeneutics in his emphasis on Being itself after the turn. Yet even here Bonhoeffer's objection that Heidegger does not posit radical transcendence holds, if Bonhoeffer is correct in anticipating Levinas's argument that human transcendence occurs only in personal and social, that is, in ethical, categories.

Already in *Act and Being,* and long before Levinas, Bonhoeffer levels this important hermeneutical argument against Heidegger: he can only answer the question of self-understanding and achieve the unity of act and being because he posits a finite world, closed in on itself in its atheistic refusal of looking beyond the finite: "Heidegger's philosophy is a consciously atheistic philosophy of finitude. . . . That finitude is viewed as closed in on itself is decisive for the existential analysis of Dasein. This being-closed-in can no longer be separated from finitude" (DBW 2, 66). In other words, Bonhoeffer challenges Heidegger's phenomenological presumption actually to have hit upon the deepest ontological structures of Being. Bonhoeffer implies that Heidegger's hermeneutical cards are stacked, as it were, against theology through the arbitrary closing of the hermeneutic circle by positing being toward death as the greater whole of the hermeneutic circle of self-understanding. Conceptions about God are now viewed from within this enclosed circle, so that even Heidegger's pretensions to open up a space beyond onto-theology for a new conception of God turns out to be merely another form of "conceptual idolatry," as Marion puts it, another stance anterior to God's own coming, another self-made idea of how God should come to mind.[34]

The end result of this conceptual idolatry, which obviously remained unknown to Bonhoeffer, is Heidegger's conception of human being as the herdsman or shepherd of Being, which was already, as Heidegger tells us, the sole purpose of *Being and Time*.[35] Standing in the clearing of Being, straining a listening ear to its voice in language, poetry, and even technology allows glimpses at human self-understanding, but any substantial content concerning the purpose of human life or the nature of God is rejected as metaphysical or onto-theological nostalgia. The later Heidegger shares here with other postmodern prophets of transcendence such as Jacques Derrida and Jean-Luc Marion the notion that true self-understanding and knowledge of God have no real presence in the realm of ontology. Bonhoeffer, however, was one of the first to call this supposed radical openness to Being into question by arguing that its assumed openness turns out, upon closer inspection, to be an arbitrary foreclosure of the hermeneutical circle.

What can we then conclude concerning Heidegger's influence on Bonhoeffer? Already determined to find an expression of the Christian faith on a relational basis, determined by God's revelation, and as holding together ontological participation and reflective unfolding, Bonhoeffer encounters in Heidegger's philosophical framework congenial elements. It is hard to tell whether Bonhoeffer actually learned from Heidegger, or whether he knew from the first reading of *Being and Time* that Heidegger's closed system is philosophically inadequate to arrive at genuine self-understanding, and theologically useless because of its self-enclosed hermeneutical circle. For Heidegger, "Dasein is always already guilty, it can call itself out of the world to itself in conscience, but it always already finds itself as guilty. To regard this always-already-being-in-guilt analogously as mode of being of faith is impossible . . . because faith is not a possibility of human being as such, and therefore also not a being in which existence can already find itself" (DBW 2, 94).

Bonhoeffer's analysis of Heidegger ends with a direct challenge to philosophy's priority over theological reflection on what it means to be human. His theological work is driven by the conviction that the incarnation posits the possibility of being human in a new and liberating way that recognizes the social structure of human self hood and reflection. Philosophy, argues Bonhoeffer, cannot by default, as it were, arrive at true self-knowledge because it does not know radical transcendence. Since it will always be a question of giving priority to either philosophical or theological categories, Bonhoeffer's ultimate position is that, since the incarnation provides the only true model of being human, it also provides the only authentic categories for thinking about human existence. Heidegger has provided him with a coordinating vision of act and being, but this vision fails in the end. It is important to see that this vision fails not simply because it is atheistic and hence offends theological sensibilities. Rather, this vision fails because its atheistic horizon of being toward death offers merely a fragmented human existence. Heidegger cannot reconcile genuine transcendence with a unified human identity. Moreover, while Bonhoeffer appreciates Heidegger's reconciliation of ontology and reflection, and the demand for human authenticity, he also criticizes that in Heidegger's philosophy ontology finally does get swallowed up by reflection, so that the self once again winds up understanding itself out of itself, and hence authenticity remains inauthentic precisely for this reason: it is self-induced and in this individual romantic existential heroism lacks any objective measure of real humanity.

While Bonhoeffer did not know the later Heidegger, his judgment in *Act and Being* allows a fairly certain conjecture as to how he would have reacted both to the notion that humanity's dignity and purpose lies in its role as the herder or shepherd of Being and to Heidegger's continued refusal to say something positive about God. Heidegger's later attempt to think Being more directly, "without regard to the justification of Being through existing things,"[36] essentially confirms Bonhoeffer's judgment that Heidegger's openness will always remain closed to revelation because it insists, despite all assurances to the contrary, on a ready-made definition of openness to Being that continues to reject the Christian God and theology as ontic entities.

Bonhoeffer's Answer to Heidegger: Participatory Ontology

Bonhoeffer, in the end, rejects Heidegger's solution to dualism and subjectivism on philosophical and theological grounds. Heidegger's philosophy, as we have seen, arbitrarily forecloses the hermeneutical circle, whereas Bonhoeffer wants to configure self-understanding and interpretation in relational terms which remain open to an address from God. Nonetheless, Bonhoeffer's Christian ontology shares fundamental elements with Heidegger's analytic of Dasein. Like Heidegger, Bonhoeffer rejected psychology as the deepest layer of self-understanding, based on Luther's insight that "man is psychologically impenetrable. . . . [M]an cannot understand himself out of his own psychic experience" (DBW 2, 98). Both thinkers recognize that the hermeneutics of self-knowledge require a vantage point of unity, a hermeneutic whole in light of which individual existence makes sense. The human mind and self-reflection on its own cannot arrive at such unity. The early Heidegger set this unity artificially as being toward death, but later emphasized more strongly that Being has to be thought as much as possible on its own. Finally, Bonhoeffer's Christian ontology with its revelational emphasis begins where the later Heidegger ended up, namely with the realization that human subjectivity is an inadequate starting point for authentic self-knowledge.

In contrast to the Heidegger of *Being and Time,* however, Bonhoeffer does not first go to existential structures to establish the nature or authenticity of human existence. For him, the only place where such unity is found is outside of human existence in God:

> This unity of human existence is derived solely from the Word of God. This Word allows man to understand himself as existing in Adam or in Christ, as being in the community of Christ, so that the foundation of unity through the Word is identical with the foundation of unity through the being in Adam or in Christ. This too is not merely a datum of experience but is given as revelation to faith. Only in faith does the unity, the "being" of the person become evident. (DBW 2, 99)

Bonhoeffer conjoins act and being while upholding God's otherness in this correlation by defining authentic human existence as "being-in" Christ. To put it more philosophically, Bonhoeffer suggests a participatory ontology based on God's revelation as person, which is experienced and reflected on communally in the church. Bonhoeffer's overarching goal to arrive at a theologically accurate notion of human identity begins with God's self-revelation in Christ through participation in this event. Bonhoeffer's starting point is the incarnation: God in complete freedom entered ontology, being, history, and time in order to tie himself to humanity. In the incarnation, God affirms (becoming human), judges (the cross), and redeems humanity toward its ultimate fulfillment in the eschaton (resurrection).

Christian faith is participation in this incarnational event. Bonhoeffer recovers the dogmatic concept of *fides directa* for his participatory ontology of belief. The idea of *fides directa* guards the relational character of faith as encounter with another person. Like any personal encounter, faith as being-in-relation-to is a conscious act that nonetheless precedes rational reflection. In the context of Bonhoeffer's ecclesially oriented epistemology, this means that faith "rests objectively on the event of revelation in Word and Sacrament; [this] dependence on Christ need not become conscious of itself but is entirely taken up into the event [of faith] itself (*den Aktvollzug selbst*)" (DBW 2, 158). Faith is therefore first of all a mode of existence as participation in God's revelation, a mode of being that is passively received rather than created by faith:

> Faith meets with an existence prior to its act [of reflection], it is suspended from this existence, because it knows itself drawn into a special determination of this existence. This mode of being is not dependent on faith, on the contrary, faith knows this existence's independence from itself.... All depends on this that faith understands itself as not somehow determining or creating [this existence] but precisely as being created and determined by this existence. (DBW 2, 114)

The unity of human existence and hence its continuity lies in Christ, the wholly other in whom each believer participates and hence participates as community (DBW 2, 115). Thus, like Heidegger, Bonhoeffer avoids the dualism of act and being, but unlike Heidegger he succeeds in uniting transcendence and immanence with a genuinely holistic understanding of the self by defining faith as a mode of being in Christ as community out of which the *actus reflexus*, that is, preaching, sacraments, dogma, and theology "as the mind of the church," arise (DBW 2, 127–29).[37] Because Christian existence is being in Christ, who is a particular person and also creator and sustainer of the believer's new existence, "Dasein remains in backward looking reflections and future oriented projections determined by transcendence, it 'is' 'between' transcendence" (DBW 2, 126).

The new human being exists collectively in the Trinitarian pattern of difference in unity as the church. Act and being, in other words, come together in the communal existence of the church. Here participation in God occurs through preaching and the sacraments. God is here concretely present as the person Jesus Christ within every member, each of whom has been drawn into the event of God's self-revelation, that is, not into a propositional assent, but into a relation with Christ through God's grace. Here the entire person in its social relations, in its facticity, in its entire humanity, is addressed and brought into relation with the authentic human being, Christ himself. Any other notion of authenticity, "including the 'authentic existence of Heidegger,' is inauthentic" (DBW 2, 113). Authenticity is only the new humanity in Christ, "the historical human being who knows himself transposed from old into the new humanity, who is what he is through membership in the new humanity, as new person created by Christ, which 'exists' only in its enacted relation to Christ, and whose 'being-in-relation-to-Christ' is grounded in his being-in Christ, in the [church] community, so that act is 'taken up' into being just as in turn being is not without act. Personhood as act-being synthesis is always both in one, *individual* and *humanity*" (DBW 2, 117).

Incarnational Christology and faith as participation in this event thus makes possible what current post-metaphysical discussions about God cannot envision: the correlation of identity and difference. Because faith is being in Christ, the inauthenticity or untruth of human being is drawn into relation with the divine-human person who is truth: "because here untruth is placed into truth, therefore the disproportionate is perceived through the disproportionate" (DBW 2, 133). In Christ, the new human being finds all that which Heidegger's philosophy had lacked. True humanity is not the guardian of an impersonal Being with questionable ethical content but rather exists in relation to the definite word of life, who gives a definite image and purpose of human being without the relieving of the interpretive task to work out this image in particular cultural scenarios. The definite word of Christ himself as person and his message of neighborly love remains the definite "meaning, the clear word, but not as if this 'given' meaning would ultimately still allow the possibility of autonomous self-understanding. But in this means of 'meaning' the unequal reveals himself to the unequal, Christ the crucified and risen to the human being who lives to himself. It is in being known by God that human beings know God. But to be known by God means to become a new human being" (DBW 2, 133). Not as the Shepherd of Being but as being in the Shepherd does human being stand open to the possibility of true self-understanding.

Bonhoeffer's incarnational Christology and its participatory ontology offer important insights for contemporary discussions about God and Christianity within continental philosophy. We will end by briefly sketching out the most important contributions Bonhoeffer can make.

Bonhoeffer's Contribution to Post-Heideggerian Thinking about God

In 1954, Heidegger told a circle of evangelical theologians, "Philosophy only conducts thinking, of which man is capable by himself; where he is addressed by revelation, such thinking stops." With the arrival of revelation, so Heidegger, the thinker may as well "close up his workshop."[38] Bonhoeffer challenges this view on two counts. We have already seen that Bonhoeffer repudiates any neutral phenomenology and stresses the participatory nature of human knowing, what Michael Polanyi has called the indwelling of tacit assumptions, or what has become known in hermeneutic philosophy as the axiom that all understanding proceeds from a kind of faith. Hence, Bonhoeffer's theology links up with current understandings of hermeneutics as formulated, for example, by Richard Kearney, against pure events, whether in the service of theology (Marion) or of scientific phenomenology (Janicaud): "Whereas I would argue that there is no pure phenomenon as such, that appearing—no matter how iconic or saturated it may be—always already involves an interpretation of some kind."[39]

Bonhoeffer also challenges Heidegger's equation of revelation with reification of thought. As we shall see below, Bonhoeffer counters Heidegger's separation of theology and philosophy by stating the existence of all thought within the Logos of God. The divine Logos is always already before and hence in such philosophical thinking: No Christ, no workshop. On the basis of his Christological ontology, Bonhoeffer's interpretation of human existence addresses a number of important prejudices which continue to cloud the dialogue between theology and post-Heideggerian philosophy. These issues are, in the order of importance: the equation of traditional Christian theology with metaphysics and its consequent denunciation as onto-theology, the fear of conceptual idolatry in objectifying divine and human others in the name of ethics, and the consequent desire for radical hermeneutics or unconditional hospitality in the name of peace. We can only briefly deal with each in turn.

Bonhoeffer's incarnational Christology should effectively dispel the common prejudice that equates Christian theology with metaphysical onto-theology. No lesser philosopher than Heidegger himself started this misunderstanding. Heidegger argued in *Introduction to Metaphysics* that Christianity's Logos doctrine is another form of objectifying thinking which obfuscates the original Greek concept of logos as "gathering." Nothing less is at stake for Heidegger in this question than the very essence of what it means to be human. Metaphysics, he argues, including the Christian Logos concept, has obscured the openness of this question with the distorting, objectifying lens of whatness. Instead, Heidegger contends, logos should be understood with the early Greeks as "the original collecting collectedness which is in itself permanently dominant."[40] This sense of logos as original gathering and its importance for a historical understanding should reshape, according to Heidegger, the question about the nature of human being from "what is man" to "*who* is man."[41] Heidegger's entire project pursues the relation between thinking and being in the name of our true humanity. Against the Western tendency to define humanity as rational animal, he sets the need for ontology—not in order to collapse thinking into being, that "thinking and being are the same," but to find the "reciprocal bond between apprehension and being."

This is the very context of Bonhoeffer's theological efforts too, but how different the response! Bonhoeffer, equally opposed to objectifying definitions of our humanity,[42] believes that true humanity and Heidegger's "reciprocal bond between apprehension and being" is found precisely in the Christian definition of Logos that Heidegger suspects of onto-theological collusion with Platonism. Bonhoeffer rejects metaphysics in the name of Christ because any area of human being metaphysics claims for itself is already occupied "*by someone else, namely by Christ*" (DBW 2, 54).

Bonhoeffer's understanding of Christ as the center of reality, toward whom all history moves and in whom all things are connected, not only fulfills Heidegger's demand to define logos as "collecting collectedness," but actually endows it with substantive ethical features.[43]

Contrary to any metaphysical objectification of human being, Bonhoeffer's understanding of Christ as Logos offers a Dasein with flesh and blood, truth we can participate in but not possess, *Mitsein* at the heart of being rather than as camouflage for philosophical piety,[44] and a definite ethical ontological structure of human existence as freedom in being-for-others. Which belief, which piety offers a more human self-understanding? As Bonhoeffer has shown us, this question cannot be answered abstractly, but must be enacted in a Christian philosophy operating out of the greatest mystery of being in the history of thinking.

Secondly, Bonhoeffer's participatory ontology frees post-metaphysical thinking about God from the fear of idolatry. Especially, the ethically motivated religious phenomenology of Levinas, which has greatly influenced other thinkers such as Jean Luc Marion and Jacques Derrida, is marked by the fear of ontology as idolatry. Levinas is right, of course, as Bonhoeffer had also conceded to Barth: only personal transcendence absolutely limits human thought and so protects otherness. Barth had rightly urged divine transcendence, and correctly stressed the "non-objectivity of God" (DBW 2, 89). But his ultimate refusal to grant God any *real* ontological presence enforces a dialectical Christian existence, a fragmented dualism between two spheres of existence, hence Barth's relentless criticism of religion as cultic action and his ultimately non-sacramental theology. For Barth (the Barth whom Bonhoeffer knew), God is ever arriving, but never the God who actually is.[45]

Similarly for Levinas too, ethical transcendence may protect otherness from conceptual mastery, but it also renders communion with the human other impossible. Bonhoeffer addresses this problem in reviewing the theologians Gogarten and Knittermeyer, who already proffered the radical personal transcendence of personal encounter. Like Levinas, these theologians already relocated the encounter of transcendence from the eternal divine into the concrete historical proximity of the other's face. Bonhoeffer's concern about this position anticipates Levinas's hyperbolic construct of ethical substitution. He warns that "here the thou is absolutized. Should it turn out, however, that here the claim of the self's absolute sovereignty is only transferred to the thou, and not Him who is above both and above the absolute, we seem not only merely to steer towards an ethicizing understanding of the gospel but also to lose clarity concerning definite concepts of history and theology, and that means we lose sight of revelation" (DBW 2, 81).

Bonhoeffer's Christian ontology avoids absolutizing of the other and so allows intersubjective relation without trauma. Christian ontology allows for a self-identity in which difference relates to difference. In contrast to Levinas, Bonhoeffer's encounter with the other is no longer a traumatic barrier of difference, but communion with the divine other through the mediation of Christ, in whom "the unequal reveals himself to the unequal, Christ the crucified and risen one to the human person" (DBW 2, 133).

God gives himself through Christ to the church as the new humanity, without losing his otherness or transcendence. In him we also relate to every other member of the community and to humanity as a whole. This existence, however, is not merely the traumatic imposition of an ethical law, but derives from an actual participation in the very Logos who created the universe, and defined and affirmed humanity by becoming human. Christologically configured, Levinas's desired asymmetrical relation, the "relation without relation," becomes actual personal relation whose asymmetry is contoured by Christ as being-for-the-other.

Finally, Bonhoeffer's incarnational Christology speaks to the hermeneutical dispute in post-Heideggerian God talk which pits radical or deconstructionist hermeneutics against more moderate interpretations of Christian belief.

Following Levinas, continental philosophy has emphasized difference, and has often rejected hermeneutics as crypto-totalitarianism which seeks to assimilate difference into sameness in order to understand better and ultimately, to understand oneself. As Derrida had formulated it in his first official encounter with Gadamer, hermeneutics pursues "context-related coherence,"[46] on the basis of a common experience which could be expanded or translated in dialogue with others. Derrida, by contrast, favors the breach, which he later, as he becomes increasingly Levinasian in his thinking, grounds in the other "who speaks in us" before all interpretation.[47] John Caputo once interpreted deconstruction as "that passion of non-knowledge and structural blindness," which "is the most salutary form knowledge can take."[48] For Bonhoeffer, by contrast, structural blindness cannot pass as hermeneutic humility but constitutes irresponsible atheism which closes its eyes to the incarnational good news that genuine being, that true ontology and hence our humanity, is determined by Christ as suffering-with-the-world.

Bonhoeffer's incarnational ontology, in other words, lays to rest the fear of presence as objectification which informs, in the wake of Heidegger, Derridean thought in its manifestations as logocentrism and its later, Levinasian, overtones upholding the ethical notions of hospitality and justice as messianic, constructs which, as Bonhoeffer puts it disapprovingly with reference to Barth, never are but are ever arriving.[49]

Bonhoeffer shares with Heidegger and his postmodern descendants the dislike for a metaphysical conception of God, but unlike them, he does not find the solution in a denial of doctrine, but in a denial of *wrong* doctrine. For Bonhoeffer, a post-metaphysical conception of God cannot be derived from the rejection of substantial doctrines sanctioned by politically correct, and hence vacuous, versions of negative theology, but can be derived solely from a properly conceived Christology. God cannot ever be encountered abstractly as an object (here Heidegger is right), nor should he be relegated into the unspeakable difference, but in Christ, God is there *for me,* act and being come together: "The being *there* for you and the being there *for you* come together. The presence of Christ as the pro me is his real being-for-me" (DBW 12, 296). Bonhoeffer, unlike some postmodern champions of God's absence, recognizes that the human desire for identity is God-given, and that such identity requires full presence. Hence he takes seriously God's designation of Emmanuel, the promise to "be with" his creation in the new covenant. For Bonhoeffer, this presence is realized within the church in the sacraments of preaching, the Eucharist, and baptism (DBW 12, 297).

Bonhoeffer thus speaks to a "Eucharistic" trend in continental philosophy. Thinkers like Jean-Luc Marion and Richard Kearney are exploring a eucharistic hermeneutic, or what Kearney also approximates with his concept of a fourth eschatological reduction, which returns us from "meta-physics to ana-physics, that is, back to the most concretely enfleshed phenomenon of the *prosopon*,"—in short to oneself-as-another.[50] This is Kearney's eucharistic version of his earlier belief that we enable God to be God when we incarnate him by helping the least of these, when we offer "the Eucharist in a morsel of Madeleine. The Kingdom in a cup of cold water."[51]

Bonhoeffer's Christology agrees with this idea, but there is no need for a new eschatology after God—unless it is as re-articulation of the ancient Christian humanist notion that in the incarnate God-man we are connected to humanity in the ontological structure of being-for-the-other. Because of God's incarnation, transcendence as such is structured ontologically as being-there-for-the-other. This is actual "experience of transcendence," and faith is "participation (*Teilnehmen*) in this being of Jesus (becoming human, cross and resurrection)" (DBW 8, 558). God's incarnation in Jesus and his death for the reconciliation of creation to God means that experiencing the divine is not some vague religious notion but is, instead, "non-religious" precisely because "our relation to God is not a 'religious one,' to a conceivable highest, almighty, supreme being—this is not genuine transcendence—, but our relation to God is a new life in 'existing-for-others,' as participation in this being (*Sein*) of Jesus. Not infinite, unreachable tasks but the respective, concrete neighbour is the transcendent" (DBW 8, 558).

Yet even within this ontological structure, Bonhoeffer never gives up the essentially hermeneutic nature of every human endeavor. Although Bonhoeffer assumes the unity of all reality in Christ as the divine Logos, he never forgets that even in the unity of the Logos, we exist in the eschatological tension of ultimate and penultimate. God's ultimate Word in Christ that we exist for the other, that we are oneself only through another, applies first of all to the indwelling of Christ, whose presence to believers defines the nature of authentic humanity in accordance with his character and redemptive action. It is precisely because of the *real presence* of God's self-revelation in the sacrament as "brother among brothers," but also as the new humanity, that participation in this presence, which is essentially "being-for-human-being," impresses his cruciform shape on the participant. Bonhoeffer makes clear that this statement is not "psychological, but theologically ontological" (DBW 12, 307).

Yet this presence resides in a fallen world, so that neither history nor nation can serve as final reference for our identity. For this reason, Bonhoeffer even rejects sacramentalism, which may all too easily lead to looking to natural structures and hierarchies as revelation. Bonhoeffer is more radically hermeneutical. "The world," he writes, "is as the natural world no longer a transparent world. Therefore is creation as a whole no longer a sacrament" (DBW 12, 301). Yet there is real divine presence, for "in the midst of the creaturely world God pronounces his full presence—in the sacraments [of the church]" (DBW 12, 304). These, in turn, nourish us not merely with possibility but with the real presence of a new creation. Partaking of the sacraments is an act of renewal through God's presence "as our creator, who makes us through this new creation into new creatures" (DBW 12, 305).

The question of how that can be, is to be changed into the question of whose existence touches us like this. And the answer is: "the historical, crucified, resurrected, and ascended Jesus of Nazareth, the God-Man, but here revealed as brother, and Lord, creature and creator" (DBW 12, 305). The strength of Bonhoeffer's position over against many other post-metaphysical approaches to God is his insistence that God *is* and that human identity *is* in him through ontological structures such as time and narrative but because of the incarnation also *before,* albeit not ever *without,* such structures: "God's '*is*' cannot be separated in any way from its concrete [personal] determination, precisely this has to remain the ontological foundation of theological concepts of being" (DBW 2, 69).

It is because of the incarnation that Bonhoeffer does not avoid the risk of hermeneutics. In his ultimate-penultimate conception of relating this new humanity to culture, he is very clear about the reciprocity between sacred and secular, which find their ultimate unity in Christ, a unity which has to be interpretively realized "ever anew in the lives of human beings" (DBW 6, 44). Human knowing, in other words, has to follow the way of the incarnation, finding the sacred only in the profane even while they are not identical. Bonhoeffer had seen too much misery and oppression in the name of *Seinsgeschick* to be tempted by such a conflation of Christology with ontology.[52] They are, however, unified in Christ, the ultimate word of reconciliation, in whom all things are gathered up, and toward whom all things in history move.

Conclusion

Our comparison of Bonhoeffer with Heidegger under the criterion of human identity shows that the more human, the more radical, the more eucharistic way of speaking about God after metaphysics is to speak about being in the Logos—the Logos who unifies and gathers up all things in himself, and whose incarnation realized God's promise that true being is communion, a being-for, and being-with the other, without trauma, without mysticism of Being. Bonhoeffer offers a sense of identity we indeed possess, not because we comprehend God, but because He knows us and we are his, as the new humanity represented by the church whose very end, as Bonhoeffer knew, "consists precisely in its being-for-the-world" (DBW 6, 407).

The God who entered ontology in the concrete God-man Jesus, has forever taken up genuine, historical human being into the Trinity, not only as a final barrier to all human egology and understanding, but to move us beyond general theories of the good toward helping one another. "Christ was not interested," concludes Bonhoeffer, "like a philosopher in what is 'generally valid,' but in that which serves real concrete human beings. Christ was not concerned about whether 'the maxim of an action' could become 'a principle of universal law' but whether my concrete action now helps my neighbor to be a human being before God. God did not become an idea, a principle, a program, a universally valid belief or a law. God became human. That means that the form of Christ, though it certainly is and remains one and the same, intends to take form in real human beings" (DBW 6, 86).

Our human dignity and identity, contrary to Heidegger's assertion, is not in our calling as shepherds of being. Human identity is not impersonal transcendence, but living out of being in Christ. Objecting every bit as much to onto-theology as Heidegger, and every bit as much against Heidegger's impersonal ontology and immanence of Being as Levinas, Bonhoeffer combines both their aspirations of ontologically rooted transcendence and ethics:

> Who is God? . . . Encounter with Jesus Christ. Experience that here a reversal of all human existence is given to us in that Jesus exists only "for others." This "being-for-others," of Jesus is experience of transcendence as such. Our relation to God is not a "religious one," to the highest, most powerful and best being possible—that is not real transcendence—but our relation to God is a new life as "existing-for-others," in participation [*Teilhabe*] in the being of Christ. Not the eternal, unreachable tasks, but the respectively given and reachable concrete neighbor is the transcendent. (DBW 8, 558)

Nor do we have to defer our identity and knowing who we are in the name of some masochistic passion of non-knowing. "Who am I," asked Bonhoeffer in Tegel prison, and the answer came, "[W]hoever I am, you know me, I am thine" (DBW 8, 514). Some time before this poem, he wrote in his *Ethics:* "to be conformed to the one who has become human—that is what it really means to be human." This is to be cruciform through the presence of him who died for the life of the world. Here alone lies the promise of true humanity both for theology and for philosophy, if either wants to be true to its name.

Notes

1. Not as a new religion canvasses for adherents (that is an image of later times), but God established the reality of the church, the pardoned humanity in Jesus Christ (DBW 1, 97).

2. "The new human being [*Mensch*], who is drawn into the community of God" (DBW 1, 113).

3. Unless otherwise indicated by referencing the English source, all translations from the German are my own.

4. Bonhoeffer also emphasizes this in his summary of his habilitation in his inaugural university lecture in 1930. The title of this summary lecture, "Die Frage nach dem Menschen in der gegenwärtigen Philosophie und Theologie" (The question concerning humanity in contemporary philosophy and theology), also indicates Bonhoeffer's general focus on the question of human identity (DBW 10, 377).

5. Bonhoeffer argues that Christ's nature is to be in the middle of things, of our existence, of history, and of nature, with, obviously, important implications for church-state relations in DBW 12, 307. Especially in the sections titled "positive Christology," Bonhoeffer emphasizes the importance of keeping the mystery of the

incarnation constantly before us, in order to ensure a proper ecclesial understanding of the new humanity as Christians (DBW 12, 340–48).

6. Bonhoeffer writes that the whole reality of the world is in Christ, and hence in the church. Hence "this realm of the church is not something that exists for itself but something which always already stretches far beyond itself, precisely because it is not the arena of a cultic club [*Kultvereins*] which has to fight for its existence in the world but because it is the place which witnesses to the foundation of all reality in Jesus Christ" (DBW 6, 49).

7. Heidegger already had attacked humanism in his Plato lectures of 1931–32, in which he makes Plato's understanding of truth the beginning of humanism as an anthropocentric metaphysic that occludes Being and man's true essence. See Martin Heidegger, "Platons Lehre von der Wahrheit," in *Wegmarken* (Frankfurt am Main: Vittorio Klostermann, 1996), 236–38. We find the same assessment in Heidegger's essay "Zeit des Weltbildes," in *Holzwege*: "It comes as no surprise that humanism arises only where the world turns into a world-picture. But as little as such a world-picture was possible in the great age of Greek philosophy, as little could a humanism manifest itself back then. Therefore humanism, in a narrower historical sense, is nothing but a moral-aesthetic anthropology" (93, my translation).

8. Martin Heidegger, *An Introduction to Metaphysics* (New Haven, Conn.: Yale University Press, 1987), 205.

9. See William J. Richardson's *From Phenomenology to Thought* (New York: Fordham University Press, 2003), 45–46, for an excellent description of the problem that gave rise to Beaufret's question. If Dasein is an ontological structure prior to man rather than man himself, then what is the relation between the two? "For that matter, what man are we talking about? There is an obscurity, then, not only concerning the relationship between There-being and Being but concerning the relationship between There-being and man. If one retains a purely ontological (vs. anthropological) inter-pretation of There-being, one can see that Jean Beaufret's question becomes plausible, even inevitable: 'How give sense to the word humanism?'" (46).

10. "Brief über den Humanismus," in *Wegmarken*, 317.

11. "Letter on Humanism" in *Basic Writings*, 199–200; *Wegmarken*, 319.

12. "Letter on Humanism" in *Basic Writings*, 201; *Wegmarken*, 321.

13. Ibid.

14. Ibid., 210; *Wegmarken*, 330.

15. Gadamer has always understood Heidegger's work as a move out of subjectiv-ism and toward transcendence. Gadamer makes clear that his project is in regard to art while Heidegger's was with regard to metaphysics—not how metaphysics understands itself but what it actually is. Heidegger has been misinterpreted to say that understand-ing human existence out of the horizon of time means that Dasein understands itself completely in terms of its own time and its future. This, however, would not be a cri-tique of subjectivism but merely an existential radicalization of it. Heidegger, however, wants to overcome subjectivism from the subject itself. By asking what the Being of self-understanding is, the question transcends the horizon of this self-understanding. By opening up the hidden ground of time in which self-understanding moves, Heideg-ger doesn't preach a blind engagement out of nihilistic despair but opens a new dimen-sion, the thinking from the experience which transcends the subject, an experience Heidegger calls Being (*das Sein*). See *Wahrheit und Methode*, 105. See also Gadamer's reminiscence in "Heidegger im Rückblick: Hermeneutik und ontologische Differenz,"

where he recalls Heidegger's answer to Gadamer and his fellow student's inquiry how one can achieve the ontological difference: "Aber nein, diese Unterscheidung wird doch nicht von uns gemacht." The ontological difference is not something we make; rather we are placed (*gestellt*) into this distinction, this difference, and it is this difference which is taken up by deconstruction and held open (Hans Georg Gadamer, *Gesammelte Werke,* 10 vols., vol. 10: *Hermeneutik im Rückblick* [Tübingen: Mohr Siebeck, 1995], 58–70). Likewise, William Richardson tells us that Heidegger's hermeneutic of facticity originated as the attempt to articulate transcendence, to articulate "the Being of beings in its *difference* from beings. So it happened that 'hermeneutic' came to mean the entire effort to let Being be manifest, sc. to achieve a more original assumption of Being in order to lay the groundwork of metaphysics." In this sense, hermeneutics *is* phenomenology for Heidegger; the interpretive analysis of phenomena with an eye to trace Being itself in its manifestations is the process of letting things be (631). This basic orientation of Heidegger's though has never changed, and so "the whole effort remains as hermeneutic as ever," says Richardson (633).

16. For Heidegger, this is a thoroughly positive development which elevates human being. In his *Letter on Humanism,* he insists that thinking against values is thinking against subjectivism and against degrading God and human being: "Every valuing, even where it values positively, is a subjectivizing. It does not let beings be. Rather, valuing lets beings be valid solely as the objects of its doing. The bizarre effort to prove the objectivity of values does not know what it is doing. When one proclaims 'God' the altogether 'highest value,' this is a degradation of God's essence. Here as elsewhere thinking in values is the greatest blasphemy imaginable against Being. To think against values, therefore, does not mean to beat the drum for the valuelessness and nullity of beings. It means rather to bring the lighting of truth of Being before thinking to prevent subjectivizing beings into mere objects" (*Basic Writings,* 228).

17. "Letter on Humanism," in *Basic Writings,* 204.

18. Ibid.

19. Ibid., 213.

20. Ibid., 229–30.

21. Ibid., 210.

22. As do, following Eberhard Bethge's biographical comments, Hans Richard Reuter in his foreword to DBW. Dietrich Bonhoeffer, *Akt und Sein* (Munich: Christian Kaiser Verlag, 1988), 7; Charles Marsh, "Bonhoeffer on Heidegger and Togetherness," *Modern Theology* 8, no. 3 (July 1992): 1; and Martin Rumscheidt, "The Formation of Bonhoeffer's Theology," in *The Cambridge Companion to Dietrich Bonhoeffer,* ed. John de Gruchy (Cambridge: Cambridge University Press, 1999), 65. Wilhelm Lütgert himself notes in a letter to the ministry that Bonhoeffer, coming from Seeberg to him, has "developed independently, following Heidegger" (DBW 12, 113). In an article about the theology of Karl Heim, Bonhoeffer gives a succinct formulation of his position on Heidegger. He speaks of an ontological reduction of the being of beings which understands the issue of meaning as a mode of being of an existent so that it is taken up into the existent, "although it is the case, as it is with Heidegger, that the question of meaning swallows up the question of Being and Being is raped by the Dasein existing as the question of meaning" (DBW 12, 215).

23. In *Schöpfung und Fall* (DBW), Bonhoeffer alludes to Heidegger's notion of nothingness (which we know only through the copyist's note) but in general terms to subordinate it under a theological understanding of nothingness as something

employed by God rather than opposed to him (32). Heidegger's fundamental ontology appears a little later again in the same lecture (61), and Bonhoeffer repeats his criticism of Heidegger's being toward death on page 153. In *Nachfolge* (DBW 4) Heidegger's concept of existence as holistic makes one appearance as philosophical backing for the total claim of Christ's calling on a person (46). In *Ethik* (DBW 6), Bonhoeffer revisits and criticizes briefly Heidegger's notion of nothingness (119) and mentions more positively (Heidegger's?) being toward death as transcendent freedom: "Only because man is free towards his death can he risk his bodily life for a higher good" (192). The first draft of "History and the Good" contains another reference to the historicity of human existence (219). In the second draft, Bonhoeffer employs but also critiques Heidegger's notion of conscience as failing to provide actual content to the notion of authenticity, which is, again, a re-use of material from *Act and Being*. A faint echo of the same argument is found at the beginning of "Die Liebe Gottes und der Zerfall der Welt" (301). The editors of the Tegel Literary Fragments consider Bonhoeffer's reference in the Drama to "willing nothing than what expects them already, their death," a reference to Heidegger's being toward death (DBW 7, 60).

In Bonhoeffer's prison letters we find his father's reference to Heidegger's *Phänomenologie des Zeitbewusstseins,* but no such text by Heidegger actually exists. The closest possibility is a later text which cannot have been meant here ("Über das Zeitverständnis in der Phänomenologie und im Denken der Seinsfrage," in Helmut Gehrig (Hrsg.), *Phänomenologie—lebendig oder tot?* Veröffentlichungen der Katholischen Akademie der Erzdiözese Freiburg, Nr. 18. [Karlsruhe: Badenia Verlag, 1969]). Our options are therefore Husserl's writings as edited by Heidegger (Edmund Husserl, *Vorlesungen zur Phänomenologie des inneren Zeitbewußtseins, Jahrbuch für Philosophie und phänomenologische Forschung* 9, 1928), or Heidegger's treatises "The Concept of Time" ("Der Begriff der Zeit," GA 64) and "A Brief History of the Concept of Time" ("Prolegomena zur Geschichte des Zeitbegriffs," GA 20). According to Ernst Feil, it is most likely that Bonhoeffer was more interested in Husserl's notion of time consciousness than in Heidegger's. Ralf Wüstenberg does not mention Heidegger as influential in shaping his Tegel theology in any way. F. Burton Nelson in his article on Bonhoeffer's life in the *Cambridge Companion to Dietrich Bonhoeffer* repeats this list offered. Another echo of Heidegger may be the mentioning of "Care" (*Sorge*) as an existential aspect of human existence (DBW 8, 478). In his inaugural lecture, Bonhoeffer offers a short summary of his position on Heidegger, whom he understands here clearly as asking the question of human existence, which Heidegger answers by offering being as understanding of Being (DBW 10). Repeating his criticism of *Act and Being*, Bonhoeffer rejects the notion that man carries in himself the possibility of wholeness and of self-understanding out of his own potentiality. Heidegger is charged with neglecting the world, which is not intrinsically important for self-understanding. "The Question of Man is finally still answered by man himself to himself" (DBW 10, 364). Bonhoeffer turns Heidegger's accusation that Christians cannot seriously think on its head and replies, "Man, in the final analysis, knows about himself; the question has no ultimate seriousness" (DBWE 10, 397). In a seminary paper on "The Theology of Crisis and Its Attitude toward Philosophy and Science," Bonhoeffer accuses Heidegger of immanentism, of pulling all reality into the circle of understanding (DBW 10, 445—a similar charge is later made by Levinas against Heidegger). Bonhoeffer repeats this verdict in a thesis fragment on Grisebach and Heidegger when he writes, "In Heidegger the pre-given is taken up into understanding Dasein and thus robbed of its pre-givenness" (DBW 11, 214). Bonhoeffer reasserts in this fragment the incarnation of theology in philosophy, which means also the transformation of philosophy (DBW 11, 215). In his article on Karl Heim (WS 32/33) Bonhoeffer sums up his criticism of Heidegger, charging him with an "ontological reduction of beings to being," with the consequence "that the question of the meaning of Being swallows up the question of Being, and Being itself is raped by Dasein in its existence as the question of meaning; in this process the reciprocal movements of being are pulled into the meaning seeking subject and Being as issuing forth [*heraustreten*] into the meaning seeking subject should be thought as infinitely reproducing themselves" (DBW 12, 215). We find another echo of Heidegger's philosophy in Bonhoeffer's "Bibelarbeit über Versuchung," in which he rejects Heidegger's abstract notion of decision in favor of the concrete understanding of existence and decision making the Christian exercises in his relation with God (DBW 15, 373). Finally, in prison, Bonhoeffer commenced to write an essay on truth telling, where his notion of truth as contextual and concretely addressed to another with consideration of all circumstances induced the editor to suggest Bonhoeffer touches here on Heidegger's participatory notion of truth as being in the world (DBW 16, 623).

24. In a note to the sponsor of his dissertation, Paul Althaus, Bonhoeffer explained: "For me there are essential topical [*sachliche*] connections between these two works, which deal basically with nothing but the church" (cited in Hans-Richard Reuter's preface to DBW 2, 12). See also Bonhoeffer's conclusion to his inaugural lecture, in which he summarizes his findings of AB and concludes, "Only as thinking of the church does theological thinking ultimately remain only thinking which does not rationalize reality through the category of the possible. In this way not only does every single theological problem point back to the reality of Christ's church, but theological thinking recognizes itself in its entirety as one that belongs to the church alone" ("Die Frage nach dem Menschen," in DBW 10, 378).

25. "By asking about himself man comes up against the limit of transcendence. He finds himself transcended in himself. In this situation inquiring man has the choice, which cannot be forced through logic, between two decisions: either man acknowledges that he has met with an insuperable limit, that the self he seeks can never appear as a given to reflection, but that his essence consists in his relation to the questioning self, that is, in relation to transcendence; the essence of humanity then rests not in man himself but in each enacted moment of his relation to transcendence. The other possibility is to draw the transcendent questioning 'I' itself into the question and to master it, to see in this coming-to-itself of the self the central process of all mental reflection. If it is characteristic of the first decision that man can only be understood in relation to his limits, the second decision is defined by man's basic ability to be accessible and transparent to himself, to understand himself by himself; he finds in himself the point of unity from which his being can be unlocked. The thinking of the own self as a thinking from unity becomes here the original position of all philosophy. Philosophy now means the unity of the question about human nature and its answer. . . . Man understands himself out of his very own [*ureigensten*] work" (DBW 10, 359).

26. Levinas takes this term from Husserl as exemplary of philosophy's general tendency to obliterate difference: "The I's identification, its marvelous autarchy, is the natural crucible of this transmutation of the Other into the Same. Every philosophy is—to use Husserl's neologism—an egology" ("Philosophy and the Idea of the

Infinite," in Adriaan Theodoor Peperzak and Emmanuel Levinas, *To the Other: An Introduction to the Philosophy of Emmanuel Levinas* [West Lafayette, Ind.: Purdue University Press, 1993], 96–97).

27. For an excellent description of Bonhoeffer's project in *Act and Being,* see Ernst Feil, *Die Theologie Dietrich Bonhoeffers: Hermeneutik, Christologie, Weltverständnis,* 5, Aufl. ed. (Berlin: LIT Verlag Berlin, 2005), 38–52.

28. "Idealism and Materialism lie right next to each other" (DBW 2, 34).

29. "The most fundamental, innermost identity of I and God is here, as in Idealism as a whole, the sole expression of the sentence: same is only understood by same (*das Gleiche wird nur durch Gleiches begriffen)*" (DBW 2, 47).

30. "Bonhoeffer on Heidegger and Togetherness," *Modern Theology* 8, no. 3 (July 1992): 263–83, 267. Marsh rightly points out Bonhoeffer's appreciation of Heidegger for overcoming the dualism of act and being (ibid., 264).

31. "In Heidegger, the pre-given (*das Vorgegebene*) is taken up into Dasein which understands and so is robbed of its pre-givenness" (DBW 11, 214).

32. "Anyone for whom the Bible is divine revelation and truth has the answer to the question [the question of all questions] 'Why are there beings rather than nothing?' even before it is asked: everything that is, except God himself, has been created by Him. . . . One who holds to such a faith can in a way participate in the asking of our question, but he cannot really question without ceasing to be a believer and taking all the consequences of this step" (*Introduction to Metaphysics),* 6–7.

33. Emmanuel Levinas, *Alterity and Transcendence,* European Perspectives (New York: Columbia University Press, 1999), 49.

34. Jean-Luc Marion, *God without Being: Hors-Texte,* Religion and Postmodernism (Chicago: University of Chicago Press, 1991), 42–43.

35. "Human being as the shepherd [*Hirte*] of Being. Toward this alone was the thinking of *Being and Time* directed, when ecstatic existence is experienced as Care" (Martin Heidegger, *Wegmarken,* Unveränd. Text. ed., Gesamtausgabe; Bd. 9: Abteilung 1, Veröffentlichte Schriften 1914–1970 [Frankfurt am Main: Klostermann, 1996]), 331.

36. Heidegger describes his later thinking as an attempt, "which thinks Being heedless of how one might ground Being in beings" ("der das Sein ohne Rücksicht auf eine Begründung des Seins aus dem Seienden denkt"). See "Zeit und Sein" in Martin Heidegger, *Zur Sache des Denkens* (Tübingen: Niemeyer, 1988), 2.

37. "Theological knowledge is not existential knowledge; it has its object in the events stored in the community's memory of Bible, preaching, and sacrament, prayer, confession; in the words of the Christ person, which are preserved as existents [*Seiendes*] in the historical church" (DBW 2, 128).

38. *Anstösse.* Berichte aus der Arbeit der Evangelischen Akademie Hofgeismar. 1 Jahrgang 1954. Heft 1–6, 33.

39. "Hermeneutics of Revelation" in *After God: Richard Kearney and the Religious Turn in Continental Philosophy,* ed. John Panteleimon Manoussakis (New York: Fordham University Press, 2006), 319.

40. Martin Heidegger, *An Introduction to Metaphysics* (New Haven, Conn.: Yale University Press, 1987), 128.

41. Ibid., 144.

42. See, for example, *Akt und Sein* (DBW 2), 151–53. Bonhoeffer rejects metaphysical understandings of human being which try to define his being there without his existential mode of being, the "how." He insists that "in the Christian doctrine

of being all metaphysical ideas of eternity and time, being and becoming, living and dying, essence and appearance must be measured against the concepts of being of sin and the being of grace or else must be developed anew in light of them." Theology requires an understanding of humanity as creature and, "no metaphysical deductions and distinctions (existential, essential, ens), no ontological existential structures adequately describe the 'thereness' of creaturely being. Being-as-Creature means Dasein through and for God in faith, that is, as being touched by revelation."

43. The notion of Christ as center (*Mitte*) is found in SC and AB, and runs through most of the *Ethics*. In the prison letters, Bonhoeffer retains this idea, referring to St. Paul's and Irenaeus's notion of "recapitulation."

44. Gadamer in one of his last interviews explains that "*Mitsein* is a concession Heidegger had to make, but which he held without real conviction. Already back then, when he developed this concept, he wasn't really talking about the other. . . . Care (*Sorge*) is always caring for one's own existence, and *Mitsein* is in actuality a very weak thinking about the other, it is more a letting-the-other-be than an actual being-turned-towards him." Gadamer adds that Heidegger acknowledged this difference: "He acknowledged that I connected more with the thought about the other than he did with the idea of *Mitsein*. Being-with is a weakening, because the 'with' leaves open whether the other is also a Dasein; this 'also' functions, so to speak, as justification for his conscience" (*Lektion des Jahrhunderts* 27).

45. "God remains always Lord, always Subject, so that, who wants to possess him as object, ends up not having the real God; he is always the arriving, never the God of being there [*der daseiende Gott*]" (DBW 2, 79).

46. See Diane P. Michelfelder and Richard E. Palmer, "Three Questions to Gadamer," in *Dialogue and Deconstruction: The Gadamer-Derrida Encounter,* Suny Series in Contemporary Continental Philosophy (Albany: State University of New York Press, 1989), 53.

47. Jacques Derrida, *Der ununterbrochene Dialog: Zwischen zwei Unendlichkeiten, das Gedicht,* trans. Martin Gessmann, Christine Ott, and Felix Wiesler, Manuscript 2003, abridged version, *Neue Zürcher Zeitung* 44 (February 22, 2003): 69.

48. John D. Caputo, *More Radical Hermeneutics: On Not Knowing Who We Are,* Studies in Continental Thought (Bloomington: Indiana University Press, 2000), 5.

49. One is reminded of Kafka's sentiment that "the Messiah will come only when he is no longer necessary; he will come only on the day after his arrival; he will come, not on the last day, but on the very last."

50. John Panteleimon Manoussakis, *After God: Richard Kearney and the Religious Turn in Continental Philosophy* (New York: Fordham University Press, 2006), 7.

51. Ibid., 3.

52. Yet this view of a gathering Logos does not forget about the ultimate transcendence of God, unlike Gianni Vattimo's recent conflation of the incarnation with a weak or nihilistic ontology which reduces God's kenosis to an impersonal historical principle, to some kind of *Seinsgeschick*. Gianni Vattimo expounds his incarnational ontology especially in *After Christianity,* Italian Academy Lectures (New York: Columbia University Press, 2002). He articulates the equation of Christianity with his reading of Heidegger as Christian Nihilism in Richard Rorty, Gianni Vattimo, and Santiago Zabala, *The Future of Religion* (New York: Columbia University Press, 2005).

PART THREE

Regarding "Religionless Christianity"

SIX

Philosophical Influences on Bonhoeffer's "Religionless Christianity"

RALF K. WÜSTENBERG

In May 1944, Bonhoeffer wrote to his friend Eberhard Bethge from Tegel prison: "I am thinking about how we can reinterpret in a 'worldly' sense (. . .) the concepts of repentance, faith, justification, rebirth, and sanctification" (LPP 286–87).[1] In the following correspondence the two friends discussed those concepts that would subsequently become so well-known to us: the conviction that a *religionless time* had arrived, and that the *world had come of age* since it began to exist without God as a *stop-gap* for the incompleteness of our knowledge. In introducing these terms, Bonhoeffer wanted to provide an interpretation whereby Christ would become Lord of the world again. This approach, implying that religion is no longer a condition of justification, was given both a *worldly* and a *nonreligious* interpretation. However, Bonhoeffer did not mean a metaphysical form of interpretation, but rather the reinterpretation of *biblical concepts*. So what, then, does it mean to interpret biblical concepts in a nonreligious way? What are the philosophical roots that gave rise to his ideas on religionless Christianity? To what extent were European philosophical approaches involved?

A large number of publications, especially in the 1960s, simply ignored such questions. For speaking about a religionless time, some interpreters, such as Harvey Cox, have called him an "atheist," others a "secularist" (A. Loen).[2] John Macquarrie believed that Bonhoeffer himself had a "religious nature,"[3] while for William Hamilton and others, Bonhoeffer was the "father of the God-is-dead theology."[4] Such interpretations clearly reflect the religious or the secular perspectives of the interpreters rather than Bonhoeffer's own assumptions.

Many of the misinterpretations of Bonhoeffer in the 1960s are due to the failure to take into account how profoundly his theology was informed by his Christology. As Thomas Torrance stated:

> [T]he tragedy of the situation is that . . . instead of really listening to Bonhoeffer many . . . have come to use Bonhoeffer for their own ends, as a means of objectifying their own image of themselves. . . . In this way Bonhoeffer's thought has been severely twisted and misunderstanding of him has become rife, especially when certain catch-phrases like "religionless Christianity" and "worldly holiness" are worked up into systems of thought so sharply opposed to Bonhoeffer's basic Christian theology, not least his Christology.[5]

Ignoring the Christological core in Bonhoeffer's theology means misconstruing him altogether. The same rule applies to the nonreligious interpretation of biblical concepts. Gerhard Ebeling was ultimately right to presume that the nonreligious interpretation meant for Bonhoeffer a Christological interpretation.[6] This basic insight has often been quoted in the publications of the last four decades, but it has not been put into concrete terms. In order to do so it is imperative to analyze Bonhoeffer's philosophical roots, the key to understanding religionless Christianity in a more concrete way.

In what follows I shall analyze Bonhoeffer's "religionless Christianity" in dialogue with his readings of philosophy, beginning with observations on his uses of the word "religion," followed by analyzing his criticism of religion against the background of dialectic theology (Karl Barth) in connection with transcendental philosophy (Kant), pragmatism (William James), and life-philosophy (Wilhelm Dilthey).

Categorizing Bonhoeffer's Uses of the Term "Religion"

If we take into account all of Bonhoeffer's statements, we can see three quite distinct views of religion. Firstly, there is the *positive* view, which appears in his early writings and is based on the influence of liberal theology. As a student,[7] Bonhoeffer adopted a positive understanding of both religion and culture from his teachers, notably Adolf von Harnack and Reinhold Seeberg. After 1925 Bonhoeffer came under the influence of Karl Barth. Discovering dialectical theology meant changing his opinion of religion as well. So, secondly, there is Bonhoeffer's *critical* view of religion, which appears for instance in his doctoral dissertation, *Sanctorum Communio*. The year of its publication, 1927, marks the change from a positive to a more critical view of religion. But Bonhoeffer went further. From his critique of religion he developed, thirdly, his *non-religious* interpretation. Assuming that the time of religion was finished, he proclaimed a religionless Christianity. Bonhoeffer did more than criticize religion in a *theological* way; he supposed that the time of religion had run its *historical* course. So he proposed a Christian faith that is not "anti-" but "a-" religious.[8]

In his writings, then, Bonhoeffer speaks about "religion" in three different ways—positively, negatively, and historically—as a phenomenon that has run its course. Statements reflecting these three different ways of perceiving religion appear unsystematically and at times even side by side. Bonhoeffer does not establish a theory of religion. For him, religion was never a problem *of* or *within* theology; he wanted to speak of God without religion—in "nonreligious terms."

Bonhoeffer used the word "religion" in such a way that its content cannot be clearly determined. To put it dogmatically, the meaning of religion in Bonhoeffer's writings is not "univocal." In fact, it seems that Bonhoeffer had no interest in describing the meaning of religion. In a lecture he gave in 1931 he explicitly said that the time for theology to use a *concept* of religion was over ("keinen allgemeinen *Begriff* von Religion (kann es) mehr geben").[9]

In not integrating religion into a theological system he distinguished himself for instance from the dialectical theology of Karl Barth.[10] On the other hand he did not underestimate the dimensions of worship and prayer, asking, "What is the place of worship and prayer in a religionless situation?" (LPP 281). If in a religionless situation religious practices like worship and prayer have lost their meaning, how can that vacuum be filled? Bonhoeffer answers such questions with reference to the "discipline of the arcane"—the secret—or *disciplina arcana*. He believed that the rediscovery of this ancient discipline would help to save such religious praxis from profanation. Religious practices such as worship and prayer, he argued, should not be given up but should be performed secretly, in terms of the *disciplina arcana* (discipline of the secret).

At the same time, worship and prayer in "secret" ought always to be followed by responsible action in the world. If the discipline of the secret was one side of the dialectic,[11] the other was Bonhoeffer's nonreligious interpretation of Christianity. He proposed, thus, a dynamic dialectic of dogmatics and ethics, of indicative and imperative, of faith and deed. You cannot, he argued, have one without the other. Likewise you cannot agree with religionless Christianity and not accept prayer and worship. In the language of the prison letters: the discipline of the secret is to religionlessness as prayer is to righteous action (LPP 300); or, in the words of the *Ethics,* as "the last things" are to "the things before the last" (E 146–70).

In a first step exploring the meaning of religionless Christianity, I have viewed the field by drawing attention to Bonhoeffer's own statements on religion, concluding that he neither defines religion systematically nor develops a theory of religion. This means two things for our understanding of religionlessness. Firstly, it means that we cannot deduce its meaning merely from Bonhoeffer's view of religion, simply because for him a *Religionsbegriff* does not exist. Secondly, it means that we have to go a step behind the sources and ask for both the philosophical and the theological roots. Where do the critique of religion and the proposal about religionless Christianity come from? What was Bonhoeffer reading when he developed his thoughts on religionless Christianity?

German Idealism, Karl Barth, and Kant's Phenomenalism

Bonhoeffer, who was born in 1906 in the late German *Kaiserreich,* anticipated philosophical thinking as he felt it was presented to him. He read philosophers of the nineteenth century such as Schopenhauer, Kierkegaard, Feuerbach, and (during his imprisonment) Wilhelm Dilthey in the light of their criticism of German idealism (Fichte, Hegel, Schelling). Throughout the nineteenth century and particularly in the early twentieth century we come across a movement that was trying to establish Kant anew, that is to say, the *Neukantianer.* The Marburg wing of the *Neukantianer,* among whom Paul Natorp was a leading philosopher, highly influenced Karl Barth's view on Kant.

Generally speaking, nineteenth-century *liberal theology* was influenced by idealist philosophy. Ferdinand Christian Baur from Tübingen, for instance, used Hegelian dialectic to explain the development of the early Church. Friedrich Schleiermacher could be regarded as a half-Kantian and a half-idealist philosopher. This precluded his not becoming a target of criticism against idealist theology in the nineteenth century. Against this background it is easy to understand that to criticize idealism at the same time meant to criticize theology (see Feuerbach against Hegel or Engels against Schelling's existential philosophy or Kierkegaard against Fichte's *absolutes Ich*).

By 1929 when Bonhoeffer wrote *Act and Being* he was fully integrated into a movement that he had first come across several years earlier, in 1924 in the teachings of Karl Barth—an encounter that had been to him like "a liberation."[12] This experience had enabled him to discover Kantian philosophy anew and to link it with Barth's theology in a way that with *Act and Being* he gave up liberal theology and thus idealist philosophy altogether. Bonhoeffer's reading of Karl Barth started with the essay-collection *Das*

Wort Gottes und die Theologie, in which Barth declares (1920): "Jesus has simply nothing to do with religion" ("Jesus hat mit Religion einfach nichts zu tun").[13] For Barth, the "Word of God" meant the judgment of all religious efforts. The "freedom of God" stood for Barth in opposition to "human religion."[14] "Religion" was for Barth the opposite of grace.[15]

In essays that Bonhoeffer wrote as a student for his seminars in 1925–26 there are a number of references to Barth's *Römerbrief,* particularly with regard to this distinction between grace and religion. In *Sanctorum Communio* (1927), his doctoral dissertation, the influence of both Barth and liberal theologians such as Albrecht Ritschl is evident.[16] Dialectical and liberal theology coexisted. But with *Act and Being,* Bonhoeffer's *habilitations-thesis* in 1930, things had begun to change. I shall demonstrate this with reference to the term "religious a priori."

As Bonhoeffer understood it, Reinhold Seeberg took a Kantian approach to theology in arguing that "God is the supramundane reality transcending consciousness, the Lord and creator." How, then, can man understand God? "This is where Seeberg's theory of the religious *a priori* comes into play." According to Seeberg, "there is a mould in human beings into which the divine content of revelation may pour. In other words, revelation must become religion; that is its essence. Revelation is religion. But that is a turning away from pure transcendentalism toward idealism" (AB 57–58).

Kant had sought to show that human understanding is limited to the phenomena of sensory experience. Transcendent objects, such as God, freedom, and immortality, lie beyond human modes of perception and so are unknowable. Bonhoeffer detects a lack of logic in Seeberg's Kantian approach in introducing Troeltsch's idea of a religious a priori. This, Bonhoeffer argues, is idealist thought according to which God could be understood by human beings on the basis of their religious a priori rather than through God's revelation in Jesus Christ. The distance between God and human beings was bridged by the religious a priori: however, for Bonhoeffer the deep gulf between God and human beings can be overcome only through God's self-revelation. This, of course, is not Bonhoeffer's insight alone but reflects the influence of Barth's "word of God" theology in its opposition to liberal theology.

For Barth, God as he is in himself *(an sich)* cannot be recognized except through self-disclosure. The gap between God and humanity can be overcome only by God. Where Hegel mixes revelation with religion and Seeberg uses the human term "religious a priori," Barth focuses solely on God's revelation in his Word, Jesus Christ. By 1929, when Bonhoeffer wrote *Act and Being,* he had become fully initiated into the dialectical theological movement.

In his first lecture that Bonhoeffer gave at Berlin University he stressed the antagonism between philosophy and theology, particularly in terms of the separation of those following the strains of idealist philosophy such as existentialism and phenomenology (Heidegger/Scheler) from the followers of *theology of crisis* (Barth).[17] The most striking aspect in this lecture is that Bonhoeffer rejects all philosophical approaches to theology apart from one, namely Kantian transcendental philosophy. Bonhoeffer follows Barth's *Dogmatics in Outline,* which used Kantian terminology in order to oppose idealist philosophy and the 19th-century *Liberal theology* that went with it: "God remains the eternally other, the eternally distant, even and precisely where he comes near to man in revelation. Barth says, 'The man to whom God reveals himself is the man to whom God cannot become manifest' (Dogmatik I p.287). (...) Barth supports this train of thought from the Kantian idea of man, who only is in reference to transcendence" (DBW 10, 371). It is evident—in sum—that every critical statement on religion that can be found in Bonhoeffer's writings is based upon Barth's theology. The critique that Bonhoeffer learned from Barth is the critique of the "Word of God" on religion, the antagonism between religion and grace. Through Barth and his dialectic theology Bonhoeffer discovered the importance of Kantian terminology and philosophy for theological statements, particularly with respect to revelation. Then, in New York in the early 1930s, Bonhoeffer became familiar with a different philosophical strain.

New York, Pragmatism, and William James

It is worthy of mention right at the beginning of this section that a certain antagonism between philosophy and theology that Bonhoeffer stressed in 1929 (*Act and Being*) and then in 1930 (first lecture) still appears during his research stay at Union Theological Seminary in 1930–31. In an article that he wrote for *The Journal of Religion,*[18] Bonhoeffer describes the difference between philosophy and theology in the following way: "Philosophical thinking attempts to be free from premises (if that is possible at all); Christian thinking has to be conscious of its particular premise, that is, of the premise of the reality of God, before and beyond all thinking" (DBW 10, 424–25).[19] Bonhoeffer generalizes his attitude toward philosophy from 1929 and 1930, when he argues, "God is subordinated to the ego. That is the strict consequence of the idealistic, and, as far as I see, of all exact philosophical thinking which tries to be autonomous" (DBW 10, 424). Bonhoeffer obviously includes Kantian thinking in the antagonism between idealist philosophy and theology. Now, this seems to be something new that we should take into account. We could ask whether or not this suggests that Bonhoeffer is moving toward a different philosophical framework that he might have found more adequate for theology as early as 1931.

On the other hand he is certainly following Barthian theology in his article. Bonhoeffer picked up his arguments in *Act and Being*, when he states in the same article, "The basis of all theology is the fact of faith. Only in the act of faith as a direct act is God recognized as the reality which is beyond and outside of our thinking, of our whole existence" (DBW 10, 425–26). Bonhoeffer continues, "Theology, then, is the attempt to set forth what is already possessed in the act of faith. Theological thinking is not a construction a priori, but a posteriori as Karl Barth has maintained. Therefore it has to be conscious of its limitations" (DBW 10, 426). With regard to Barth, it is interesting to notice that Bonhoeffer focuses his criticism of philosophy on idealistic philosophy (as in 1929–30), "The idealistic philosophy conceives of history as of the realization of ideas, values, etc. History becomes a 'symbol,' transparent to the eternal spirit" (DBW 10, 428). Against the background of idealistic philosophy dialectic theology argues, "History in its essence does not enter our system of ideas and values. On the contrary, it sets for us our limitations" (DBW 10, 429).

Apart from the observation that Bonhoeffer in this article does not entirely seem to follow a Kantian approach to theology, it seems interesting to note some parallels to later statements from his prison cell: "Justification is pure self-revelation, pure way of God to man. No religion, no ethics, no metaphysical knowledge may serve man to approach God" (DBW 10, 433). This criticism of a metaphysical framework is significant for Bonhoeffer's late theology. It may suffice to understand parts of what Bonhoeffer was writing in 1931 both in terms of a continuity from 1929 onward and in terms of a discontinuity from 1944 backward. The continuity pertains to Barth and the rejection of idealist philosophy, the discontinuity to a condemnation of philosophy altogether and to his prison-cell terminology.

At Union Seminary Bonhoeffer discovered the philosophy of William James. In a book review on William James's *Varieties of Religious Experience*,[20] Bonhoeffer commented:

> 1. It is not true to say that the religious individual does not care as much about the reality as about the efficiency of God. The reality of God is, of course, for most religious people not a philosophical question but a basic

conviction. 2. Concerning the term "subconsciousness" we must ask if sub-consciousness is to be satisfactory for the religious experience of the outside, then it must be considered really outside of the individual person. But if it is not really outside then the religious experience of the outside is an illusion; if it is really outside then the term subconsciousness seems to be misleading, and we must ask why we do not say: God; which would of course show that the apparent contact with science is illusive. So it seems to me not possible to find a mediating term between religion and science. (DBW 10, 410)

Particularly evident in his second comment on James's book: Bonhoeffer was obviously missing the transcendental aspect, the "really outside" as he puts it. The subconscious *and* the "really outside" do not go together and cannot be linked within a philosophical framework. The link for Bonhoeffer is: God *and* "really outside," which leads us back to both Kantian philosophy and Barthian theology. Bonhoeffer is obviously making two points here. First of all, he is trying to defend the theological insights that he became convinced of in the late 1920s against a very different philosophy, namely pragmatism. Secondly, Bonhoeffer seems open to new philosophical ideas. Otherwise he would hardly have read almost all the writings of William James. In sum, the year 1931 indicates a turning point in Bonhoeffer's adaptation of philosophy: Bonhoeffer started reading William James, whose thought was labelled as "pragmatism." James argues that if religion is true, it has meaning in life, but if it has no meaning in life, then it is false. This pragmatic argument is important for Bonhoeffer because of the value that James attributed to life and, more generally, of the earthbound-ness of pragmatism as a philosophy of life. From here the way leads to Wilhelm Dilthey.

What about Feuerbach and Kierkegaard's Influences on Bonhoeffer's "Religionless Christianity"?

In secondary literature, particularly in the English-speaking world, Bon-hoeffer's dependency on philosophy has been stressed. Henry Mottu,[21] for instance, interprets Bonhoeffer against the background of Ludwig Feuer-bach. He argues that "everything suggests that Bonhoeffer was, and still is, the Feuerbach of what is called . . . 'the new theology.' "[22] Mottu sets his ar-gument in the larger framework of philosophy and theology when he states, "We are concerned here with the analogy between the Hegelian system and the mature Barth, between Feuerbach's iconoclasm and Bonhoeffer's criti-cism of religion, between the situation of the early left-wing Hegelians and our own—an analogy, in other words, between more or less conscious structures of thought and actual historical and philosophical situations."[23] Bonhoeffer and Feuerbach were put into the larger context of Barth and Hegel.

It is already here that we have to ask whether Mottu is right to interpret Barth against a Hegelian background rather than against a Kantian one. And if Mottu were not right in assuming a link between Barth and Hegel, there would be—according to Mottu's argument—no link between Bonhoeffer and Feuerbach either. Why is it that Mottu argues within such a large framework? To me it seems that Mottu's aim is to position Bonhoeffer against Barth, and in doing so, he uses the antagonism between Feuerbach and Hegel on a philosophical level.

According to Mottu, the suggested antagonism between Barth and Bonhoeffer finds its strongest expression in Bonhoeffer's late writings. "The originality and interest of the Letters and Papers [from Prison] seem to me to lie precisely here in this transition from a Barthian view of the problem (which sets the theological in opposition to the religious) to a new standpoint which detects the ideological even in the theological."[24] The difference in Barth's and Bonhoeffer's Christology could be understood against their philosophical backgrounds: "whereas Barth very deliberately ties in his Christology with God's Trinitarian being, Bonhoeffer appears so to concentrate theology on Christology that the latter seems to end up displacing theology. Thus (. . .) Bonhoeffer's procedure here is typically Feuerbachian."[25] In detail Mottu argues that, for instance, Bonhoeffer's thoughts in his letter of July 18, 1944, were dependent on Feuerbach. In this letter Bonhoeffer describes religion in terms of its particularity: "To be a Christian does not mean to be religious in a particular way, to make something of oneself (a sinner, a penitent, or a saint) on the basis of some method or other, but to be a man—not a type of man, but the man that Christ creates in us. It is not the religious act that creates the Christian, but participation in the sufferings of God in the secular life" (LPP 361). The fact that Bonhoeffer describes religion in terms of its particularity does not indicate mere Feuerbachian thinking. Life-philosophy stresses the same point; it is the understanding of the wholeness of life that fascinated Dilthey most, and that became the basis of his philosophical approach.

I would agree with Mottu that to some extent Feuerbach influenced Bonhoeffer, as did other nineteenth-century philosophers who opposed idealistic philosophy (such as Kierkegaard or Nietzsche). Bonhoeffer explicitly quotes Feuerbach in his *Letters and Papers from Prison,* but only took up one aspect of his philosophy. He had referred similarly to Feuerbach in his lecture on the "History of Systematic Theology in the 20th Century" at Berlin University in the winter term 1932–33.[26]

In 1944 Bonhoeffer did not adopt a philosophical framework like Feuerbach's completely. Dilthey, as we will see, was the only philosopher besides Kant who helped Bonhoeffer to articulate his theological ruminations throughout his imprisonment. But before we develop this idea let us have a brief look at two further pieces of secondary literature.

David Thomasma's essay could be regarded as a supplement to Mottu's text, for he argues that Kierkegaard and Nietzsche influenced Bonhoeffer's theology.[27] "With Kierkegaard, Bonhoeffer demands a total commitment to God; yet with Nietzsche, he celebrates the death of God!"[28] The most interesting point that Thomasma makes concerns the evolving nature of Bonhoeffer's philosophical thought. Bonhoeffer adopted not a single philosophical school but a variety of schools. The form of the philosophical argument he used is dependent on the stage of his life and work. Using a Hegelian dialectic, Thomasma observes a development in Bonhoeffer's use of philosophy between 1939 and 1944: in 1939, while writing *The Cost of Discipleship,* Bonhoeffer was under the influence of Kierkegaard.[29] In Hegelian terminology he was articulating the "thesis." In 1942, when he started writing his *Ethics,* Bonhoeffer was adopting Nietzsche. In Hegelian terminology this means that he was articulating the "antithesis" to his earlier book. In 1944, finally, Bonhoeffer found in his *Letters and Papers from Prison* the "synthesis" between "godly" and "ungodly," "theistic" and "atheistic." Although Thomasma's argument showing the development in Bonhoeffer's philosophical thought (between 1939 and 1944) is clear, he fails to explain what philosophical reflections actually moved Bonhoeffer in 1944. It is insufficient to reduce Bonhoeffer's statements on religionless Christianity to a mere "synthesis" coming out of Kierkegaard and Nietzsche.[30]

Stuart Picken was convinced that Bonhoeffer's late statements on a world that had come of age were highly influenced by Kant.[31] Picken argued that there is a link "between Kant's rejection of rationalist metaphysics, in the first Kritik, and his later discussion of man's coming adulthood in *Die Religion.*"[32] "His first Kritik was an attempt to face this problem, to admit that traditional metaphysics was doomed, but to leave room yet to speak about God and human freedom. (. . .) [H]e found it necessary to deny knowledge in order to make room for faith" (ibid.). "In *Die Religion,* Kant predicted a time when 'religion will gradually be freed from all empirical determining grounds.'"[33] Picken comes to the conclusion, "the thought of Bonhoeffer (. . .), like that of Kant, is grounded in a deep perception of European thought since the Renaissance."[34]

German Historism, Life-Philosophy, and Wilhelm Dilthey

In trying to determine more precisely the philosophical basis of Bonhoeffer's observations about a "religionless Christianity," we are now able to summarize that there were only three philosophers of special importance for Bonhoeffer, namely Kant, James, and Wilhelm Dilthey. We noticed a development in Bonhoeffer's adoption of philosophy, from his reception of Kant in the 1920s, to his discovery of James in 1931, to Wilhelm Dilthey, whom he read during his imprisonment in 1944.

Dilthey himself could be regarded as a second Kant, for he developed a critique of historical reason in accordance with Kant's critique of pure reason. Unlike Kant, however, Dilthey explained human autonomy *historically*. According to Dilthey's philosophy of life, humans began to think autonomously from the time of the Renaissance and the Reformation. They no longer used God as a stop-gap (*Lückenbüßer*), as a matter of convenience, but used autonomous reason to explain politics (as, e.g., Niccolo Machiavelli), law (e.g., Hugo Grotius), natural sciences (e.g., Galileo Galilei), and other subjects.

While reading Dilthey, Bonhoeffer started to comment on theological problems such as the criticism of religion within a historical framework, whereby he stopped setting revelation up against religion (as Barth had done) but felt more fundamentally that the *time of religion* was over: "The time when people could be told everything by means of words, whether theological or pious, is over, and so is the time of inwardness and conscience—and that means the time of religion in general" (LPP 279).[35] Bonhoeffer learned from Karl Barth to criticize religion in the light of faith on the basis of the antagonism between religion and grace. Yet in Tegel prison things changed. Writing to his friend Bethge, he remarked: "The 'religious act' is always something partial; 'faith' (. . .) is involving the whole of one's life." Bonhoeffer thus understood faith as an act of life. He continued: "Jesus calls men, not to a new religion, but to life."[36] The antagonism between religion and grace had now become an antagonism between religion and "life." Faith was interpreted in the light of "life"; the concept of faith had become a concept of life. He wrote, "I believe that we ought so to love and trust God in our *lives,* and in all the good things that he sends us."[37] The quest for the "Good" brings us back to Bonhoeffer's *Ethics,* but in his view of worldliness and autonomy, Bonhoeffer moved further in his letters from prison. Whereas in a manuscript from the *Ethics* the world, which is in the process of "coming of age," was regarded negatively in terms of "nihilism," in the prison letters Bonhoeffer reflects positively on the autonomy of the world, humanity, and life. What caused his view of autonomy to change? Between the *Ethics* and these positive statements in the *Letters and Papers from Prison,* Bonhoeffer had read Wilhelm Dilthey.

Scholars have only marginally discussed the question of Dilthey's influence as a *philosopher of life.* After Eberhard Bethge's and then Ernst Feil's initial, general references to the significance of the philosophy of life for Bonhoeffer, it was T. R. Peters who provided the first concrete initiative, pointing out that Bonhoeffer's appropriation of Dilthey's thought was not limited to the latter's historicism, but included his philosophy of life as well.[38] Peters did not, however, examine thoroughly the possibility of Bonhoeffer having appropriated elements of Dilthey's philosophy of life, and reckoned instead with the continuing significance of Nietzsche's philosophy of life for the entirety of Bonhoeffer's work. It was only the study of K. Bartl and that by Hans-Jürgen Abromeit that took things further.[39] Bartl demonstrates Dilthey's relevance to Bonhoeffer's "understanding of reality" as *one* reality, and shows that Bonhoeffer stands close not only to Dilthey's "presentation of history," "but already to his basic concept of life."[40] Bartl does not, however, apply this insight to the understanding of religion in the *Letters and Papers from Prison,* and instead sticks to the theme of his study, namely, "Theology and Secularity." Abromeit also adduces Dilthey's significance for Bonhoeffer as a philosopher of life, working out the significance of various currents of the philosophy of life for the *Ethics;* in the *Ethics,* however, Dilthey was not yet providing Bonhoeffer with any new impulses. Only in the *Letters and Papers* does Bonhoeffer's appropriation of Dilthey emerge through Bonhoeffer's own systematic reading. Abromeit does not address the significance of Dilthey's philosophy of life for the *Letters and Papers,* though he does coin the term "life theology" for the later Bonhoeffer, demonstrating thereby the close connection with the philosophy of life, a connection consisting, he alleges, "in the interdependence of understanding and experience undergirding the two."[41] In summary, we can note that these two initiatives do not throw any new light on the connection between the philosophy of life on the one hand, and the critique of religion on the other; commensurately, they also do not illuminate the significance of Dilthey's *concept of life* for the non-religious interpretation. However, they certainly do raise the pertinent general question about the possibility of Dilthey's significance for Bonhoeffer as a philosopher of life.

The following discussion will concentrate exclusively on the text by Dilthey that Bonhoeffer studied beginning in March 1944 during his incarceration, namely: *Weltanschauung und Analyse des Menschen seit Renaissance und Reformation.*[42] Herein Dilthey combines the concept of life with that of history into a certain interpretation of history, namely, historicism.[43] To acknowledge the interdependence of *history* and *experience,* reference is also made here to Dilthey's conception of a *historical philosophy of life* (*historische Lebensphilosophie* or *Historismus*).

In working through *Weltanschauung und Analyse,* Bonhoeffer probably proceeded chronologically. Several considerations suggest this; for example, the citations from Giordano Bruno on friendship and from Spinoza on the affections in Bonhoeffer's "Thoughts on Various Things"[44] come from the end of Dilthey's volume (*Weltanschauung und Analyse*).[45] Bonhoeffer cites these sentences in July 1944, that is, also at the end of his own reading of Dilthey. We can assume that at this time the *whole* of Dilthey is present. In this context, mention of the philosopher and scientist Cardano in the *Letters and Papers* and *Weltanschauung und Analyse* is also revealing. In a letter at the end of April 1944, Eberhard Bethge draws his friend's attention to Cardano's significance.[46] Bonhoeffer answers Bethge at the beginning of May 1944, that is, upon beginning to read Dilthey, "I am not familiar with Cardano. Has he been translated into German?" (DBW 8, 420). In the middle of June, Bonhoeffer then remarks to Bethge in an aside: "By the way, Dilthey writes quite a bit about Cardano" (DBW 8, 492). In *Weltanschauung und Analyse,*[47] Dilthey first mentions Cardano on page 284. From this one can directly conclude that by mid-June, Bonhoeffer has already read over half—if not more—of *Weltanschauung und Analyse,* while at the beginning of May he is quite obviously just beginning to read Dilthey; in any event, he quite obviously had not come across Dilthey's discussion of the Renaissance philosopher.

Bonhoeffer's mention of Cardano shows in an exemplary fashion how carefully he was reading Dilthey's *Weltanschauung und Analyse.* At this point, I would like to mention other names that acquired significance for Bonhoeffer as he read Dilthey: Herbert of Cherbury, Hugo Grotius, Jean Bodin, Michel de Montaigne, Giordano Bruno.[48] This selection is limited to the significant letter of July 16, 1944; Bonhoeffer associates these names with certain themes with whose aid the "*one* great development [. . .] toward the autonomy of the world" (DBW 8, 530) becomes discernible. These themes include "theology" (representative: Herbert of Cherbury), "morality" (names: Montaigne, Bodin), and "politics" (representative: Machiavelli); the name of Grotius is mentioned in connection with the theme "autonomy" in "human society."[49]

Bonhoeffer is quite obviously systematically organizing *Weltanschauung und Analyse* according to certain themes and name grouping from the perspective of autonomy and coming of age. In the letter of July 16, 1944, he then brings together various historical reflections in the different sections of *Weltanschauung und Analyse* (cf. also the parallel letter of June 8, 1944). Our previous overall examination of *Weltanschauung und Analyse*, however, revealed that nowhere in his volume does Dilthey himself actually analyze "autonomy" or "coming of age" as concepts in and for themselves.[50]

As an example, let us see how Dilthey understands Grotius. He saw how in the first three decades of the sixteenth century Pierre Charron, Francis Bacon, and Herbert of Cherbury establish the line of thought that Grotius would then carry forward: the "natural system of the moral world" (WA 276) is established. Dilthey examines the "task" (WA 277), "method" (WA 278), and "concepts" (WA 279) of Grotius and finds that the "universally valid concepts" (WA 278) are "life concepts" (WA 279). These concepts "inhere in the entirety of life and draw from life their persuasive power" (WA 279). The "legal concepts" thus deduced (= "life concepts") (WA 280), following Grotius, are concepts whose "validity does not depend on faith in their grounding within a teleological order resting in God. 'Even if there were no God,' the principles of natural law would maintain their independent and universal validity" (WA 280).

The famous citation of Grotius, which Bonhoeffer renders in Latin,[51] thus appears in the immediate context of the philosophy of life. Dilthey adduces Grotius as a Renaissance legal thinker who takes the concepts of life as his point of departure, thereby renewing "the true intention of Roman jurisprudence" (WA 279); the concept of justice is a life concept. This also directly explains why Bonhoeffer speaks about *life* without God and why his historical excursuses on the striving for autonomy in various areas basically all end up talking about life.[52]

From Dilthey, Bonhoeffer saw that the statement from Grotius is a statement about life, and "that we must *live* in a world 'etsi deus non daretur.'"[53] What we find here in the case of Grotius applies as well to the other themes and names mentioned above.[54] A larger examination of Dilthey's work reveals that all the names enumerated here are associated with the philosophy of life.[55] Regardless of the sphere in which Dilthey observes the striving to come of age or to attain autonomy, he always begins with human life as it is actually lived in a given epoch. The maturity of the world derives from the maturity of life in the world. Life as a cognitive-theoretical maxim becomes the historical understanding of a given epoch. The autonomy of life becomes the autonomy of human beings and of the world. Bonhoeffer consciously goes along with this progression, beginning thetically with the conclusion: "(. . .) it is one great development that leads to the autonomy of the world" (DBW 8, 529–30). When Bonhoeffer speaks elsewhere about the autonomy of human beings and of life, he lets us know that he is interpreting Dilthey's cognitive-theoretical position—namely, life—Christologically: The "appropriation of the world come of age through Jesus Christ" (DBW 8, 504). In the preceding sentence of the letter just cited, Bonhoeffer demands that "the entirety of human life" must be claimed by Christ. The conceptual pairs "mature world" and "worldly life" as well as "world come of age" and "mature life" can thus be used alongside one another.

Bonhoeffer's formulation of the theme of his Tegel theology progresses from the general to the particular, from the initial Christological question to the appropriation of earthly life. We can discern the following development in Bonhoeffer's Christological understanding of life (my emphasis):

1. Initial question: "[W]ho *Christ* really is *for us today*" (April 30, 1944; DBW 8, 402)
2. Basic theme: "*Christ and the world come of age*" (June 8, 1944; DBW 8, 479)
3. Ethical theme: The "*appropriation of the world come of age through Jesus Christ*" (June 30, 1944; DBW 8, 504)
4. Theme of life: "*Jesus lays claim to the entirety of human life for himself*" (June 30, 1944; DBW 8, 504)
5. Theme: The biblical "blessing is the *appropriation of earthly life for God*" (July 28, 1944; DBW 8, 548)
6. Ecclesiological conclusion: The church "must tell people of all vocations what *life with Christ* is, what it means 'to be for others'" (*Outline for a Book*; DBW 8, 560)

From his initial Christological question (1), Bonhoeffer formulates the basic theme of his Tegel theology (2), applies it ethically (3) (also with respect to "life," 4), and finally gives the theme an exclusive concrete orientation toward life (5), including the ecclesiological conclusion of this Christology of life (6). The essence of the various formulations is thus: Christian life and life come of age.

When we said that Bonhoeffer applies Dilthey's philosophy of life Christologically, this alludes to the particular accentuation Bonhoeffer gives to his own reading of Dilthey. Our examination of *Weltanschauung und Analyse des Menschen seit Renaissance und Reformation* repeatedly encountered Dilthey's concept of religion, one he obviously draws into his own philosophy of life. His intention is to show the relationship between life and religiosity in their various manifestations during the Renaissance and Reformation. For example, Ulrich Zwingli's "religiosity" is allegedly "true life" (WA 226). Dilthey raises the question of "true religion" in connection with Jean Bodin (WA 151), and also admires "the religious vivacity of Luther" (WA 231). On the whole, Dilthey is inclined to engage in criticism whenever religion and life are isolated and opposed to one another (WA 137). The *whole* of life is for him *religious* life: "God wants to be enjoyed" (WA 160). Religion is to be asserted "in life" (WA 237), and Dilthey thus demands a "livable" religion, that is, a religion of the here and now. Dilthey's *Weltanschauung und Analyse des Menschen seit Renaissance und Reformation* contains no critique of religion, something we already pointed out in connection with other Dilthey writings; nor, according to Dilthey, can any religion*lessness* come about.[56] In substance, a critique of religion and the notion of religionlessness as two significant motifs of Bonhoeffer's own understanding of religion do *not* derive from Wilhelm Dilthey, although the *critique of metaphysics*—as a further basic motif of Dilthey's *Life-philosophy*—exerted considerable influence on Bonhoeffer. Bonhoeffer emphatically followed the critique of metaphysics as grounded in the philosophy of life. The critique of religion, however, is in Bonhoeffer grounded on the critique of religion presented by Karl Barth.[57] Where Dilthey finds an antithesis between *life* and *metaphysics*, Bonhoeffer juxtaposes *life* and *religion*. Where Dilthey interprets *life and inwardness* from a mutually inclusive perspective, Bonhoeffer does the same with *life and Jesus Christ*.

Under the influence of Bonhoeffer's systematic reading of Dilthey, the concept of life becomes the basic cognitive-theoretical concept.[58] From the philosophy of life, Bonhoeffer acquired an important impulse for his understanding of life, and the theological understanding of life remains determinative for his reading of Dilthey. So, in conclusion, we have to put Gerhard Ebeling's argument in a more concrete form: to interpret non-religiously implies a Christological form of interpretation that is made concrete by taking into account the decisive concept of life. "Non-religious" interpretation means a form of interpretation by which modern *life* that has come of age in the modern era and Christian *faith* are brought together in a new relation. In his fragmentary Tegel theology, Bonhoeffer equipped us with the guiding questions regarding the correct relationship between life come of age and Christian faith—that was his theme, and was the essence of the question of nonreligious interpretation. Both the church and theology will have to struggle ever anew to find the appropriate answer.

Notes

1. Letter to Eberhard Bethge from May 5, 1994. Cf. DBW 8, 416.

2. A. E. Loen, *Säkularisation: Von der wahren Voraussetzung und angeblichen Gottlosigkeit der Wissenschaft* (Munich: Chr. Kaiser Verlag, 1965), 205–207.

3. B. Jaspert, *Frömmigkeit und Kirchengeschichte* (Erzabtei St. Ottilien: EOS

Verlag, 1986), 76–77; John Macquarrie, *God and Secularity* (London: SCM, 1968), 72–74.

4. William Hamilton, "A Secular Theology for a World Come of Age," *Theology Today* 18 (1962): 440; A. T. Robinson, *Honest to God* (London: SCM, 1963).

5. Thomas F. Torrance, "Cheap and Costly Grace," in *God and Rationality* (Oxford: Oxford University Press, 1971), 56–85, 74.

6. Gerhard Ebeling, "Die 'Nicht-religiöse Interpretation biblischer Begriffe,'" *Zeitschrift für Theologie und Kirche* 5, no. 2 (1955): 296–360; quotation from *Die Mündige Welt*, ed. Eberhard Bethge, vol. 2 (Munich: Chr. Kaiser Verlag, 1956), 12–73, 20–21.

7. See Bonhoeffer's essays "Luthers Stimmungen gegenüber seinem Werk in seinen letzten Lebensjahren. Nach seinem Briefwechsel von 1540–1546," in DBW 9, 271–305, 300; also "Referat über historische und pneumatische Schriftauslegung," ibid., 305–23, 321. See English translation. DBWE 9, 257–84; 285–300.

8. R. Bernhardt, *Der Absolutheitsanspruch des Christentums. Von der Aufklärung bis zur pluralistischen Religionsauffassung*, 2nd ed. (Gütersloh: Gütersloher Verlag, 1993), 68.

9. "Die Systematische Theologie des 20. Jahrhunderts," in *Vorlesung aus dem Wintersemester* 1931/32, ed. Eberhard Bethge, *Gesammelte Schriften* vol. 5 (Munich: Chr. Kaiser Verlag, 1972), 181–227, 219.

10. See Karl Barth, *Church Dogmatics* I, 2, §17.

11. Andreas Pangritz, "Aspekte der 'Arkandisziplin' bei Dietrich Bonhoeffer," *Theologische Literaturzeitung* 119 (1994): 755–68, 765.

12. Cf. Eberhard Bethge, *Dietrich Bonhoeffer: Theologe, Christ, Zeitgenosse* (Munich: Chr. Kaiser Verlag, 1986), 104: "Mit dem Durchbruch der dialektischen Theologie trat bei Bonhoeffer an die Stelle eines gewissen ruhelosen Schweifens eine selbstgewissere Bestimmtheit. Er gewann erst jetzt eigentlich Freude an der Sache; es war wie eine Befreiung" (cf. the English edition of Bethge's biography, *Dietrich Bonhoeffer: Theologian, Christian, Contemporary*, London: Collins, 1970).

13. Karl Barth, *Das Wort Gottes und die Theologie* (Munich: Chr. Kaiser Verlag, 1924), 94.

14. Karl Barth, *Der Römerbrief*, 13th ed. (Zürich: Zollikon, 1984), Beleg 236.

15. Ibid., 212.

16. See SC 153n76 (editor's footnote) and Albrecht Ritschl, *Rechtfertigung und Versöhnung* 3 (Bonn, 1888), 508: "Jede gemeinsame Religion ist gestiftet."

17. "Die Frage nach dem Menschen in der gegenwärtigen Philosophie und Theologie." Antrittsvorlesung in der Aula der Berliner Universität am 31.Juli 1930 (Man in contemporary philosophy and theology), in DBW 10, 357–80.

18. "Concerning the Christian idea of God. 1931," in DBW 10, 423–33; originally published in *Journal of Religion* 12, no. 2 (April 1932): 177–85.

19. Ibid., 424–25.

20. "Kurzreferat über William James, Varieties of religious experience," in DBW 10, 408–10.

21. H. Mottu, "Feuerbach and Bonhoeffer: Criticism of Religion and the Last Period of Bonhoeffer's Thought," *Union Seminary Quarterly Review* 25, no. 1 (1969): 1–18.

22. Ibid., 1.

23. Ibid., 3.

24. Ibid., 8.

25. Ibid., 13.

26. "Die Geschichte der systematischen Theologie des 20. Jahrhunderts," in DBW 11, 139–213.

27. D. Thomasma, "Dietrich Bonhoeffer: Religionless Christianity," *Revue de l'Université de Ottawa* 39 (July–September 1969): 406–25.

28. Ibid., 407.

29. Volume editors' note: Thomasma seems to overlook the fact that Bonhoeffer finished writing *Discipleship* in 1937.

30. Thomasma, "Dietrich Bonhoeffer," 410.

31. S. Picken, "Kant and Man's Coming of Age," *Scottish Journal of Theology* 26, no. 1 (1973): 63–70.

32. Ibid., 68.

33. Ibid., 69, with regard to Kant, *Die Religion*, 112.

34. Ibid., 70.

35. Ernst Feil has shown that the term "inwardness," like "metaphysics," was directly taken by Bonhoeffer from Wilhelm Dilthey; see E. Feil, "Der Einfluß Wilhelm Diltheys auf Dietrich Bonhoeffers *Widerstand und Ergebung*," *Evangelische Theologie* 29 (1969): 662–74.

36. Ernst Feil, *The Theology of Dietrich Bonhoeffer* (Philadelphia: Fortress Press, 1985), 362.

37. Ibid., 168.

38. Cf. Eberhard Bethge, "The Challenge of Dietrich Bonhoeffer's Life and Theology," *Chicago Theological Seminary Register* 51, no. 2 (1961): 1–38; Ernst Feil, *Die Theologie Dietrich Bonhoeffers* (Munich: Chr. Kaiser Verlag, 1971), 132n20 [note omitted in English translation, *The Theology of Dietrich Bonhoeffer* (Minneapolis, Minn.: Fortress, 1985)];T. R. Peters, *Die Präsenz des Politischen in der Theologie Dietrich Bonhoeffers* (Munich: Chr. Kaiser Verlag, 1976), 133–35.

39. Karl Bartl, *Theologie und Säkularität: Die theologischen Ansätze Friedrich Gogartens und Dietrich Bonhoeffers zur Analyse und Reflexion der säkularisierten Welt* (Frankfurt am Main: Lang, 1990); . Hans-Jürgen Abromeit, *Das Geheimnis Christi: Dietrich Bonhoeffers erfahrungsbezogene Christologie* (Neukirchen: Neukirchen-Vluyn, 1991).

40. Bartl, *Theologie und Säkularität*, 204.

41. Abromeit, *Das Geheimnis Christi*, 126.

42. Cf. Wilhelm Dilthey, *Gesammelte Schriften*, vol. 2 (Leipzig/Berlin: Verlag Teubner, 1921).

43. See, for more detail, my study *A Theology of Life: Dietrich Bonhoeffer's Religionless Christianity* (Grand Rapids, Mich.: Eerdmans, 1998), and "Dietrich Bonhoeffers theologische Rezeption der Lebensphilosophie Wilhelm Diltheys," in *Dilthey-Jahrbuch* 2000 (Göttingen: Vanderhoeck and Ruprecht, 2000), 260–70.

44. DBW 8, 550–52.

45. *Weltanschauung und Analyse des Menschen seit der Renaissance und Reformation* (abbreviated hereafter as WA), 341–42.

46. Cf. DBW 8, 394–96.

47. He then speaks more extensively about Cardano in *Weltanschauung und Analyse des Menschen seit der Renaissance und Reformation*, 416–17 and 429–32. Since Bonhoeffer says he is reading *a great deal* about the philosopher, it is also conceivable that he is already referring to these later passages.

48. Cf. WA 248ff., 279–80, 274–75, 263–64, 297–98 = DBW 8, 529.

49. Cf. DBW 8, 530.

50. Scholars have repeatedly noted that Bonhoeffer, too (motivated by Dilthey), variously concluded his historical excursuses by focusing on the thematic material of life (cf. my discussions of the letters of June 8 and July 16, 1944).

51. Scholars have not determined the source from which Bonhoeffer derived the Latin version "etsi deus non daretur." Dilthey (WA 280) cites this in a German version (English: "as if there were no God"). The original version in H. Grotius, *De jure belli ac pacis libri tres*. Prolegomena 11,7, reads: "etiamsi daremus, quod sine summon scelere dari nequid, non esse deum" (= "Even if we were to grant—which cannot be done without great sacrilege—that there is no God"). Bonhoeffer used a construction with Latin "datur"; Grotius also used "datur" twice. I conclude that Bonhoeffer was familiar with the citation in its longer, original Latin version, and under the influence of the (shortened) German rendering in Dilthey constructed the Latin form that we now have from him.

52. Cf. Bonhoeffer, DBW 8, 533.

53. DBW 8, 530; my emphasis.

54. One notices that the mention of names is important for both Dilthey and Bonhoeffer. Dilthey explicates his "historical philosophy of life" with the aid of such names (Bruno, Montaigne, Bodin, etc.), while Bonhoeffer similarly explicates his "nonreligious interpretation" with the aid of such names, whereby biblical names acquire significance alongside the philosophers taken from Dilthey, e.g., Paul (306–307, 369), Cornelius, Jairus, Nathanael (396), etc.

55. See my study *A Theology of Life*, 68–90; 104–12.

56. Cf. Dilthey, *Einleitung in die Geisteswissenschaften* [German edition], 138, according to which the notion of a "religiousless condition" is historically incomprehensible.

57. See my study *A Theology of Life*, 31–99.

58. Here the Tegel theology differs from the fragments of the *Ethics*. Although both in and prior to his *Ethics* Bonhoeffer appropriates elements of the philosophy of life, he does not yet understand these as motifs integral to cognition. The ethical theme is: Christ and the good. It is only in the *Letters and Papers from Prison* that this becomes the theme of Christ and the world come of age. In this context, we encounter *discontinuity in continuity* in Bonhoeffer's understanding of religion. We discern continuity in his Christological questions, and discontinuity with respect to his understanding of the world and of autonomy. In the *Ethics,* Bonhoeffer evaluates mature life and autonomy negatively as apostasy from God, while in the *Letters and Papers* he poses the question of Christ and a world come of age. In Tegel, the ethical alternative "Christ or an autonomous world" becomes the relation "Christ *and* the world come of age." Parallel to this discontinuity, the continuity in Bonhoeffer's initial Christological question is maintained: *Christ and/or* life come of age.

SEVEN

The Non-religious Interpretation of Christianity in Bonhoeffer

PAUL RICOEUR

A Few Words about the Man

Dietrich Bonhoeffer was the most outstanding of Karl Barth's disciples. Having begun, while extremely young, a body of scientific work on a few theological themes, he was immediately thrown into the struggle for the Confessing Church, vehemently opposed Nazism, was expelled from Germany, and taught abroad. As soon as the declaration of war was evident, he chose to take the last ship back to Germany from the United States in order to be among his people and to commit himself to the resistance. Coming from Christian pacifism, he passed at once into armed conflict and even terrorism[1] (this posed a considerable problem), since he had chosen to kill the tyrant.

Here is something written by a prisoner who spent several months with him in prison before his execution: Bonhoeffer "was all humility and sweetness; he always seemed to me to diffuse an atmosphere of happiness, of joy in every smallest event in life, and of deep gratitude for the mere fact that he was alive. . . . He was one of the very few men that I have ever met to whom his God was real and ever close to him."[2]

He was executed a few hours after delivering his last sermon before his fellow prisoners. The guards waited for him at the door and he left tranquilly, saying farewell to his community. It is important to have this background in mind. What we have before us here is not a systematic elaboration but rather, if one can say it, a striking out in unknown directions.

Here, in all its brutality, is the theme just as it appeared for the first time in his letters from prison:

> What is bothering me incessantly is the question what Christianity really is, or indeed who Christ really is, for us today. The time when people could be told everything by means of words, whether theological or pious, is over, and so is the time of inwardness and conscience—and that means the time of religion in general. We are moving towards a completely religionless time; people as they are now simply cannot be religious any more. Even those who honestly describe themselves as "religious" do not in the least act up to it, and so they presumably mean something quite different by "religious." Our whole nineteen-hundred-year-old Christian preaching and theology rest on the "religious *a priori*" of mankind. "Christianity" has always been a form—perhaps the true form—of "religion." But if one day it becomes clear that this *a priori* does not exist at all, but was a historically conditioned and transient form of human self-expression, and if therefore man becomes radically religionless—and I think that that is already more or less the case (else how is it, for example, that this war, in contrast to all previous ones, is not calling forth any "religious" reaction?)—what does that mean for "Christianity"? (LPP 279–80)

And a little further:

> How can Christ become the Lord of the religionless as well? Are there religionless Christians? If religion is only a garment of Christianity—and even this garment has looked very different at different times—then what is a religionless Christianity? (LPP 280)

What Dies Today as Religion

It is therefore this unusual problem of non-religious Christianity that now occupies us.

Karl Barth posed this question first in 1919 and in 1923, in the first two editions of his epistle to the Romans, when he said: "Christianity is not a religion." In the second preface to this commentary, he even says: "Christianity is the death of religion."[3] But Bonhoeffer thought that Barth had withheld the logical conclusion of his discovery because of what he called Barth's "positivism of revelation," which turned his theology into "a restoration."[4] The logical conclusion is this question:

> What do a church, a community, a sermon, a liturgy, a Christian life mean in a religionless world? How do we speak of God—without religion, i.e. without

the temporally conditioned presuppositions of metaphysics, inwardness, and so on? How do we speak (or perhaps we cannot now even "speak" as we used to) in a "secular" way about God? In what way are we "religionless-secular" Christians, in what way are we the ἐκ-κλησία, those who are called forth, not regarding ourselves from a religious point of view as specially favoured, but rather as belonging wholly to the world? In that case Christ is no longer an object of religion, but something quite different, really the Lord of the world. But what does that mean? What is the place of worship and prayer in a religionless situation? (LPP, 280–81)

From these extremely scattered notes, which are like flashes of light in the dark, I have tried to extract a few questions that I have grouped together in a slightly more systematic order.

First of all an initial question: "What is religion?" or "What dies today as religion?"

This question goes much further than that of Bultmann's treatment of mythology, which was a much more limited question, in as much as mythology was only the vision of the world from an epoch that is no longer ours. Here, it is a millennial—perhaps a plurimillennial—structure leading right up to the present day.

Metaphysics: Dualism of the Sacred and the Profane

Bonhoeffer, in this regard very Barthian, places religion under two headings: metaphysics and interiority. Several times he says: "Religion, i.e., metaphysics and interiority."

By metaphysics he means approximately that which Feuerbach one hundred and thirty years ago, and Nietzsche more recently, called "metaphysics," "religion," and sometimes "Christianity"—namely, adding God, as a reality, to reality. God as a supplement of reality. It is this dualism of visible and invisible, of this world and another world, that constitutes metaphysics. This dualism takes several forms. At the level of common culture, it is the distinction between sacred and profane, a distinction that ramifies in multiple ways in our culture:

- the distinction between places: profane places and sacred places
- the distinction in time: between profane, working days, and sacred days and festivals
- the distinction between personages: secular men and priests
- the distinction between sentiments: profane love and sacred love

· this distinction also between religious respect and all human
sentiments, etc.

It is therefore the cultural covering for the development of metaphysics,
which is like its rationalized form.

The God of Metaphysics Is Dead

In a narrower and more technical sense of the word, what was called metaphysics is the appeal to "God" (Bonhoeffer always puts this "God"—the "God of the
philosophers and scholars," as Pascal said—between quotations marks) as a
final explanation, a first cause, a sovereign thinker, a rational end for the world.
All the proofs of the existence of God refer to this "God" and depend on the
search for a necessary connection that would lead us from this world toward
the other. But, says Bonhoeffer, this "God" constantly retreats as knowledge
advances. We are in a phase of culture when "God" has been pushed back to the
outer edges of the world. And then, in the last phase, one tries to retain "God"
as a "stop-gap" explanation, as an answer to unsolvable questions, a resolution
of questions without answers; in other words, one appeals to this "God" in
the boundaries of experience and when the resources of experience have been
exhausted, or when it fails. It is therefore truly the *deus ex machina,* that is, that
to which one has recourse in order to wrap up an unresolved intellectual situation. But, says Bonhoeffer, the human being has come of age in the sense that
he has learned to grapple with all of the important questions without resorting
to this "God" as a working hypothesis. In science, in art, in ethics, in politics,
everything proceeds without "God," and just as well as before. "God" relegated
to the exterior of life, in a narrower and narrower margin, appears as the most
remote and the most reduced.

It is then that religion has a second resource. We said metaphysics *and*
interiority.

The Man Come of Age and the "God" of Interiority

Indeed, when "God" was relegated outside of the world, outside of the public
sphere of life, he was retained in the sphere of personal, intimate, private
life. And the "God" who was supposed to resolve the unsolvable problems
of knowledge is here again the one of the boundaries of human experience.
The "God" of the gaps of the world is also the "God" of the limit experiences

of the human being: death, sin, suffering. But we are approaching the day when these ultimate questions of humanity are also resolved without the "God" of metaphysics.

In this manner we are seeing the behavior of the religious man become apparent: he is the one who searches furiously to reserve a place for God, and today this place is at the boundaries. When we read the positive passages of Bonhoeffer's investigation, we will see him say, "I should like to speak of God not on the boundaries but at the centre, not in weaknesses but in strength; and therefore not in death and guilt but in man's life and goodness" (LPP 282). We will return to this when we discuss Bonhoeffer's faith. But for now, we see it expressed in his contempt regarding every Christian apologetic founded on the failure of the mature human being.

> The attack by Christian apologetic on the adulthood of the world I consider to be in the first place pointless, in the second place ignoble, and in the third place unchristian. Pointless, because it seems to me like an attempt to put a grown-up man back into adolescence, i.e. to make him dependent on things on which he is, in fact, no longer dependent, and thrusting him into problems that are, in fact, no longer problems to him. Ignoble, because it amounts to an attempt to exploit man's weakness for purposes that are alien to him and to which he has not freely assented. Unchristian, because it confuses Christ with one particular stage in man's religiousness, i.e. with a human law. More about this later. (LPP 327)

Nothing is more dishonorable, he says, than this choice: either Christ or despair. In some very Nietzschean passages, Bonhoeffer says in substance: I do not like the priests who sniff around the sins of human beings in order to capture the sinner. It is the revolt of the base.[5]

What is so Barthian here is the critique of the desire of God, where pious interiority is defined as an individual concerned with his salvation. Every individualistic conception of salvation is born of this culture of interiority, of a Christianity conceived as a way of passing through the world— the "vale of tears"—without danger, a Christianity of escape and flight. But the Bible does not distinguish the interior and the exterior. It knows only the total human being. According to Bonhoeffer the discovery of interiority is a recent discovery—that of the Renaissance, of Petrarch, perhaps. In the Bible the human heart is not an interior human, but the real human, the concrete human, the entire human in relation with God.[6]

I finish this first section on the question "What is religion" by reading an extremely vehement text of Bonhoeffer: "God as a working hypothesis in morals, politics, or science, has been surmounted and abolished; and the same thing has happened in philosophy and religion (Feuerbach!). For the sake of intellectual honesty, that working hypothesis should be dropped, or as far as possible eliminated. A scientist or physician who sets out to edify is a hybrid" (LPP 360).

Atheism of the Philosophical God and Theology of the Suffering God

If we continue reading this text, there is a turn leading toward the second section concerning the possibility of a post-religious Christianity. We read there something extraordinarily obscure, enigmatic, which is this:

> And we cannot be honest unless we recognize that we have to live in the world *etsi deus non daretur*. [as if there were no God]. (LPP 360)[7]

The text continues:

> And this is just what we do recognize—before God! God himself compels us to recognize it. So our coming of age leads us to a true recognition of our situation before God. God would have us know that we must live as men who manage our lives without him. The God who is with us is the God who forsakes us (Mark 15.34). The God who lets us live in the world without the working hypothesis of God is the God before whom we stand continually. Before God and with God we live without God. God lets himself be pushed out of the world on to the cross. He is weak and powerless in the world, and that is precisely the way, the only way, in which he is with us and helps us. (LPP 360)

This text clearly indicates an orientation toward an atheism of the philosophical God and a theology of the suffering God, and it is this conjunction that we must try to intercept.

THE POSSIBILITY OF A POST-RELIGIOUS CHRISTIANITY

The Time of Silence

Bonhoeffer believes that we are in the time of silence, when that which must die is not yet dead, and when a new word can therefore not yet be heard in its purity. He often reiterates that "we must live in this time of silence in prayer and in simple brotherhood with men." This is why we find many more questions than positive statements. But this may be, and for my part I believe it, our way of being Christian today; I would say a sort of problematic Christian offered to other human beings, rather than a dogmatic Christian separated from other human beings. In this second section I have tried to arrange Bonhoeffer's notes around a few themes, in spite of the fact that they will become entangled all over again.

The Opposition of Faith and the Law in the Gospel

First of all an initial group of notations surrounding this question: How can we find in the gospel itself the possibility of a non-religious interpretation? This theme takes us the closest to the opposition of faith and law in the gospel. It is the central theme where Bonhoeffer is not for that matter original, but where he is Lutheran, Barthian, Bultmannian: this gospel in the gospel, which has always served each radicalization of the Reformation—the opposition of the gospel and the law. But what Bonhoeffer attempted was to think theologically the non-religious, post-religious age, by beginning with this opposition. That is the original, penetrating thing. Thus we return to Barth, but in order to go further than him. If Barth is right, if faith is not *a* religion, not *the* religion, then it is necessary to make the second step, which is this: true preaching is preaching to the non-religious man and not to the religious man. In this way, Christ preached to the unrighteous and not to the righteous, in this way he preached, as Scripture says, "to the lost sheep of the house of Israel"—in all likelihood the people who did not go to the temple—and not to the Sadducees and the Pharisees, that is, the faithful of the Jewish religion.

Putting the Gospel and the
Non-religious Man in Direct Relation

For us, this must mean that it is the non-religious man who is the true addressee of preaching, and who discovers faith for what it is: faith. Hence this anticipation of a new preaching that would put the gospel and the non-religious man directly in relation, passing over the death of the philosophical God, beyond the end of metaphysical and individualistic discourse. Is it possible? It is possible—we are strictly in the order of possibility here—if one radicalizes for the twentieth century what Luther attempted to radicalize for the sixteenth century: the distinction between the gospel and the law.

In sum, Luther had begun this radicalization, since St. Paul was thinking of some fairly specific laws when he said that circumcision is not the condition of faith. Well, let us transcribe that for the twentieth century: religion is not the condition of faith. I quote Bonhoeffer: "Freedom from circumcision [περιτομή] is freedom from religion" (LPP 281).

We should discuss, perhaps, what the superposition of these two problems means: the opposition *law-gospel* in St. Paul and Luther, and the opposition *religion-faith* in Barth and Bonhoeffer. For Bonhoeffer, a non-religious interpretation means an interpretation that distinguishes law and gospel. But he adds that we cannot make use of this distinction as a preliminary key, as a prepared framework, because we do not yet know precisely what the distinction between law and gospel is. We discover it in its fullness today only when we understand it as the opposition of religion and faith.

With this first theme we find the common element in Bultmann, Ebeling, and, in short, in the post-Barthians as a whole: to say a liberating word today, to humans such as they are, that is, to non-religious humans, is the way to be present. This is the way for an ancient word to be preached anew. At this point it is no longer an explanation of the world and of history, but a word that opens the space of life, of language, of communication between human beings.

The God of Jesus Christ

What becomes of the word "God," the name of God? The reply that Bonhoeffer gives is radical: the God of metaphysics and interiority is dead. In this sense Nietzsche is right when he says: God is dead. All that remains for us then is the God of Jesus Christ. A theology is something that we can no longer do; but what we must do is a Christology, and it is this Christology that can give us a theology. But, says Bonhoeffer, the Christian should not be surprised by this. Is it not true—what we heard again through the Reformation and through Barth—that the God of Jesus Christ has nothing to do with what we think God must be?[8] And yet the Christian is surprised: he believes that this spells the end when he hears the words: God is dead. Why? Because he has not dared to take on the fundamental insight—namely, that we know God only in his total weakness on the cross. And we can speak of the power of God only through the word that transforms the defeat of the cross in human life, in the whole of life. But this word of life cannot be established by a metaphysics of omnipotence, because it exists only if it is preached and if it opens life, if it gives life.

Let us go back to the text that I set aside because it was too dense:

The God who lets us live in the world without the working hypothesis of God is the God before whom we stand continually. Before God and with God we live without God. God lets himself be pushed out of the world on to the cross. He is weak and powerless in the world, and that is precisely the way, the only way, in which he is with us and helps us. Matt. 8.17 makes is quite clear that Christ helps us, not by virtue of his omnipotence, but by virtue of his weakness and suffering. Here is the decisive difference between Christianity and all religions. Man's religiosity makes him look in his distress to the power of God in the world: God is the *deus ex machina*. The Bible directs man to God's powerlessness and suffering; only the suffering God can help. To that extent we may say that the development towards the world's coming of age outlined above, which has done away with a false conception of God, opens up a way of seeing the God of the Bible, who wins power and space in the world by his weakness. This will probably be the starting point of our "secular interpretation." (LPP 360–61)

Faith in the Atheism of the Metaphysical God

This text is absolutely fundamental: " . . . only the suffering God can help. . . . This will probably be the starting point of our 'secular interpretation'" (LPP 361). I personally attach a great deal of weight to this text. It is here, in my opinion, that faith and atheism meet, that they come together and in some respects become indiscernible. I believe that we are moving toward a time when faith and atheism will no longer be two worlds, nor two species of human beings, but will produce something new: faith in the atheism of the metaphysical God. The atheism of Marx, the atheism of Nietzsche, the atheism of Freud, signify the death of the metaphysical and moral God. We have to acknowledge this large cultural process that Nietzsche called nihilism. But this nihilism is the major movement of clearing out of which Bonhoeffer speaks.

Once again, it is necessary to remember that in writing this, he is in prison, cut off from everything, exposed before the radical possibilities of the human being, and confronted with other dying humans. It is in this situation that he has the courage to carry this insight through to its end.

The Word "God Is Dead" Has Nothing To Do
with the Word "God Does Not Exist"

It may be that for a long time this commingling will make it impossible to distinguish between a problematic faith and an atheism that will itself become problematic once again—instead of being dogmatic and undisturbed.

Ours is without doubt the time when the whole of human beings is connected to God by his silence and his absence. But is it not the Psalm that says: "How long will you remain silent, Lord?" Is it not Jesus on the cross who cries, "My God, my God, why have you forsaken me?" If I assume all of this modern culture, and live—if I dare to say—out of the absence of God, then I can hear the word "God is dead" not as a triumphant thesis of atheism—because I will say that the word "God is dead" has nothing to do with the word "God does not exist"—but as the modern expression, on the scale of an entire culture, of what the mystics had called "the night of understanding" (*la nuit de l'entendement*). "God is dead" is not the same thing as "God does not exist." It is even the total opposite. This means to say: the God of religion, of metaphysics and of subjectivity is dead; the place is vacant for the preaching of the cross and for the God of Jesus Christ.

THE LIFE OF FAITH IN A WORLD WITHOUT RELIGION

But we must take a third step: How do we live faith without religion? Not simply the possibility, not simply the word "God," but the life of faith. And here Bonhoeffer is always questioning more, in a manner that alienates secularists: "How do we claim a world come of age for Christ? How can Christ become the Lord of the non-religious human being?"

We bring together some scattered, but dazzling, notes, which one can place under the general title of a "worldly Christianity," or a "Christianity for this world," or perhaps—I thought of it in relation to a text of Emmanuel Mounier, who in my opinion perceived something of this in the *Hope of the Desperate*—of a "Christianity of the strong."

Christ Is the Center of Life

These are only indications, because Bonhoeffer was unable to live them out in freedom. First of all this one: "God is in the centre of life, not at the periphery." We saw that the God of metaphysics had been pushed back little by little. He is in the margins. He is becoming invisible. To which responds the movement of faith: "God is beyond in the midst of life" (cf. LPP 282). This is not the "stop-gap" God of explanation; it is not the God who shows up to give an answer to our weaknesses. He is the one who is, if I dare to say, the affirmation of our affirmations. Once again a very beautiful text, where he says of this continual retreat of the stop-gap God:

It is now possible to find, even for these questions, human answers that take no account whatever of God. In point of fact, people deal with these questions without God (it has always been so), and it is simply not true to say that only Christianity has the answers to them. As to the idea of "solving" problems, it may be that the Christian answers are just as unconvincing—or convincing—as any others. Here again, God is no stop-gap; he must be recognized at the centre of life, not when we are at the end of our resources; it is his will to be recognized in life, and not only when death comes; in health and vigour, and not only in suffering; in our activities, and not only in sin. The ground for this lies in the revelation of God in Jesus Christ. He is the centre of life, and he certainly didn't "come" to answer our unsolved problems. From the centre of life certain questions, and their answers, are seen to be wholly irrelevant (I'm thinking of the judgment pronounced on Job's friends). In Christ there are no "Christian problems." (LPP 311–12)

The Christian Is the Entirely Human Man

Moreover, I see this as the response to Nietzsche. All of his life Nietzsche denounced in Christianity precisely what metaphysics and interiority had made of it—namely, a sort of transcendence foreign to man and a desire to leave this life in order to live a spiritual and celestial life. There we have on the contrary the theme of the resurrection, which reintegrates us in the world, which returns us to the world, in order to live in fullness.[9] Thus this idea—still more audacious—is the most extreme expression of this "Christianity of the strong": "The Christian adds nothing to the human; the Christian does not add anything more to the human than God adds to the world. The Christian is the human being, the entirely human man." He says again, a short time before his execution:[10]

> During the last year or so I've come to know and understand more and more the profound this-worldliness of Christianity. The Christian is not a *homo religiosus,* but simply a man, as Jesus was a man—in contrast, shall we say, to John the Baptist. I don't mean the shallow and banal this-worldliness of the enlightened, the busy, the comfortable, or the lascivious, but the profound this-worldliness, characterized by discipline and constant knowledge of death and resurrection. I think Luther lived a this-worldly life in this sense.
>
> I remember a conversation that I had in America thirteen years ago with a young French pastor. We were asking ourselves quite simply what we wanted to do with our lives. He said he would like to become a saint (and I think it's quite likely that he did become one). At the time I was very impressed, but I disagreed with him, and said, in effect, that I should like to learn to have faith. For a long time I didn't realize the depth of the contrast. I thought I could acquire faith

by trying to live a holy life, or something like it. I suppose I wrote *The Cost of Discipleship* as the end of that path. Today I can see the dangers of that book, though I still stand by what I wrote.

I discovered later, and I'm still discovering right up to this moment, that it is only by living completely in this world that one learns to have faith. One must completely abandon any attempt to make something of oneself, whether it be a saint, or a converted sinner, or a churchman (a so-called priestly type!), a righteous man or an unrighteous one, a sick man or a healthy one. By this-worldliness I mean living unreservedly in life's duties, problems, successes and failures, experiences and perplexities. In so doing we throw ourselves completely into the arms of God, taking seriously, not our own sufferings, but those of God in the world—watching with Christ in Gethsemane. (LPP 369–70)

The Experience of the Weakness of God in the Strength of Man

What is very difficult to grasp—and I believe that this is what Bonhoeffer pursued—is the conjunction of these two themes: to meditate on the weak God, the suffering God, in the experience of the fullness of life. One could say that this is precisely the inverse of what Nietzsche hated in Christianity, that is, an omnipotent God opposite a weak human being. In a certain way Bonhoeffer anticipated something that would be the strong and mature human being living in communion with the sufferings of the weak God. Here he was unable to push further. But this was, in my opinion, the horizon of Bonhoeffer's faith.

It seems to me that here in Bonhoeffer there is an approach that consists in taking the Nietzschean idea to its end, in order to reverse it, as it were, by adopting it entirely. This appears again even more clearly in a letter from Bonhoeffer to his friend:

> The poem about Christians and pagans contains an idea that you will recognize: "Christians stand by God in his hour of grieving"; that is what distinguishes Christians from pagans. Jesus asked in Gethsemane, "Could you not watch with me one hour?" That is a reversal of what the religious man expects from God. Man is summoned to share in God's sufferings at the hands of a godless world.
>
> He must therefore really live in the godless world, without attempting to gloss over or explain its ungodliness in some religious way or other. He must live a "secular" life, and thereby share in God's sufferings. He *may* live a "secular" life (as one who has been freed from false religious obligations and inhibitions). To be a Christian does not mean to be religious in a particular way, to make something of oneself (a sinner, a penitent, or a saint) on the basis of some method or other, but to be a man—not a type

of man, but the man that Christ creates in us. It is not the religious act that makes the Christian, but participation in the sufferings of God in the secular life. (LPP 361)

CHRISTIANS AND PAGANS

1

Men go to God when they are sore bestead,
Pray to him for succour, for his peace, for bread,
For mercy for them sick, sinning, or dead;
All men do so, Christian and unbelieving.

2

Men go to God when he is sore bestead,
Find him poor and scorned, without shelter or bread,
Whelmed under weight of the wicked, the weak, the dead;
Christians stand by God in his hour of grieving.

3

God goes to every man when sore bestead,
Feeds body and spirit with his bread;
For Christians, pagans alike he hangs dead,
And both alike forgiving. (LPP 348–49)

The Polyphony of Life

How do we live what I have dared to call, in terms that may be a little forced, the experience of the weakness of God in the strength of the human being? We see some scattered expressions of it in the tranquility and joy that Bonhoeffer's fellow prisoners had recognized on his face and in his everyday gestures. This is what he continually called the polyphony of life. Several times he speaks of this multidimensional and polyphonic life, against the man of only one idea, or the man of only one experience. "Jesus reclaims for himself and for his kingdom," he says, "a full life in all of its manifestations and not only in the weakness and distress of man." This is a theme, I might add, which had been perceived several times by Goethe and also by Nietzsche—that the fullness of human experience in joy and in suffering, this polyphony, is the true experience of "walking with God." In a very beautiful text Bonhoeffer, taking a musical image, says that the presence of God is the *cantus firmus,* the bass singing, underneath the diversity of human experience. It is therefore the direct opposite of a Christianity of condemnation and obligation. It is a sort of detached participation in everything, in the sense when St. Paul said, "weeping as though not weeping, being all things to all men" (*pleurant comme ne pleurant pas, étant tout à tous*).[11]

A Church for Others

I will stop there, with a question that also remained a question for Bonhoeffer: What does this mean for the church? Here we only have a few words from Bonhoeffer. He says that this means at least one thing for the church: to be "a church for others." He likes to say that Christ is the man for others. The true church is the church for others. Often, he says, it has fought for its preservation. But it exists only in pronouncing a word of reconciliation for all human beings. Or again: "The measure of preaching is the non-religious human being. Attending to the non-religious human being measures the faith of the church." But then perhaps this was, if not its last word, in any case, its last silence: yet Bonhoeffer thought that the church will have to pass through a very long time before being able to pronounce this word. This is why in the period of our culture in which we live, when men are brought back to God in his absence and in his silence, the church may be unable to speak until it has regained this freedom and invented this new language.

†

We reproduce here the main part of the discussion that followed the above lecture.

Q. = Question or intervention.
R. = Paul Ricoeur's Response.

Q. What do you think of this kind of phrase, which one hears in the churches: "You are sinners; you must be redeemed in order to have eternal life"? What do you do with these notions of sin and eternal life?

R. I believe that it's necessary to redeem the sinner in this original sense, namely that this isn't a moral category. If we define sin as an infraction of commandments, we would be defining it according to law. But, as St. Paul says, the law and sin are dead. Consequently I believe that it's necessary to recover the non-moral sense of sin, which is the absence of God. It's necessary to de-moralize the notion of sin in order to restore to its meaning the notion of sin that is not measured by an individual transgression, a sort of personal impurity, but as the state of a community that is not in friendship with God. In the Old Testament, the fundamental notion is this "covenant," which is much more important than that of "law." Elsewhere in the Old Testament the notion of law has a positive sense, as instruction, as Torah and not as categorical imperative. It is therefore necessary to rediscover what I would call the existential dimension of sin.

Secondly then, you say "eternal life." But eternal life is the fullness of the present (*la plénitude du présent*). Eternity is not an infinite time; it's a full moment. I believe what philosophers and theologians have always said. It's the imagination that carries eternity forward into a sort of duration without end, a sort of before time or after time. Eternity is the fullness of the present.

Q. I would like to say something regarding Nietzsche. Nietzsche took Christianity to be a form of nihilism, which is to say, a form of condemnation of life. This is because the Christian is a man who does not accept suffering, who does not accept death, who does not accept travail—all that which is negative in life, such that he conjures up a compensation in the idea of a Savior, of an anti-world in which these things would no longer exist. And in the name of that world, of course, he condemns this life. The existence of that world is the best proof that this life is detestable. And that is why it is a form of nihilism.

But I believe that what Nietzsche proposes is a sort of Dionysianism— that is, the full acceptance of life, the negative aspects as well as the positive. But just now you spoke of a reversal of Nietzschean thought. But what I saw there instead was a total acceptance, in as much as you spoke of the polyphony of life, of the negative and of the positive.

R. I wanted to speak more precisely of a reversal in the conception of Christianity such as it was condemned by Nietzsche. In that case, as you have said, this reversal is in a certain sense in agreement with Nietzsche's condemnation. Nietzsche spoke in the nineteenth century, in a moment when this vision of a Christianity of evasion was still triumphant, albeit wounded, and this is indeed what he attacked. I have always been struck that in Nietzsche, there is never an attack on Christ. It isn't even the same as when he happens to become insane, he cites: "The crucified or Dionysus."

I don't want to say that Bonhoeffer would represent this as the only Christianity that is possible. But he wanted to go to the opposite extreme of what appeared to him to be the historical vice of Christendom: Christendom presented as a sort of spiritual hospital for the wounded of life. Then that is the reality of life. If we truly preach creation, incarnation, and resurrection, this means three successive ways of preaching that glorify life.

Q. I would also say that, more than Mounier, what you have said makes me think of Béguin. Béguin meditated on agony as being a sort of radiating center . . .

R. Well, I'm not in a position to tell you—since I myself am on the threshold of this thought—what this total identification between the agony of Christ and the joy of life might mean. If this conjunction could be understood, I believe we would grasp there the type of Christianity that Bonhoeffer was on the way to discovering, or perhaps of inventing.

Q. There is *The Birth of Tragedy*, by Nietzsche, which goes in this direction . . .

R. That's very intriguing, because one would find a new agreement with Greek thought. It happened with Plato, for ten centuries. It happened with Aristotle for six centuries. And here one would return to tragedy, to the Presocratics. Incidentally, in his book Bonhoeffer makes some notes on *The Gods of Greece*. In certain places he says: "Well, I prefer this to the God of the Christians" (which means: what the Christians have made of God).[12]

He also spoke of the O.T., saying that it is necessary to return there against the Gnostic aspects of the N.T., because there we have a God of the earth. The promised land, the soil, is this earth. The O.T. does not speak of Heaven, but always of the earth: "I will give to you a land . . . , You will be a people." Not an interiority, but a people; not a Heaven, but a land . . . Simone Weil had seen that. There is something to be done on "Bonhoeffer and Simone Weil."

If it's necessary that the church returns to the Old Testament, it is therefore, according to Bonhoeffer, in order to root its preaching in a worldly manner, against the temptation to create a celestial message, a religion of salvation, in the sense of the religions of salvation of the Hellenistic world— that is to say, a way of withdrawing from the world in order to be incorporated in an invisible world. What we find in the Old Testament is a worldly meaning of life, a return to the soil, to this world, in order to exist there and in order to act there in a human community.

Q. In all that you say, is there a central point from which one can radiate?

In what way do you acknowledge Christ? Is he a historical given, do you accept him under a positive form, or is he a model for a way of life, of thought?

R. I am trying to understand Bonhoeffer. He thought very exactly about the Christ to whom the primitive Church testifies, without which we could, with certitude, piece together the historical person, the Jesus of history. But with him there is a kind of adhesion of the Christ of faith to the Christ of history at a determinate point, which is the cross as the giving of life for others.

Q. Then it's the cross that is at the center . . . ?

R. Yes, it's the cross that is at the center. It's the resurrection as well since it isn't a distinct event, but the return of the meaning of the cross, which is no longer the defeat of one man, but the opening of life for all. The resurrection is this meaning of life that takes up the event of the cross. There aren't two events: the cross and the resurrection. There is only one of them, which, as defeat, signifies life. The good news is that this defeat of the cross is my life. I believe Bonhoeffer understands things in this way. Then from this I am a free man, who lives, who's not going to mortify himself, since life is truly stronger than death.

Q. What still remains very problematic for me is Bonhoeffer's assertion, according to which the human being that we know today, the human being as we are today, is a human being come of age. If I think that one can't be in deep accord with his aggressiveness against the stop-gap God, the God of metaphysics and interiority, to what extent can one really talk about the human being strictly the way he presents him? To what extent is the human being not also, always and at the same time, this weak creature who needs help? I noted what you said at the same time concerning the weakness of God in the strength of man. Why oppose the two? Why say that it is necessary to speak strictly of the weakness of God and of the strength of man and not of the inverse? Because St. Paul spoke of the inverse as well. It seems to me that here there is a shortcoming in Bonhoeffer's perspective. There is an absence of dialectic, which finally unbalances all of his message. It is necessary to receive it as profoundly questioning for the church, to be sure. But the gospel is also the declaration of the strength of God offered to the weakness of man, because we are at the same time one and the other, strong and weak.

R. Yes, Bonhoeffer says: That is what always happened, and that is what has falsified Christianity by turning it into a hunt for the miserable. Elsewhere he has some very curious passages on psychotherapists. He must have been thinking about all these people who use the discovery of neuroses to stir people up and capture them in the sacristy,[13] by means of the clinic: "You think you're well? It's not true, you're sick."

I don't make a church father out of him: But I do believe that this may mean something for both believers and unbelievers; I would even mix them in order to make matters more complex. One can no longer know who is who, inside, and that may be absolutely fundamental at this moment of our culture. More and more I forbid myself to use "believers" and "nonbelievers" in order to make categories of human beings. It may not even be necessary to make use of these categories anymore. I do not want to know who is believing, who is not believing. I simply want to know if there is a Word that still speaks. It's the only thing that counts.

Q. That doesn't make the problem of the church easier. What is the church and how should it live as the church today?

R. There are all sorts of passages that I have not presented—passages that would be much thornier, and would confuse things more. Because at the same time, one sees him who says, "Today, I read the text of the day." Bonhoeffer is a man who prays like a child, who reads the texts of liturgical lists of his church, who writes an admirable text to his godson for his baptism, who writes to his friend: "You should preach today on such and such passage; it is a beautiful text." On the one hand, he thinks that it is necessary, if one thinks one should be part of it, to make the parishes live so that preaching exists; but on the other hand the parish must be the place where religion dies so that there is continually born a word that can be heard by all. It's the confessing community as the base for preaching to man himself. But that permits me at no moment to say that the one who doesn't take part is an unbeliever. I know nothing of it. No more than I will say the one who runs the parish is a believer. I know nothing of that either. We have to leave that as a total unknown about which we shouldn't make pronouncements.

Q. Several times there is the word "prayer." What does that cover?

R. Certainly not the prayer of demands, this begging of the weak, but very certainly, for Bonhoeffer, the recognition of being alive, or if you like, a way of remaining "before God," as he often says. It is an expression that returns without ceasing: "Being before God, as if God did not exist." It is again an extraordinary paradox, this "being before God." It doesn't necessarily mean that one mumbles sentences. But it may be a psychological, educational support to be before God. Prayer doesn't simply turn itself back into giving a little speech to God.

Q. It's easy to say, "Religion is dead, God is dead." It's easy to say this to people who know what religion is, who can understand what we are talking about when we talk about God. But when one addresses children, how do you think one must present these things? Too often we distort things from the start by speaking to children like we do.

R. I think that this consists first of all in not saying a certain number of things, in never initiating them with the metaphysical God, but only, for example, telling them biblical stories. It isn't necessary to present a theoretical, speculative catechism on providence. They should be initiated only with conduct, with characters, like Abraham, the prophets, the life of Jesus . . .

So first of all a catechism without metaphysics; this seems to me important. Then secondly, to point toward the other and not toward interiority. In each case, what Bonhoeffer forbids is to turn the catechism into an apologetic, as a kind of conquest of souls.

Q. Isn't it in maturity, in the state of the adult man, that one has the most profound experience of solitude?

R. The human being who faces God is not only an abstract construct of the human being, but the entire human, the concrete human, and by consequence the strength and the weakness, the joy and the pain. It's the wholeness of human experience.

Q. Isn't it also the dialectic of the one and the other?

R. Yes. There is a very beautiful text, where he says, "Sorrow and joy are twin brothers." In Teilhard, by contrast, it seems to me that there is a sort of new theological positivism, in the sense that if you observe the fossils well you will see there the mark of the divine. It is a *néofinalisme*.

But it is necessary to add, if one wants to speak of dialectic in Bonhoeffer, that things return at precisely the moment when all seemed lost. I want to say that it is in the moment even when the metaphysical God grows more distant, as an explanation of which one has less and less need, that a certain proximity of the suffering God of the cross is achieved. I believe that's what he heard when he spoke of "the beyond in the midst of our life."[14] But I don't know very well what this means. This is one of these formulas that have such a force of radiation that they blind before they enlighten: "A suffering God can help"!

In any case, they become serious again if faith has its point of impact in this world and not another. Then we take things seriously, since here Christ is called "the man for others," and it's said that the only church that is possible is a church for the world. At this moment we can no longer take refuge in a sort of interior garden of piety, in order to shelter ourselves from war, from injustice, from apartheid, etc. On the contrary, everything becomes serious; because nothing is serious if we say that this life is a sort of examination to traverse for the sake of another life that would alone be important.

Q. But the beyond, as life after death—do you make an abstraction of it, or how do you conceive of it?

R. I answer you here very precisely that I know nothing of it. Every movement of Bonhoeffer's thought is to lead us, as he says, on this side of death, for the seriousness of a life resurrected here and now. I think that in the current state of our culture the question of the beyond cannot yet be posed . . .

Translated by Brian Gregor

Notes

This chapter originally appeared in *Les Cahiers du Centre Protestant l'Ouest*, no. 7 (November 1966): 3–20. Ricoeur delivered it at the Centre Protestant de l'Ouest on the weekend of June 4–5, 1966. Thank you to Catherine Goldenstein and Le Fonds Ricoeur for permission to publish this translation. Also, thanks to Richard and Anne Kearney for their help and suggestions.

1. Ricoeur's word choice here ("la lutte armée et même au terrorisme") conveys a slightly inaccurate impression regarding Bonhoeffer's involvement in the anti-Nazi resistance and the plots to assassinate Hitler, since he himself did not take up arms.—Eds.

2. S. Payne West, *The Venlo Incident* (New York: Hutchinson, 1950), 180.

3. None of the prefaces to Barth's *Der Romerbrief* contain this statement. Later in the text Barth does speak of religion "dying," insofar as it comes under God's judgment and is unable to stand before God as an independent human possibility. See *The Epistle to the Romans*, trans. Edwyn C. Hoskyns (London: Oxford University Press, 1933, 1968), 130–31, 233, 238.—Eds.

4. "Barth, who is the only one to have started along this line of thought, did not carry it to completion, but arrived at a positivism of revelation, which in the last analysis is essentially a restoration. For the religionless working man (or any other man) nothing decisive is gained here" (LPP 280).

5. Here Ricoeur is distilling a letter from July 8, 1944: "The displacement of God from the world, and from the public part of life, led to the attempt to keep his place secure at least in the sphere of the 'personal', the 'inner', and the 'private'. And as every man still has a private sphere somewhere, that is where he was thought to be the most vulnerable. The secrets known to a man's valet—that is, to put it crudely, the range of his intimate life, from prayer to his sexual life—have become the hunting-ground of modern pastoral workers. In that way they resemble (though with quite different intentions) the dirtiest gutter journalists. . . . From a sociological point of view this is a revolution from below, a revolt of inferiority" (LPP 344).—Eds.

6. Cf. LPP 346.

7. Volume editors' note: Ricoeur includes a French rendering—"comme si il n'y avait pas le Dieu"—of this expression, which Bonhoeffer appropriates from Grotius.

8. Cf. LPP 391.

9. Cf. LPP 336–37.

10. This letter is actually from July 21, 1944 (LPP 369–70).—Eds.

11. Volume editors' note: Here Ricoeur seems to be combining two passages from Paul's first epistle to the Corinthians: 1 Cor 7:29–31 ("Voici ce que je dis, frères, c'est que le temps est court; que désormais ceux qui ont des femmes soient comme n'en ayant pas, ceux qui pleurent comme ne pleurant pas, ceux qui se réjouissent comme ne se réjouissant pas, ceux qui achètent comme ne possédant pas, et ceux qui usent du monde comme n'en usant pas, car la figure de ce monde passé."), and 1 Cor 9:22 ("J'ai été faible avec les faibles, afin de gagner les faibles. Je me suis fait tout à tous, afin d'en sauver de toute manière quelques-uns.").

12. "I'm at the present reading the quite outstanding book by W. F. Otto, the classics man at Königsberg, *The Gods of Greece*. To quote from his closing words, it's about 'this world of faith, which sprang from the wealth and depth of human existence, not from its cares and longings.' Can you understand my finding something very attractive in this theme and its treatment, and also—*horribile dictu*—my finding these gods, when they are so treated, less offensive than certain brands of Christianity? In fact, that I almost think I could claim these gods for Christ?" (LPP 333).

13. Volume editors' note: Ricoeur uses a hunting metaphor here, speaking of "*rabatteurs de sacristie*." A "rabbatteur" is one who beats bushes in order to scare game in the direction of the hunters. Thus "*rabatteurs de sacristie*" are those religious people who use the psychoanalytic discovery of neuroses to send people in the direction of the sacristy, where they can be captured by the church. See LPP 326, 341, 346.

14. See LPP 282.

EIGHT

Bonhoeffer's "Religious Clothes": The Naked Man, the Secret, and What We Hear

KEVIN HART

On the train from Berlin to Munich on June 25, 1942, Dietrich Bonhoeffer wrote to Eberhard Bethge about how his recent activity had been largely "in the worldly [*weltlich*] sector." He was amazed, he said, that "I am living, and can live, for days without the Bible"; it was an "authentic experience" that he did not want to falsify, even though he was going against what he had written and published. There had been richer times "in the 'spiritual' sense," he admitted, and then made an important remark. "But I sense how an opposition to all that is 'religious' is growing in me. Often into an instinctive revulsion—which is surely not good either. I am not religious by nature. But I must constantly think of God, of Christ; authenticity, life, freedom, and mercy mean a great deal to me. It is only that the religious clothes they wear make me so uncomfortable. Do you understand? None of these are new thoughts and insights at all. Because I believe that I am on the verge of some kind of breakthrough, I am letting things take their own course and do not resist."[1]

That some kind of theological breakthrough took place for Bonhoeffer has not been doubted, but exactly what it was, what its roots are, and what follows from it have been much debated. Is it a matter of patching "religious clothes" or changing them for a suit and tie, of recognizing, as the redoubtable Diogenes Treufelsdröch did before him in his *Die Kleider, ihr Werden und Wirken* (1831), that "all Symbols are properly Clothes; that all Forms whereby Spirit manifests itself to sense, whether outwardly or in the imagination, are Clothes"?[2] In that case Bonhoeffer is committed to a natural supernaturalism, and God and Christ could be translated without loss into authenticity, life, freedom, and charity. Or is it a question of recognizing that "religious clothes" cover true Christianity, inhibiting any Christian who wears them? The two questions indicate quite different ways in which Bonhoeffer has been read, and I will begin by briefly considering them.

The first question implicitly sees Bonhoeffer as inheriting from a rich tradition in which positive religion is regarded as having largely been played out. ("None of these are new thoughts and insights" in history is significant for this interpretation.) The tradition has many roots, though two of the deepest and most enduring of them are Kant's attempt to rethink religion within the limits of bare reason, and hence to promote ethics over doctrine and ritual, and Hegel's argument that *Geist* no longer fully discloses itself in religion—not even in Christianity, the consummate religion—but in philosophy.[3] Whether the analysis is purely conceptual (as with Kant) or conceptual-historical (as with Hegel), the conclusion is the same: a mature understanding of Christianity requires one to recognize that, if one still wishes to talk of God, one must do so in terms negotiated by philosophy, and on behalf of a philosophical anthropology. And if one does not wish to talk of God, the other conversations in which one takes part will become possible and attractive partly because the negotiation has been forgotten, or sidelined by a growing sense of the disenchantment of the world. Religion becomes, as Philip Larkin puts it so well, "That vast moth-eaten musical brocade."[4]

A world "come of age," as Bonhoeffer has it, is one in which we must recognize that our responsibilities are in the world and to the world, not the beyond. One must be "this-worldly," Bonhoeffer says, by which he means "living unreservedly in life's duties, problems, successes and failures, experiences and perplexities" (LPP 370). To be "this-worldly" is "to throw ourselves completely into the arms of God, taking seriously, not our own sufferings, but those of God in the world—watching with Christ in Gethsemane" (LPP 370). What may well seem evangelical in tone is Hegelian in substance: in the Passion "the life of God" has known "the seriousness, the suffering, the patience, and the labor of the negative."[5] And remembering how Hegel's words tremble before the hermeneutical violence of both the right and the left, we may suspect that "God in the world" is perhaps no more than the reconciliation of religion and worldliness by way of ethics understood as *Sittlichkeit*.[6] This reading turns on Bonhoeffer's provocative formulation "religionless Christianity" [*Religionsloses Christentum*], and it links him in the past to German idealism and in the future to the "secular city" and the "death of God" movements, for whom Jesus became, in a way, all the more important with the rumored demise of his Father.[7]

The second question is oriented more surely by another of Bonhoeffer's formulations, one that occurs more often in his last writings than "religionless

Christianity"; it is "non-religious interpretation of Scripture" [*nicht-religiöse Interpretation*], and it leagues him now with Karl Barth and now with Rudolf Bultmann.[8] It has roots in his own writings—"'religion' is really superfluous," he notes in 1939 in the context of a failure of American theologians to shift decisively from religion to the Word—which gives a personal sense to "None of these are new thoughts and insights" (WF 230).[9] The link with Barth is clearly the fierce criticism of "religion" in the second edition of *The Epistle to the Romans* (1922) and the more subtle, Hegelian treatment of the topic in *Church Dogmatics*, 1: 2 (1938), §17, "The Revelation of God as the *Aufhebung* of Religion." I will return to it in a moment. The connection with Bultmann is hinged to Bonhoeffer's comment on May 5, 1944, that in demythologizing the New Testament Bultmann did not go "'too far,' as most people thought, but that he didn't go far enough." Where Bultmann located "the 'mythological' concepts, such as miracle, ascension, and so on" as problematic, the real difficulty for Christians is in "'religious' concepts generally" (LPP 285). Bonhoeffer rightly saw that the concepts regarded as mythological "are not in principle separable from the concepts of God, faith, etc.," and so it comes as no surprise to read him saying a month later that "the full content, including the 'mythological' concepts, must be kept—the New Testament is not a mythological *clothing* [my emphasis] of a universal truth; this mythology (resurrection etc.) is the thing itself." Indeed, "the concepts must be interpreted in such a way as not to make religion a precondition of faith" (LPP 329).

On this reading, less common in the United States than in Germany, Bonhoeffer is more radical than Bultmann, not by finding deeper, more hidden resources in liberal theology than the old Marburger had used, but by repudiating the program of liberal theology while retaining and extending Bultmann's methodological insight. Bonhoeffer is to be read as offering a thoroughgoing hermeneutic that preserves Christianity without talking, in terms made familiar by Ludwig Feuerbach and Adolph von Harnack, of an "essence" of the faith.[10] We might say that in refusing a reduction of Christianity to its supposed *Wesen*, Bonhoeffer seeks to retain the *eidos* of the faith. That is, he keeps the principles that structure Christianity as a whole (incarnation, cross, and resurrection, among others) and that are distinct in theory from its religious coverings.

Neither of these readings of Bonhoeffer is entirely persuasive, partly because the context of his final writings is fragmentary and incomplete, partly because it is unclear to what degree, if any, the final writings cohere with the earlier ones, and partly because each reading needs some nourishment from the other. That said, the two readings are not of equal merit. Not that they are entirely commensurable: the first is largely descriptive, based on a historical account that something has happened, while the second is largely normative, turning on proper theological procedure.[11] Nonetheless, the second one accounts for more of Bonhoeffer's theology than the first one. Even if this judgment is accepted, however, it is difficult to see the later and earlier writings in their proper relation because we cannot always determine the true value of motifs in the later writings, and even if we could do so we would still not be in a good position to link them to other values. For example, we know that the notion of a "world come of age" is central to Bonhoeffer, but we do not know the extent to which he was aware of quoting the same expression in Barth's *Church Dogmatics* 1: 2 (1938), where it has a somewhat different flavor.[12] More complex is the question of how we are to hold together the theologies of Finkenwalde and Tegel. Equally difficult is the question of how we are to balance Bonhoeffer's Christology ("I must constantly think of God, of Christ") with his late absorption in Wilhelm Dilthey's *Lebensphilosophie* ("authenticity, life, freedom, and mercy mean a great deal to me").[13] In terms of influence, it is evident that Hegel is behind the notion of "religionless Christianity," though so too is Kierkegaard, if only one looks at the notion in another light, that of Christianity without Christendom. And in terms of conclusions, it is clear that Bonhoeffer prizes ethics, although it should be apparent that it is a *Christian* ethics, one that cuts its figure against all philosophical ethics, including Kant's.[14] Finally, in terms of theological structure, it is plain that liberal theology is rejected; and yet it needs to be recognized that it is rejected twice, in its positive shaping of Bultmann's program and in its negative shaping of Barth's neo-orthodox dogmatics.

In general we might ask are those clothes, from *Sanctorum Communio* to *Life Together* and beyond, to be patched or are they to be replaced? Or, if all clothes are no more than the forms of the Spirit manifesting itself to sense, do we need them at all? Do Christians need to wear garments that are shot through with religious threads? If not, one image that might fit the late Bonhoeffer is provided by the gospel. We recall the scene. Jesus has been praying in Gethsemane, throwing himself completely into the arms of God, and is now being taken away to the high priest; it is the first stage of what will be his Passion. At just that moment Mark relates a strange incident that interrupts his narrative:

> And there followed him a certain young man [νεανίσκος τις]
> having a linen cloth [σινδόνα] cast about *his* naked *body;* and the young men laid hold on him;
> And he left the linen cloth [σινδόνα], and fled from them naked. (Mk 14:51–52, KJV)

There are various theories about this young man, including whether he is Lazarus or even Mark himself. Most likely, he is coming from a secret meeting, perhaps having been just baptized.[15] For us, reading the story and trying to make it hang together with the rest of the gospel, we may be inclined to see Mark hinting that baptism is a form of death, that the entire life of a Christian is a sacrifice of oneself in one's worldly dimension in the hope of resurrection. We remember that Christ left a cloth (*sindon*) in the cave on Easter Sunday, and therefore can easily iron out the wrinkle in Mark's story by associating the young man with the resurrection.[16] If we think along these lines, the vignette hardly fits the theology being worked out in Tegel, a theology turned resolutely toward the world. Yet we get closer to what is happening in the narrative if we recall the seventeenth-century expression that Bonhoeffer uses in Tegel, and the concept behind it that had been on his mind since Finkenwalde in 1937: *disciplina arcani* or *Arkandisziplin*, the discipline of the secret.[17] "What is the place of worship and prayer in a religionless situation?" Bonhoeffer asks, "Does the secret discipline . . . take on a new importance here?" (LPP 281).

Attempts to assimilate Bonhoeffer to the "secular gospel" and "death of God" camps overlook or reduce his remarks on the *disciplina arcani*, and so do those readings of the *Letters and Papers from Prison* that see Bonhoeffer's theological breakthrough exclusively in hermeneutic terms. I want to suggest that if we give due weight to the discipline of the secret we can grasp the concept "religionless Christianity" or "non-religious interpretation" more firmly, and see what follows for us from this theology if we choose to see ourselves in its wake. Giving "due weight" to something means recognizing the gravity to which it is subject, and in the world of nineteenth- and early twentieth-century theology that is given by the concept "religion," which draws all things down to earth, no matter how high they had been placed in the heavens. The positing of religion rather than God as the proper object of theology begins in the Enlightenment. The vogue of natural religion is important, needless to say, but so too is the colonial engagement with positive religions other than Judaism and Christianity, and the desire to explain their differences and to find common ground between them.

Over the same period of Enlightenment, philosophy untwines itself from theology and considers questions arising from theology entirely on its own, first under the heading of *theologia rationalis,* and then with Kant's influential lectures of 1783–84, published as *Vorlesungen über die philosophische Religionslehre* (1817). God was made by philosophers to cede pride of place to religion, and the object of the new subject "Philosophie der Religion" was to bring the positive religions into line with the critical philosophy. Hegel would color this picture in his own way, arguing that we can know God as *Geist,* while nonetheless folding talk of God into a broader conversation about religion. "It will be evident," he said while lecturing in 1824, "that God can only be genuinely understood in the mode of his being as spirit, by means of which he makes himself into the counterpart of a community and brings about the activity of a community in relation to him; thus it will be evident that the doctrine of God is to be grasped and taught only as the doctrine of *religion*."[18] Schleiermacher would see things differently, yet through a fisheye lens of religion that he had ground independently of the arch-philosopher in his *Speeches on Religion* (1799). And Troeltsch would continue to look in the same general direction (with a glance seeking approval from Kant) in his "On the Question of the Religious *A Priori*" (1909).

The living context of Bonhoeffer's retrieval of the discipline of the secret is Barth's abrupt refusal of "religion" as the master metaphor of theology. No more so than Barth, though in a quite different way, does Bonhoeffer simply include Hegel in this rejection: Christ remains for him the very life of community. Equally important as a qualification is that Bonhoeffer comes to see Barth's notion of "revelation," which in effect replaces "religion," as overly narrow. It allows Barth to pass from the criticism of "religion" to the doctrine of God and to establish, precisely, a *church* dogmatics, a theology for those who already belong to and participate in a determinate ecclesial structure. Reluctant at the end to take this path, Bonhoeffer moves from a criticism of "religion" to an affirmation of living in the world without it (but nonetheless with Christ). This requires us to think more deeply about what Bonhoeffer calls "the world" and the relation to it one must adopt if one is to be a Christian. Before engaging in a second detour, though, some remarks on the discipline of the secret are in order.

The New Testament tells us that the mysteries of the faith were not to be taught to initiates all at once. Paul reminds the Corinthians that, carnal as they are, they have been unfit to learn spiritual truths, and so he has had to feed them milk and not meat (1 Cor 3:1–2); and much the same is said in Hebrews 5:12–14. Certainly those aspiring to belong to the church were not allowed to participate in or even view the celebration of the Eucharist: hence early references to the *missa catechumenorum*.[19] If this was to safeguard the sacred mysteries from the eyes of the profane, it was also, before the faith was free from persecution, to minimize the chances of spies infiltrating the young religion. What Tertullian called "the fealty of silence" would prevent absurd rumors about the Eucharist being spread, absurd because they confused natural and sacramental truths; while Basil, Gregory of Nazianzus, and Cyril of Jerusalem all point out that a clear line is to be drawn between those who partake of the mysteries and those who do not.[20] In the "Pro-catechresis" Cyril tells those who wish to be baptized, "Make sure that you don't talk carelessly, not because what you are told isn't fit to talk about, but because your listener isn't fit to hear it."[21] Catechumens were told of the Trinity and the Eucharist at the last stage of instruction before baptism, and were required to learn the Paternoster only days before receiving the sacrament. The *disciplina arcani,* then, has nothing to do with an esoteric teaching or a gnosis reserved for the spiritually elect (it is not a "secret discipline") but has everything to do with the reserve of the faithful in a period of converting the heathen and being persecuted by the Romans.

Doubtless the discipline of the secret came to Bonhoeffer in Tegel because the Confessing Church was being persecuted like the Christians of the first centuries. Yet the "new importance" he ascribes to it does not come by way of a return to it but by a rethinking of it. The danger for the church now is profanation of the mysteries not by those outside the community but by those within it, by followers of "unconscious Christianity" (FTP 106).[22] Too many Christians are good merely in the "citizenship [*bürgerlich*] sense," he says, and have yet to become conscious of what the faith actually teaches and demands of them (FTP 106n39). Think of Direktor Warmblut's widow in the novel that Bonhoeffer wrote while in prison. Returning home from Sunday morning service, she tells Frau Brake about the sermon she has just heard. The minister said "that everyone should live the way they see fit and then it will be the right way, and it doesn't matter that much to the dear Lord whether the little one is baptized or not, right, Frau Bürgermeister? And it really doesn't matter that much at all whether my little Hilde goes to church or not. We're all free people, after all, that's how he expressed it. Oh, what a wonderful idea! So liberating, so deep, and why shouldn't it be, right, dearest Frau Bürgermeister? In fact, he had a Bible passage . . ." (FTP 78). To which Frau Bürgermeister responds pointedly, "My dear Frau Direktor, did it escape you again that the pastor said what you wanted to hear, but didn't preach the word of God?" (FTP 79).

The passage from the novel is worth keeping in mind when we turn to Bonhoeffer's sermon of roughly the same time on the baptism of his godson, Dietrich Wilhelm Rüdiger Bethge. Bonhoeffer tells the child and his family, "Our church, which has been fighting in these years only for its self-preservation, as though that were an end in itself, is incapable of taking the word of reconciliation and redemption to mankind and the world" (LPP 300). Christians have been confusing vehicle and tenor. "Our earlier words are therefore bound to lose their force and cease, and our being Christians today will be limited to two things: prayer and righteous action among men" (LPP 300). When young Wilhelm has grown up, his godfather says, the church will have changed by dint of this prayer and this action. The word of God will be spoken differently. "It will be a new language, perhaps quite non-religious, but liberating and redeeming—as was Jesus' language; it will shock people and yet overcome them by its power" (LPP 300). Until then, "the Christian cause will be a silent and hidden affair," a discipline of the secret (LPP 300).

Bonhoeffer's emphasis is on the importance of speech: prayer, which establishes a relationship with God; proclamation, which promotes action; and also, by implication, theological language. That new speech will become available to us only after prayer and righteous action, for only they can separate the *eidos* of Christianity as a living faith from the *Wesen* of Christianity as a religion. "I will misuse the Word in my office if I do not keep meditating on it in prayer," he writes in 1936, and his stress on prayer remains constant (WF 57).

Let me make a preliminary point about prayer. To invoke it is not merely a pious gesture on Bonhoeffer's part; it bespeaks the whole complex of Christian practice and Christian language. Only in speaking to God can we experience the awe that mystery bespeaks, and learn the proper reserve when speaking of God. And only in talking *to* God can we learn to talk properly *of* God. This simple point subtends Bonhoeffer's late theology, and recalls an enigma that generates and disturbs all theology. Anyone at any time can speak to God, and yet we all have the greatest of difficulties in knowing how to talk of God. Is "religion" needed in that talk? Is philosophy? Or can it be done purely in terms of Scripture and faith, by *analogia fidei*?

In talking of proclamation, Bonhoeffer invites us to pass from thinking of men and women in terms of the "religious a priori" to hoping to see ourselves belonging to the world yet "called forth," ek-klesia (ἐκ-κλησία), from it—in the world but at an angle to it, as it were—so that we can show our brothers and sisters that Christ addresses their problems just where they are. The language of Christianity will be one of faith, a naked language like that of Jesus' parables, without any "religious clothes," and its speaker will be critical (like Jesus) of the professionally religious, people like the priest and the Levite who passed by the man on the road to Jericho who had fallen among thieves who "stripped him of his raiment" (Lk11:30-37). His nakedness calls to the naked man or woman in each of us. Can we speak of God in ordinary language, as Jesus did? The parables do not use the vocabulary of formative ("early") Judaism—covenant and mitzvah, for example—let alone that of sin and grace, of justification and sanctification; rather, they speak of mustard seeds and lost coins, of an unjust steward and a pearl of great price, of a foolish son who leaves home and then comes home changed and a sober son who stays home and alas does not change. In such speech the Kingdom is not merely talked about but is realized in those who have ears to hear. The challenge before us, Bonhoeffer says, is to speak in the same naked language, not necessarily in parables but certainly in ways that present the humanity and otherness of God. And presumably there is an unstated coda with another challenge: to be vigilant with respect to this naked language, for it is likely to gather religious terms, natural or historical, much as a closet fills up with useless clothes over the years.

It sometimes happens that in order to clarify one's own ideas one must separate them sharply from the very ideas that have enabled them to come into being. Just so Bonhoeffer distinguishes his position from Barth's. He acknowledges that his older friend "is the only one to have started along this line of thought" but notes that he "did not carry it to completion, but arrived at a positivism of revelation, which in the last analysis is essentially a restoration" (LPP 280). In effect, the volumes of the *Dogmatics* tell their reader, "'Like it or lump it' [*Friss, Vogel, oder stirb!*]: virgin birth, Trinity, or anything else; each is an equally significant and necessary part of the whole, which must simply be swallowed as a whole or not at all" (LPP 286). This is not a biblical view, Bonhoeffer thinks. "There are degrees of knowledge and degrees of significance; that means that a secret discipline must be restored whereby the *mysteries* of the Christian faith are protected against profanation" (LPP 286). Barth's criticism of "religion" begins by insisting on the autonomy of God, yet it ends in setting church and world in opposition, whereas the New Testament teaches, Bonhoeffer thinks, that church is a being called forth from the world in order to help the world. His criticism of "religion" might be understood in this way. We do not have "religious experience," in the sense that we have distinct experiences in a part of the human spectrum of possibilities designated "religious." (Other parts of the spectrum presumably would have labels such as "domestic," "erotic," "social," and so forth.) Instead, we have what we must call "experience of God," for God can be encountered (though only as trace) intervening anywhere in the spectrum of human possibilities.

Bonhoeffer's understanding of "the world" is not all of a piece in his development as a theologian. In *Discipleship* (1937) there is a warm admiration of the monastic spirit of the late patristic era because those Christians who fled the world affirmed the costliness of grace, unlike their brothers and sisters who stayed within the increasingly secularized Church.[23] Yet this opposition of "world" and "grace" is not the most fundamental in Bonhoeffer's

thinking, early or late. To understand his sense of "the world" we must return to Adolf Schlatter, whose lectures he heard while studying at Tübingen
in 1923. One of Schlatter's steady and lonely emphases was that Judaism is not
mere background against which Christianity, a Hellenic faith, shows up in
sharp relief. Not at all: Schlatter differed from his contemporaries, especially
those in the history of religions school, in not figuring the Christianity of the
first two centuries as primarily Hellenic. The Jewish affirmation of the world
not as inherently corrupt but as natural and containing genuine possibilities
of goodness is brought out in his understanding of "the world." In his *The
History of the Christ* (1923), which came out the very year Bonhoeffer was
his student, we find him evoking "the right attitude toward the 'world,'" according to John, namely, not "in terms of things but in terms of people with
their joint expression of will and their conduct of life."[24] And in the previous
year, in *The Theology of the Apostles* (1922), it is significant that his discussion
of John's anthropology begins with the Jewish conception of "world." "The
demonstration of Jesus' divine sonship and his close association of people
with 'the world' constitute a close unity," he writes, "because the universal
scope of the message that is grounded in sonship is brought to completion
by the concept of the 'world.'"[25]

It is this sense of the world as a good work sustained by God's faithfulness to his people that was to prevent the young Bonhoeffer from thinking for long of the church as mediating the worldly and the divine. Such a
thought can be found in *Sanctorum Communio* (1930) and *Act and Being*
(1931), but not thereafter. The same sense of the world as a good work stops
Bonhoeffer from accepting a strict distinction between "church" and "world"
and affirming a false eschatology in which Christ comes *contra homines*,
and not also *ad homines* and *in homines*.[26] Also, Schlatter's resistance to
lehrbegriffliche Methode, the method of the concept of doctrine, was to play
a part in shaping Bonhoeffer's late theology. It is the unity of Jesus' work and
proclamation that is important, Schlatter taught, not simply his proclamation. What is primary is not Jesus' dogmatic teaching, his *Heilslehre*, but his
attempt to establish the Kingdom, to point to the will of God, the *Heilswille*.
Bonhoeffer did not retain the heavy shading in favor of the divine will, and
"religionless Christianity," when it started to be imagined, was to be based
on faith. Yet the "concept of doctrine" is one of the bases of "religion" for
Bonhoeffer, and its correctives are Jesus' actions and prayer.

Having pondered what Bonhoeffer learned from Schlatter, it comes as
no surprise to find that the concept of "world" comes into focus for Bonhoeffer the lecturer, not the student, in 1932, at the conclusion of his course

on Genesis, now published as *Creation and Fall*. Interpreting Genesis 3:21 ("Unto Adam also and to his wife did the LORD God make coats of skins, and clothed them"), Bonhoeffer observes, "The Creator is now the preserver; the created world is now the fallen but *preserved world*" (CF 139).[27] With this notion of a preserved world we find a distinction *in nuce* between Christians turning from the world and God coming to the world, a negative and an affirmative eschatology, and Bonhoeffer's final emphasis will be on the latter. God comes to the whole world, all its people, not just to a religious community, and comes to share their suffering and to redeem them from it. This is perhaps foreshadowed in his circular letter of September 20, 1939, written just before he left America for Germany. "In cutting across our ways, God comes to us and says his gracious 'Yes' to us, but only through the cross of Jesus Christ. He has placed this cross upon the earth. Under the cross he returns us to the earth, and its work and toil, but in so doing he binds us anew to the earth, and to the people who live, act, fight, and suffer upon it" (WF 253). I say "perhaps" because Bonhoeffer is writing here to his brethren, and we might wonder how far we can extend the range of the "our" and "us."

The concern develops into an anxiety if we place it beside a lecture of April 22, 1936. There Bonhoeffer risks the controversial statement, "*Extra ecclesiam nulla salus*," by which he means, "Whoever knowingly cuts himself off from the Confessing Church in Germany cuts himself off from salvation" because "the believer is bound to God's saving revelation" (WF 93–94). This is not a question of falling within or outside the boundary of an empirical church. "The nature of the church is not determined by those who belong to it but by the Word and sacrament of Jesus Christ which, when they are effective, gather for themselves a community in accordance with the promise" (WF 75). And Helmuth Gollwitzer underlines the distinction, pointing out that the expression "Confessing Church" can mean "the visible group of people—or the confession that gathers the congregation," and only the second interpretation can be sustained (WF 99). Even so, we may well wonder how to square the Tegel theology with this stress, entirely faithful to the Barmen Declaration, on the Christian revelation as "saving" without any reference to those who do not confess Christianity. "True, God is everywhere," Bonhoeffer says in the same piece, "'but it is not his will that you should look for him everywhere'" (WF 95). The development of his theology in Tegel includes the recognition that Christianity is a confession of faith and that faith of itself cannot draw a line between an inside and outside, a line that is required by "religion." This means that the world is not the site against which we construe transcendence, but the place where we can grasp what transcendence truly is. As Bonhoeffer says in Tegel, "The beyond is not what is infinitely remote, but what is nearest at hand" (LPP 376). And yet it also seems to mean that transcendence can be seen in one way, and one way only.

I would like to follow this issue by way of Bonhoeffer's letter of November 27, 1943, and a poem that draws on it. The poem is by Geoffrey Hill, and is called "'Christmas Trees.'" The title is a quotation from the letter. "It really is a strange feeling, to see the 'Christmas trees,' the flares that the leading aircraft drops, coming down right over our heads" (LPP 146). Here is the poem:

> Bonhoeffer in his skylit cell
> bleached by the flares' incandescent fall,
> pacing out his own citadel,
>
> restores the broken themes of praise,
> encourages our borrowed days,
> by logic of his sacrifice.
>
> Against wild reasons of the state
> his words are quiet but not too quiet.
> We hear too late or not too late.[28]

One reason I cite Hill's lyric is that it presents Bonhoeffer in the best possible light to us here and now. His cell is "skylit," illuminated from the heavens. His sainthood comes at a very high price, however. He and his cell are "bleached," turned entirely white for a moment by the flares that are dropped to give the British planes better vision for dropping their bombs. We think momentarily of the two young men encountered after the resurrection of Christ, "in shining garments" (Lk 24:4). Incarnation and resurrection are telescoped: the meaning of Christmas is not given in the religious symbol of a fir tree, one that is not even native to Christianity, but in restoring praise, encouraging others, opposing injustice, and offering oneself as a sacrifice so that others may live. The lines that most interest me, however, are the last two: "his words are quiet but not too quiet. / We hear too late or not too late." In the letter Bonhoeffer is concerned with restraint in the face of mortal danger, but Hill's poem prompts us to think more deeply about what Bonhoeffer says and how we hear him today.

Hill's Bonhoeffer speaks words that are "quiet but not too quiet": they come from a peaceful disposition although from a person who is prepared in extreme times to use violence—killing Hitler, no less—in order to restore peace. Those words are also peaceful in another sense, for they are private, secret, perhaps even disguised, although not to be kept exclusively to an inner circle. So here we return to the theme of the discipline of the secret.

"We hear too late or not too late," Hill adds, and the final line keeps in play the two senses of the penultimate line. We can hear the call of faith and act upon it before it is too late for others and ourselves, and we can hear the saving mysteries of the Christian revelation before it is too late. How we hear is a theme that Bonhoeffer addresses, and it turns on who "we" are. The church utters the call of salvation. "Of course those who are unable to hear it as Gospel hear it as law. And understood as law it carries within itself the whole hardness of the question of the extent of the church. Those who hear the church's call to salvation as law, who know that this law applies to them, protest against it and have to regard themselves as those to whom the call does not apply" (WF 78). And he adds, "Wherever the call to salvation is not heard, the church's claim becomes judgment, it divides those who hear it from those who do not hear it" (WF 78). The call of salvation itself respects and enforces no distinctions, yet those who do not answer it draw a line between themselves and the church.

What do we hear today in Bonhoeffer? We live in a world that has not come of age, a world that all too often acts in a thoroughly immature way with respect to people of other faiths. Perhaps when reading Bonhoeffer we hear that we should remove religious clothes and find a naked faith that opens us to the world; but, unlike Bonhoeffer, we find ourselves in a world that we share with persons for whom the world is differently enchanted, not only those for whom it has become disenchanted. The discipline of the secret seems at once to undercut the division between insider and outsider with respect to the secular world and to impose it on other world faiths. The issue of "religious clothes" prompts us now to consider how we can read Bonhoeffer within the frame of the theology of religions, if I may adopt Horst Bürkle's expression, and to ponder how Bonhoeffer's fragmentary late theology can be developed so that this frame does not become a prison for it.[29] At the moment it is a prison of silence. Neither Jacques Dupuis nor Paul F. Knitter even lists Bonhoeffer in his bibliography of works relating to the theology of religions.[30] As a first shot at that development, we might place Bonhoeffer's famous expression "religionless Christianity" beside another, equally well-known theological tag, "anonymous Christianity," and see if anything productive will come from their association.

Karl Rahner's idea of "anonymous Christianity" follows from his theological anthropology: all people have experience of the transcendent by dint of having transcendental experience. The position is inclusive, although we need to distinguish its first- and second-order levels. In terms of the practice of religion, Rahner holds that the good Buddhist, for example, is an anonymous Christian, and symmetrically that the good Christian is an anonymous Buddhist. There is reason to doubt that symmetry always can be found. Edward Conze, for one, maintains that a Buddhist who reads the lives of the saints could not "fully approve" one of them.[31] In terms of soteriology, Rahner maintains that the death of Christ has objectively redeemed all sinners; the subjective pole of soteriology is to be found in grace, understood as divine self-communication, which is freely offered to anyone who wishes to accept it. No symmetry takes hold at the second-order level, then: all are to be redeemed through Christ, regarded soteriologically as a final cause, regardless of whether they explicitly or implicitly believe in the saving power of the cross. "Religionless Christianity," by contrast, denies theological anthropology as an answer to the problem of secularity (and, by extension, the theology of religions). It insists on the sharp particularity of Christianity, regarded as a faith, and would object to the adjective "anonymous," since the practice of faith is an exacting discipline that should be respected.[32] This objection is forceful, and it has the effect of making it plain that, in a world that has not come of age, a theology of religions must be elaborated on a ground other than that of an inclusive theological anthropology. The Christian and the Buddhist do not look at each other, each finding his or her religious presuppositions hollowed out in the other, but rather stand together looking in the same direction (but doubtless with different intentional objects before them).

If a shared "transcendental experience" is to be put aside, it does not follow that everything held in common is to be discharged from the theology of religions. Since Justin Martyr and Augustine, Christianity has held that since God is truth, any truth stems from God.[33] The view is taken up by Barth who, in his own way, can be seen to develop one insight of theology from Tegel as well as from Hippo, in his treatment of "secular parables" in *Church Dogmatics* IV: 3. i, and the related account of world religions in his "doctrine of lights."[34] Certainly Bonhoeffer was not himself always, if ever, well disposed to the idea of there being lights other than Christ. In 1931 at least, he would have liked to "kill" everything else "beside the one great light."[35] Barth indirectly combats this triumphalism, not to mention his own tendencies in that direction, in his highly dialectical understanding of the "one Word of Christ" and the many words *extra muros ecclesiae* that bear witness to the Word.[36] As the one true Word, the light of life, Christ is held above all human words, including those we find in the Bible and in the church. Christians, like Buddhists and socialists, can only be witnesses to the truth that is given to all, and the truth of their words derives not from a natural capacity but strictly from the Word itself. All other words reflect and refract the light of the life, and the light of life illumines them, no matter where they are. Secular parables are secondary to the biblical parables: without divine illumination they would wither in the thin soil of a particular place and time. And yet we, in our place and our time, should be open to the call to repentance and their affirmation of the truth that they communicate to us, if sometimes despite their intentions.

Barth's late theology turns on a dialectical unity of reconciliation and revelation, rather than the sharp opposition between revelation and world that characterizes the theology of *Romans*. One cannot unfold Bonhoeffer's "world" so that it overlaps with Barth's "reconciliation," with its subcategories of event, history, and the life of Jesus. And yet one can think back through Bonhoeffer's procedure to find another way in which reconciliation as a central category in the theology of religions can be imagined. Such rethinking requires reversal of some ideas and re-inscription of other ideas. I propose to do both in several interrelated points.

PRIVILEGED PLURALISM

In his consideration of "world," as inherited from Schlatter, Bonhoeffer shows that we can develop Christian theology by being attentive to its living inheritance from the Jews. Readers of Bonhoeffer have the opportunity to recognize an internal pluralism in Christianity, not only in its own differing self-understandings but also in its heritage. Christianity does not have to be opened to other faiths; it is—or should be—already open in principle to them by dint of a rigorous scriptural and theological understanding of its privileged relation to Judaism. Hellenic Christianity is a faith in false clothes, and indeed the faith is itself only to the extent that it maintains a dynamic relation with Judaism, a relation without relation, as Blanchot and Levinas might say, that is, a relation that is plural, mobile, and open.[37] Bonhoeffer's recognition of the responsibility that Christians bear for the suffering of the Jews in the 1930s is a part of keeping this privileged pluralism alive, but this recognition should not be confined to guilt over non-response to particular events (November 9, 1938).[38] The Christian, Bonhoeffer teaches, is to oppose oppression wherever it is found, including the oppression of other faiths. Christians need to be kept aware that the incarnation of Christ is not something that once happened and that has been overcome by the resurrection, giving us a purely spiritual Christ. That would be as though a Monophysite Christology had finally triumphed over the formulations of the Nicene and Chalcedonian creeds. Rather, the incarnation happened once and for all eternity. Christianity is doubly displaced with respect to any claim that it can master its own religious center: Jesus Christ is eternally *Jewish* in the flesh and eternally *universal* in the spirit. The relation of Christianity to Judaism is one that must always be in play, thereby opening Christianity in principle to other religions.

DIALECTICIZE CHRISTIAN ETHICS

Like Luther and Calvin, Bonhoeffer subscribes to a divine command ethics. Christian ethics is "the critique of all ethics," since it adheres to the model of *Oben und Unten,* coming from above to below (E 299–300). Yet, in the case where this theological emphasis becomes mistakenly embedded in social structures, generating unfair privileges, Christian ethics needs the correction associated with the Enlightenment insistence "on the equal dignity of all people as ethical beings" (E 374), while remaining wary of the Enlightenment's tendency to figure human reason as an abstract principle that "dissolves and undermines all particular content" (E 374). Bonhoeffer's concern here is understandable. For unless it is properly framed, which is no easy matter, divine-command ethics courts the charge of arbitrariness: an action is moral or immoral not because of any intrinsic reason but because it is commanded from above.[39] Seen from one angle, it empties both God and human beings of virtue, for all human virtues are subordinated to obedience, while no moral virtues are associated with God.[40] Finally, it also risks rendering the ethics of other faiths unintelligible *as ethics,* since they cannot be regarded as authentic commands or they are authentic and hence presume agreement with Christianity. Yet Christian ethics, divine command ethics, is nonetheless preferable to ethics, Bonhoeffer thinks. Ethics, as he sees it, is sheer interruption—life is dissolved into a series of decisions— whereas Christian ethics is "the *flow* of life from conception to the grave" (E 384). Christian ethics contains ethics, he thinks, for the latter understands its task to create space, while the former not only gives positive content to morality ("living together") but also, as center, determines boundaries and hence performs the task that ethics would assign to itself. The dialectic needs to be taken a step further, recognizing that the God who says, "all the earth is mine" (Ex 19:5) is committed to universality. A singular revelation, if it is of a monotheistic God, must open itself to everyone. The "equal dignity of all people" is not a supplement to divine command theory; it is a part of the theory properly understood.

NO SOTERIOLOGICAL OPPRESSION

Bonhoeffer's late theology, beginning with the *Ethics*, retains from the ear-lier theology a heavy emphasis on Christ's redemptive suffering and death. The world rejects God by crucifying Jesus, and this gives us its definitive mark, "the worldliness of the world" (E 400). Only this mark has the power to reconcile the world and God. The danger here is allowing the world to remove God the Father from itself and for the universality of Christian monotheism to be subtly replaced by the universal call to the cross. That the world is reconciled to God through Christ is not in question, but what it means for God to be *in Christ* needs to be clarified. The hypostatic union of the human and divine is not the coexistence of two comparable natures, same and other. As free Creator, God is beyond "the world," beyond any distinction that can be drawn between same and other, and therefore able to be both universal and in Jesus. In this context, the expression "cosmic Christ" is exactly wrong, for Christ is not bound to the cosmos at all. That Jesus *is* the Christ is not to be doubted or downplayed by Christians; rather, it is Christ's universality, his irreducibility to anything in the world (includ-ing culture and religion), that makes him available as God to all people. The gospel is not to be figured as heard only as law by people of other faiths. On the contrary, the invitation is to recognize that God comes to the world in different ways, and to overhear parts of the gospel *in specie aliena* in the writings and actions of people of other faiths.

RETHINK THE "DISCIPLINA ARCANI"

In the world of religionless Christianity the discipline of the secret marks respect for the mystery of God. If the former notion interrupts the distinc-tion between insiders and outsiders, the latter redraws it, first with respect to the world and then, inevitably, with respect to other faiths. The discipline of the secret needs to be presented differently, not in terms of "economy," with its occasional implication of compromise or even guile, but by way of respectful reserve. At the same time it is to be expected that persons of other faiths will keep the same sort of reserve with respect to Christianity. A Christian is not always or simply perceived as a person of another faith, for it is the Christian West that brought about secularization, which is re-garded as a threat to local tradition by many persons of other faiths. Also, although the faith is open to everyone, and there is to be no secret doctrine, the faithful are to conduct themselves with reserve in conversation with people of other faiths. Brothers and sisters of other faiths are not to be seen first and foremost as objects of the church's mission. Increasingly, they are neighbors, literally as well as metaphorically, which means that "mission" must be understood anew.[41] Before anything else, they are to be regarded as already belonging to the one God and already on a path to him. To put the words of Christ before them is also to have faith that those words, once given, are active in ways that only God commands. Finally, the Christian is to understand "mission" in unity with "dialogue." Dialogue is not a right, however; it must be earned by way of unfeigned compassion for the suffering among the people with whom one wishes to talk, accompanied by unquestioning aid in their struggles. W. H. Auden says (adapting Brecht), "Grub first, then ethics."[42] It is all the more true to say, "Grub first, then religion," though in truth there should be no sequence, for faith is displayed in the sharing of food and should displace religion.

"Religious clothes" can indeed make one uncomfortable. Yet being stark naked can make others even more uncomfortable in your presence.

Notes

1. Dietrich Bonhoeffer, *Conspiracy and Imprisonment 1940–1945*, Dietrich Bonhoeffer Works, vol. 16, trans. Lisa E. Dahill, ed. Jørgen Glenthøj, Ulrich Kabitz, and Wolf Krötke, English edition ed. Mark S. Brocker (Minneapolis, Minn.: Fortress Press, 2006), 329.

2. See Thomas Carlyle, *Sartus Resartus; On Heroes and Hero Worship*, intro. W. H. Hudson (London: Dent, 1908), 203.

3. See Immanuel Kant, *Religion within the Limits of Reason Alone*, trans., intro., and notes Theodore M. Greene and Hoyt H. Hudson (New York: Harper and Row, 1960), 11, and G. W. F. Hegel, *The Phenomenology of Mind*, trans. J. B. Baillie, intro. George Lichtheim (New York: Harper and Row, 1967), DD.

4. Philip Larkin, "Aubade," *Collected Poems*, ed. and intro. Anthony Thwaite (London: Marvell Press and Faber and Faber, 1988), 208.

5. Hegel, *The Phenomenology of Mind*, 81.

6. G. W. F. Hegel, *Lectures on the Philosophy of Religion*, 3 vols., ed. Peter C. Hodgson, trans. R. F. Brown, P. C. Hodgson, and J. M. Stewart with the assistance of H. S. Harris (Berkeley and Los Angeles: University of California Press, 1985), vol. 3: *The Consummate Religion*, 342. Bonhoeffer was influenced by Reinhold Seeberg's emphasis on the presence of the Holy Spirit in the Christian community as expressed in his *Christliche Dogmatik*, 2 vols. (Erlangen, Germany: Deichert, 1924–25); he taught a seminar on Hegel at Berlin in the summer of 1936. Recent scholarship on Bonhoeffer has emphasized his debt to Hegel. See, in particular, Charles Marsh, *Reclaiming Dietrich Bonhoeffer: The Promise of His Theology* (New York: Oxford University Press,

1994), and Wayne Whitson Floyd, *Theology and the Dialectics of Otherness: On Reading Bonhoeffer and Adorno* (Baltimore: University Press of America, 1988).

7. See, for example, Harvey Cox, *The Secular City: Secularization and Urbanization in Theological Perspective* (New York: Macmillan, 1965), Paul van Buren, *The Secular Meaning of the Gospel Based on an Analysis of Its Language* (New York: Macmillan, 1963), and Thomas J. J. Altizer, *The Gospel of Christian Atheism* (Philadelphia: Westminster Press, 1966).

8. For the connection with Barth, see Andreas Pangritz, *Karl Barth in the Theology of Dietrich Bonhoeffer,* trans. Barbara and Martin Rumscheidt (Grand Rapids, Mich.: William B. Eerdmans, 2000), and for Bultmann, see Gerhard Ebeling, "The Non-Religious Interpretation of Biblical Concepts," in his *Word and Faith,* trans. J. W. Leitch (Philadelphia: Fortress Press, 1963), 98–161, and Jürgen Moltmann and Jürgen Weissbach, *Two Studies in the Theology of Dietrich Bonhoeffer,* intro. Reginald H. Fuller, trans. Reginald H. Fuller and Ilse Fuller (New York: Scribner, 1967). Ebeling notes that Bonhoeffer misconstrues Bultmann's project; see 103 and 139n2. Also see Ernst Feil, "Religionsloses Christentum und nicht-religiöse Interpretation bei D. Bonhoeffer," *Theologische Zeitschrift* 24 (1968): 40–48.

9. Bonhoeffer also notes about the same time that the *Didache* "has of itself no 'religious' character," WF 49.

10. Both Feuerbach and von Harnack wrote influential works with the title *Das Wesen des Christentums,* the one in 1841 and the other in 1900. See Ludwig Feuerbach, *The Essence of Christianity,* trans. George Eliot (Buffalo, N.Y.: Prometheus Books, 1989) and Adolph von Harnack, *What Is Christianity?* trans. Thomas Bailey Saunders, intro. Rudolf Bultmann (New York: Harper, 1957).

11. For the different senses in which Bonhoeffer uses the word "religion" in the Tegel theology, see Frits de Lange, *Waiting for the Word: Dietrich Bonhoeffer on Speaking about God,* trans. Martin N. Walton (Grand Rapids, Mich.: William B. Eerdmans, 2000), ch. 6.

12. Barth observes, "Western humanity has come of age, or thinks it has. It can now dispense with its teacher—and as such official Christianity had in fact felt and behaved," *Church Dogmatics* 1: *The Doctrine of the Word of God,* part 2, ed. G. W. Bromily and T. F. Torrance (Edinburgh: T&T Clark, 1956), 335.

13. On Bonhoeffer's reading of Dilthey in Tegel, see Ralf K. Wüstenberg, *A Theology of Life: Dietrich Bonhoeffer's Religionless Christianity,* foreword Eberhard Bethge, trans. Doug Stott (Grand Rapids, Mich.: William B. Eerdmans, 1998), 104–12.

14. See E 300.

15. See R. E. Brown, *The Death of the Messiah: From Gethsemane to the Grave. A Commentary on the Passion Narratives in the Four Gospels,* 2 vols. (New York: Doubleday, 1994), 1:298. A range of interpretations is considered by Michael J. Haren in "The Naked Young Man: A Historian's Hypothesis on Mark 14: 51–52," *Biblica* 79 (1998): 525–31.

16. The Secret Gospel of Mark also speaks of a young man "dressed only in a linen cloth" who is a witness to the Resurrection. See *The Complete Gospels,* ed. Robert J. Miller, foreword Robert W. Funk (San Francisco: HarperSanFrancisco, 1994), 411.

17. For Bonhoeffer's reflections on the discipline of the secret at Finkenwalde, see WF 151.

18. Hegel, *Lectures on the Philosophy of Religion,* vol. 1: *Introduction and the Concept of Religion,* 116.

19. See, for example, Augustine, Sermon 49: 8, in *Sermons II (20–50) on the Old Testament,* The Works of St Augustine: A Translation for the Twenty-First Century, trans. Edmund Hill, OP, ed. John E. Rotelle, OSA (Brooklyn, N.Y.: New City Press, 1990), 338.

20. Tertullian, *Apology,* vii, in *Ante-Nicene Fathers,* vol. 3: *Latin Christianity: Its Founder, Tertullian, I,* ed. Alexander Roberts and James Donaldson (1885; reprint Peabody, Mass.: Hendrickson Publishers, 1999), 23. Also see Basil, *On the Holy Spirit,* trans. David Anderson (Crestwood, N.Y.: St Vladimir's Seminary Press, 1980), ch. 27, and Gregory of Nazianzus, "Oration 11," *Select Orations,* trans. Martha Vinson, The Fathers of the Church (Washington, D.C.: Catholic University of America Press, 2003), 34.

21. Edward Yarnold, SJ, ed., *Cyril of Jerusalem,* The Early Church Fathers (New York: Routledge, 2000), 83.

22. I disagree with Kenneth Surin when he observes, in an intriguing article, that "Bonhoeffer's discipline of the secret . . . can be construed as a *contemptus mundi* for the disenchanted world." The distancing involved is with "unconscious Christianity" and not the secular world. See Surin, "*Contemptus Mundi* and the Disenchanted World: Bonhoeffer's 'Discipline of the Secret' and Adorno's 'Strategy of Hibernation,'" *Journal of the American Academy of Religion* 53, no. 3 (1985): 397.

23. See D 46.

24. Adolf Schlatter, *The History of the Christ: The Foundation for New Testament Theology,* trans. Andreas J. Köstenberger (Grand Rapids, Mich.: Baker Books, 1997), 171.

25. Adolf Schlatter, *The Theology of the Apostles: The Development of New Testament Theology,* trans. Andreas J. Köstenberger (Grand Rapids, Mich.: Baker Books, 1998), 137.

26. See Eberhard Bethge, *Dietrich Bonhoeffer: Theologian, Christian, Contemporary* (London: Collins, 1970), 34.

27. Bonhoeffer's emphasis.

28. Geoffrey Hill, *Tenebrae* (London: André Deutch, 1978), 41.

29. See Horst Bürkle, *Einführung in der Theologie de Religionem* (Darmstadt: Wissenschaftliche Buchgesellschaft, 1977).

30. See Jacques Dupuis, SJ, *Toward a Christian Theology of Religious Pluralism* (Maryknoll, N.Y.: Orbis Books, 2001), and Paul F. Knitter, *Introducing Theologies of Religions* (Maryknoll, N.Y.: Orbis Books, 2002).

31. Edward Conze, *Thirty Years of Buddhist Studies: Selected Essays* (Oxford: Cassirer, 1967), 47.

32. Vladimiro Boublik's notion of the "anonymous catechumenate" is more acceptable than "anonymous Christianity," though the expression still retains a strong sense of oxymoron. See his *Teologia delle religioni* (Rome: Studium, 1973).

33. See Justin Martyr, *Apology* 2, ch. 8, *Ante-Nicene Fathers,* vol. 1: *The Apostolic Fathers, Justin Martyr, Irenaeus,* ed. Alexander Roberts and James Donaldson (1885; reprint Peabody, Mass.: Hendrickson Publishers, 1994), and Augustine, *The Retractations,* trans. Mary Inez Bogan (Washington, D.C.: Catholic University of America Press, 1968), 12, 3.

34. See Barth, *Church Dogmatics,* IV: *The Doctrine of Reconciliation,* 3. i, ed. G. W. Bromiley and T. F. Torrance, trans. G. W. Bromiley (Edinburgh: T&T Clark, 1961), § 69. 2.

35. NRS 116.

36. See, for example, Barth's comments on the empirical life of the Jews as "unreal" in *Church Dogmatics* II: 2, ed. G. W. Bromiley and T. F. Torrance, trans. G. W. Bromiley et al. (Edinburgh: T&T Clark, 1957), 201, 301.

37. See Maurice Blanchot, *The Infinite Conversation,* trans. and foreword Susan Hanson (Minneapolis: University of Minnesota Press, 1993), xii.

38. Bonhoeffer's response to the "Jewish question" is analyzed by C.-R. Müller in *Dietrich Bonhoeffers Kampf gegen die nationalsozialistische Verfolgung und Vernichtung der Juden* (Munich: Chr. Kaiser, 1990). See Bonhoeffer's comments on the need to hurl oneself into action for the Jews in NRS 221–29. Also see Eberhard Bethge's essay "One of the Silent Bystanders? Dietrich Bonhoeffer on November 9, 1938" in his *Friendship and Resistance: Essays on Dietrich Bonhoeffer* (Grand Rapids, Mich.: William B. Eerdmans, 1995).

39. Certainly Bonhoeffer did not have available to him the subtlety of Philip Quinn in his *Divine Commands and Moral Requirements* (Oxford: Clarendon Press, 1978).

40. See ibid., 130–35.

41. See Wilfred Cantwell Smith, *The Faith of Other Men* (New York: Harper and Row, 1962), 11.

42. See W. H. Auden, "Grub First, then Ethics (Brecht)," in *About the House* (London: Faber and Faber, 1966), 33.

PART FOUR

Bonhoeffer on Ethics and the Eschaton

Bonhoeffer's "Christian Social Philosophy": Conscience, Alterity, and the Moment of Ethical Responsibility

BRIAN GREGOR

From the perspective of contemporary philosophy, one of the most interesting aspects of Bonhoeffer's thought is his claim that the self is constituted in ethical responsibility for the other person [*Andere*]. Anyone familiar with post-Kantian Continental thought is aware that the question of alterity, or *otherness,* is a prominent one. The current articulation of the problem of the other owes much to Kant and his contentious successors, Fichte and Hegel. Hegel's influence is particularly apparent in French phenomenology, where Sartre, Levinas, Ricoeur, and other theorists of alterity have made creative use of Hegel's account of intersubjectivity,[1] giving provocative descriptions of such phenomena as the exchange of gazes, the face of the other, and the call to responsibility. Even earlier than Fichte and Hegel, Jacobi formulated the statement that "the I is impossible without the Thou."[2]

Of course, the problem of otherness goes back much further in the philosophical tradition, as Plato's *Sophist* illustrates. There are also biblical roots for this problematic—a fact that Emmanuel Levinas has brought to the attention of the philosophical world with particular vigor.[3] God commands Israel not merely to care for her own, but to attend to the stranger, the widow and the orphan in her midst, since it is always too easy to forget the other within the comfort of self-identity and sameness.

Levinas is an important reference point for contemporary debates about the self and the other because of his insistence on the inadequacy of the idealist account of intersubjectivity, whether it takes its departure from Fichte and Hegel, or from Husserl's account of the constitution of the alter ego in the fifth of his *Cartesian Meditations*.[4] The idealist approach to the transcendence of the other is preoccupied with the epistemological and metaphysical problems that arise with the suggestion that there might be another subject besides myself. According to Levinas, these questions obscure the more primordial question of my ethical responsibility for the other. In the encounter with the other, the questioning subject suddenly finds itself put in question. Roles are reversed, and the constituting subject finds itself constituted—as ethically responsible rather than autonomous and isolated.[5]

Although Levinas gives a particularly influential description of the way ethical responsibility decenters the self-absorbed ego, the emphasis on the ethical transcendence of the other did not begin with him. Bonhoeffer encountered a similar discussion during the 1920s and 1930s, when German theologians were grappling with such philosophers as Hermann Cohen, Eberhard Grisebach, Martin Buber, and of course, Ludwig Feuerbach. Despite the influence of Hegel's account of intersubjectivity, one could make the case that Feuerbach is the first to emphasize the relation between concrete, existing human beings.[6] Along with his emphasis on the physical, material, and sensible as the object over against [*Gegenstand*] the subject—a realism he launched in opposition to his idealist forebears,[7] Feuerbach stressed the *Thou* as a limit that resists the *I* and thereby establishes the bond between the *I* and the world. As Karl Barth observes, the theme of the real, living human being is central for Feuerbach; in addition to eschewing abstract conceptions of the Ego or Reason, Feuerbach showed that this concrete being exists "only in community, it is found only in the unity of man with man—a unity that is supported only by the reality of the difference between I and Thou."[8] It is not surprising, then, that Buber credited his insight regarding the *I-Thou* relation to Feuerbach.[9] If Feuerbach did not entirely succeed in escaping the abstraction of idealism,[10] he nevertheless took important steps in the direction of a concrete understanding of the social.

Although it would be worthwhile to conduct a complete history of this problematic, in the present essay I will focus on Bonhoeffer's own position and the resources he offers for thinking through these issues in our contemporary context. I begin by outlining Bonhoeffer's phenomenology of the self-other relationship in *Sanctorum Communio,* his dissertation and first published work. This text is important because it contains Bonhoeffer's first articulation of the theme of ethical responsibility—a theme that continues to inform all of his subsequent thought. Bonhoeffer's analysis highlights his pertinence to the contemporary debate regarding ethical responsibility for the other, which comes into view when he is compared with such thinkers as Heidegger, Levinas, and Ricoeur. By beginning with *Sanctorum Communio,* we will also be able to demonstrate some important developments in Bonhoeffer's own understanding of the ethical relation between self and other. Bonhoeffer's early work describes responsibility in rather stark (if not severe) terms as the dominating ego submitting to the absolute demand of the other. While there is much to be gained from this account, I will argue that his later thought—particularly *Ethics*—gives a more nuanced description of the sort of resources and capabilities that the self requires in order to respond to the other. One such resource is *conscience*, which I take as a guiding theme in this essay. Bonhoeffer has a sharp critique of conscience as a hindrance to hearing the voice of the other, but he also affirms the conscience insofar as it is liberated by Christ. If Bonhoeffer provides the impetus toward a "Christian social philosophy," his critical understanding of conscience plays a crucial role therein.

Bonhoeffer's Phenomenology of Sociality in Sanctorum Communio

Although Bonhoeffer undertakes a phenomenology of sociality in *Sanctorum Communio,* he does not present his description as a presuppositionless science, à la Husserl. Nor does he make any serious effort to orient himself within the phenomenological tradition, let alone respect established methodological rules regarding phenomenological purity or rigor.[11] Instead, the preface clearly states his intention to employ a specifically and inherently *Christian* social philosophy, which proceeds on the basis of theological presuppositions. Bonhoeffer is looking for the appropriate philosophical tools to think Christianly about human sociality—specifically as a way of understanding the church—so he makes use of phenomenological tools in an ad hoc rather than systematic fashion, and continues to do so through his later writings.[12] Bonhoeffer finds phenomenology helpful because it overcomes reductionism by attending to phenomena as they are given, and also because of its attention to concrete, lived experience.[13] In *Sanctorum Communio,* Bonhoeffer insists that a distinctly Christian understanding of the person must be concrete rather than abstract. More specifically, he argues that this concrete understanding of the person depends on the encounter with alterity. Only genuine transcendence can challenge the subject's proclivity to dwell in abstraction; only that which is truly *other than* the subject can limit the subject's drive to reduce reality to ideality.

Bonhoeffer begins by setting the Christian concept of the person in relief against four philosophical models: the Aristotelian, the Stoic, the Epicurean, and the Cartesian. The problem with the first three models, in Bonhoeffer's view, is their use of a metaphysical schema that "fundamentally denies the person by subsuming the person under the universal" (SC 41).[14] In the fourth model, this metaphysical account of the person turns epistemological: with Descartes, the knowing I becomes "the starting point of all philosophy" (SC 40)—a move that Bonhoeffer locates in Kant as well as post-Kantian idealism.[15] Here the epistemological subject stands over against an object, regardless of whether that object is a thing or a person (SC 42). But to employ this subject-object opposition as the formal framework for sociality would be a category mistake. The subject-object relation can be applied to the encounter with other persons, but it would necessarily approach them as objects rather than subjects. This encounter would therefore be strictly cognitive rather than social (SC 45). The problem with the epistemological model is that it "resolves the opposition of subject and object in the unity of the mind" (SC 42). This sort of object "is ultimately no barrier" (SC 46) to the knowing subject, who grasps objects *as objects,* according to the forms of cognition. But a cognized object never attains the status of another *subject.*

Despite the differences between these four models, they share a common trait that Bonhoeffer wants to overcome: "*the concept of spirit as immanent.*" This concept of spirit "necessarily leads to the conclusions drawn by idealism," that is, the loss of the person within unity and sameness (SC 42). This is true whether the common term is a universal attribute, such as "reason," a universal imperative, or the formal principles of spirit. The intellectual, cognitive approach, whether metaphysical or epistemological, cannot lead to the transcendent, concrete existence of other persons. By contrast, the Christian concept of personhood—which is "constitutive for" and "presupposed by" the concept of Christian community—overcomes idealist subjectivity and replaces it with concrete, individual personhood (SC 44–45). If the immanence of idealist spirit is to be overcome, it requires transcendence—not simply metaphysical or epistemological transcendence, but *ethical* transcendence, in which the other person confronts the subject as a fundamental limit or barrier [*Schranke*] (SC 45–46). Only in the encounter with the other, who resists and eludes the forms of cognition, does the subject enter the sphere of sociality. And it is only in this ethical encounter with the other that the subject is constituted as a concrete, individual person.

"But what is the 'other'?" Bonhoeffer asks. In relation to the concrete, individual I, "the other is the *concrete* You" (SC 51). If the You is the living, breathing person that confronts me and calls me to ethical responsibility, then there are two things that the You is definitely *not:* First, as we have seen, the You is not merely an object standing over and against the subject.

Second, the You is not another I. In the ethical encounter, the "You-form" and the "I-form" are not interchangeable concepts. Rather, they are fundamentally different types of experience: "I myself can become an object of my own experience, but can never experience myself as You. Other persons can become objects of my reflection in their I-ness, but I will never get beyond the fact that I can only encounter the other as a You." I can never overcome the alterity of the other so as to know her the way I know myself. In short, this insurmountable barrier that we call the other is the concrete *You* who "places me before an ethical decision" (SC 51–52), thereby individualizing and constituting the concrete I.

Bonhoeffer does not want to suggest that the You holds the power to constitute the I as person. Rather, this constitution takes place when God actively enjoins the concrete I and You. God makes this encounter possible, such that the "divine You creates a human You." The human You images the divine You, who secures its claim and preserves its genuine otherness (SC 55). By identifying this role as belonging to a transcendent God, Bonhoeffer wants to distinguish the genuinely Christian perspective from that of idealism. Idealism understands *Geist* as immanent, and attributes "to the human spirit absolute value that can only be ascribed to divine spirit." For idealism, then, every other is less than wholly other, since it is ultimately reducible to the sameness of immanent *Geist*. There is therefore no barrier or limit that the ego cannot finally surmount, since no You presents a final limit to the I. Thus it is crucial that there be an infinite qualitative difference between God and humanity, because "only in experiencing the barrier does the awareness of oneself as ethical person arise. The more clearly the barrier is perceived, the more deeply the person enters into the situation of responsibility" (SC 49). For Christian philosophy, Bonhoeffer argues, the transcendence of God is necessary to preserve the ethical transcendence of the other person, since divine transcendence undermines the immanent conception of spirit that would provide a common term under which the other could be reduced to sameness.

Consequently, God is present as a mediator between the I and the You:[16] *"God or the Holy Spirit joins the concrete You; only through God's active working does the other become a You to me from whom my I arises. The other person is only a 'You' insofar as God brings it about. . . . The claim of the other rests in God alone; for this very reason, it remains the claim of the other"* (SC 54–55).[17] In saying this, however, Bonhoeffer does not want to suggest that the other is merely a proxy for God, or a stepping-stone to God. Instead, he insists on the integrity of the other, arguing that this need not strike up a rivalry in which God and the other vie for the affection of the I. God has given the other to me, and I am charged with her care. Thus my relation to God and my responsibility for the other, while distinct, are inseparable. My response to the other means my embracing God's will for the other person, and relinquishing my own. We are therefore to love our neighbor *instead of* ourselves (SC 170–71).

Note that Bonhoeffer speaks of loving the neighbor *instead of* rather than *as* ourselves: if Bonhoeffer does not see a rivalry between God and the other, he certainly detects a rivalry between the self-centered will and the call of the other. For this reason Bonhoeffer conceives the ethical response solely in terms of the ego's absolute submission to the other. As we will see, there are good reasons to question such a conception of the self-other relation, particularly because it risks suggesting that ethical responsibility requires self-abnegation or annihilation of the self. But since this theme of responsibility for others continues to motivate all of Bonhoeffer's subsequent thought, we will also see (later in this essay) that his later writings provide important qualifications of his earliest conception of ethical responsibility for the other.

Conscience and the Augenblick: Bonhoeffer contra Heidegger

According to Bonhoeffer, ethical responsibility appears in the moment (*Augenblick*) in which I am addressed by the other, and it is this ethical moment that individuates and constitutes me as a person. Bonhoeffer takes care to note that this moment is not simply an atom of time. The moment is not the shortest measure of chronological time, but rather "the time of responsibility, value-related time, or let us say, time related to God; and most essentially, it is concrete time." The concreteness of the moment is of decisive importance, for "only in concrete time is the real claim of ethics effectual; and only when I am responsible am I fully conscious of being bound to time" (SC 48). A similar conception of the decisive moment appears in several other thinkers from the early decades of the twentieth century, including Benjamin, Jaspers, and Adorno.[18] The *Augenblick* also has a distinguished philosophical and theological pedigree, tracing back to the Greek terms *kairos* and *exaiphnes*.[19] The notion would have been familiar to Bonhoeffer from his readings in Kierkegaard,[20] as well as Barth, who took up Kierkegaard's treatment of the theme in his commentary on Romans.[21] But at the time of writing *Sanctorum Communio,* Bonhoeffer had not yet studied one of the most famous twentieth-century treatments of the *Augenblick*—that of Martin Heidegger.[22]

Like Bonhoeffer, Heidegger distinguishes the "moment of vision" from the "now" of everyday temporality, in which things arise, pass away, and are present-at-hand.[23] The *Augenblick* is the ecstatic Present of authentic, resolute temporality:

> The authentic coming-toward-oneself of anticipatory resoluteness is at the same time a coming-back to one's ownmost Self, which has been thrown into its individualization. This ecstasis makes it possible for Dasein to be able to take over resolutely that entity which it already is. In anticipating, Dasein *brings* itself *again forth* into its ownmost potentiality-for-Being. (BT 388)

According to Heidegger, in the moment of vision Dasein calls itself to authenticity, resolutely taking up its potentiality as Dasein. Earlier in *Being and Time* Heidegger identifies the voice of conscience (*Stimme des Gewissens*) as that which attests Dasein's "potentiality-for-Being-its-Self" (BT 313). Conscience is a call [*Ruf*] that "has the character of an *appeal* to Dasein by calling it to its ownmost potentiality-for-Being-its-Self" (BT 314). In other words, Dasein calls itself to its *own self* (BT 315). To be sure, the phenomenon of the call is onto-logically more complex than a simple identity of caller and called—something Heidegger himself observes in his assertion that "the call comes *from* me and yet *from beyond me and over me*." But what is decisive for our present concerns is Heidegger's claim that "the call undoubtedly does not come from someone else who is with me in the world" (BT 320). There is no call from the other. Nor does the call summon Dasein directly to responsibility for the other.[24]

Despite the fact that Bonhoeffer had not yet read Heidegger, in *Sanctorum Communio* we can already discern the basis for his later critique (in *Act and Being*) of Heidegger if we contrast their different conceptions of the *Augenblick* as a response to a call.[25] For both thinkers, the call has an individualizing effect, insofar as it calls one out of anonymity and abstraction into concrete, particular existence. But who is doing the calling? We have already noted that for Heidegger, the voice of conscience sounds the call. But Bonhoeffer detects major problems with locating the call to responsibility in one's own conscience, because conscience is not fundamentally oriented toward others. Instead, Bonhoeffer consistently criticizes the voice of conscience as a symptom of the *cor curvum in se*—the heart sinfully turned in on itself. Prior to the fall, humankind exists in the image of God [*imago Dei*], "being for God and the neighbor, in its original creatureliness and limitedness." With the fall, humankind becomes like God [*sicut deus*] in its attempt to exist alone, to live out of its own resources, and to be the origin of Good and Evil for itself (CF 113). The autonomy that results is a travesty of God's aseity: the self "no longer needs any others, it is the lord of its own world." Or so it thinks. In truth, the self "is the solitary lord and despot of its own mute, violated, silenced, dead, ego-world [*Ichwelt*]" (CF 142). The apparent independence of the self is actually moribund isolation.

According to Bonhoeffer, conscience allows the self to remain locked within itself, impervious to the intrusion of the other—whether God or the neighbor. And conscience is highly effective in preserving this isolation because of its ability to feign alterity. On one level, conscience is an unintentional recognition that human beings cannot live without others. But it merely imitates the voices of God and the neighbor (CF 142). In truth, it is the self addressing itself. Conscience allows the self to determine its own responsibilities and reprimand itself for its own perceived failings, all for the sake of preserving its autonomy. In *Ethics* Bonhoeffer writes: "Conscience claims to be the voice of God and the norm for relating to other people. By relating properly to themselves, human beings think to regain the proper relationship to God and to others" (E 308). But conscience has good reason to prevent a genuinely other voice from intruding, since it can threaten the self's perception of its own unity. Hence Bonhoeffer's observation in *Creation and Fall*: "Conscience is not the voice of God within sinful human beings; instead it is precisely their defense against this voice" (CF 128). Likewise in *Ethics,* the voice of God is a threat to human beings who presume to be the origin of good and evil:

> They do not deny their own evil. But in the voice of their conscience those who have become evil call themselves back to their authentic self, their better self, to the good. This good, which consists in the unity of human beings with themselves, is now considered the origin of all good. It is God's good, it is the good for the neighbor. Bearing the knowledge of good and evil within themselves, human beings have now become the judge of God and others, just as they are their own judge. (E 308)[26]

Conscience thereby allows the self to sustain two illusions: first, that it is the origin of good and evil, and second, that it is actually in contact with genuine ethical transcendence.

It is important to note that Bonhoeffer's critique of conscience does not target Heidegger specifically. In fact, Heidegger would not recognize his position in Bonhoeffer's claim that "the call of conscience always comes in the form of a prohibition: 'You shall not. . . . You should not have . . . .' Conscience is satisfied when the prohibition is not defied. Whatever is not prohibited is permitted. Conscience divides life into permitted and prohibited. There is no commandment" (E 307). According to Heidegger, conscience is not merely or even primarily prohibitive. He explicitly distances the ontological, existent*ial* understanding of conscience from everyday, ontic, existent*iell* notions of conscience as being essentially critical or accusatory (BT 336).

Instead, Heidegger identifies conscience as fundamentally *disclosive*—that is, it discloses Dasein's ownmost potentiality-for-Being-its-Self (BT 314)—rather than *moral*. Thus if Bonhoeffer were mounting an attack on Heidegger, he would not gain much traction with his point regarding fallen humanity's desire to determine the scope of good and evil, because Heidegger sees those as ontic questions. But the prohibitive conscience is not the sole target of Bonhoeffer's critique. His more fundamental point is that conscience remains self-satisfied in all of its judgments—whether prohibitive or disclosive. Consequently, conscience remains unaware that "even in what is allowed the human being is in disunion with the origin" (E 307).[27] In other words, the Fall not only affects our guilty conscience over particular misdeeds, it also affects our fundamental self-understanding regarding every aspect of our being-in-the-world. Even our sense of our ownmost-potentiality-for-Being-our-Selves is affected by the Fall.[28] And to make matters worse, the fallen conscience is even unable to recognize the true scope of Dasein's situation, let alone correct it.

In sum, Bonhoeffer's critique of conscience does not simply concern the particulars of the good and bad conscience. It concerns the way conscience arises from the self's internal divisions and its separation from God and the neighbor (CF 128). In conscience the self judges itself, hoping to establish continuity with itself and consistency with its own convictions. But the call to responsible selfhood must come from beyond, from a truly transcendent other. Conscience cannot recognize that the self-unity it establishes "already presupposes disunion from God and from human beings" (E 307). The ultimate criterion of conscience is "unity with oneself," but this preoccupation with one's own self-relation comes at the expense of the relation to God and other persons. And even when conscience is confronted with others, it manages to preserve its sovereignty by considering itself the source and measure of its responsibility for others.

Bonhoeffer and Ricoeur on the Mediating Capacity of Conscience

Bonhoeffer's critique of conscience is definitely pointed, but it would be a mistake to conclude that he dismisses conscience altogether. He does in fact affirm conscience, albeit in a critical way. In expositing Bonhoeffer's affirmation of conscience I will bring him into dialogue with Paul Ricoeur—a dialogue that is helpful for both parties: On the one hand, Bonhoeffer also casts into relief certain limitations in Ricoeur's hermeneutics of conscience. On the other hand, Ricoeur helps illuminate the indispensability of conscience, alongside the other ethical capabilities and resources that are necessary for ethical responsibility. If Bonhoeffer's critique of conscience risks eclipsing its affirmation, Ricoeur helps to highlight Bonhoeffer's positive assertions regarding conscience.

In *Oneself as Another,* Ricoeur maintains that it is a mistake to grant absolute priority to either the self or the other. If we construe the movement between them as unilateral, it is impossible to treat the self-other dynamic correctly. This is true whether one follows Husserl's lead in the fifth of his *Cartesian Meditations,* which begins from the ego and constitutes the other by means of analogizing apperception, or whether one follows Levinas in asserting that the other alone can initiate responsibility in the self.[29] Ricoeur argues that ethical responsibility requires a self with the capacity to hear and heed the call of the other. Against the Levinasian description of the ego as fundamentally narcissistic, Ricoeur seeks a model of selfhood that would be "defined by its openness and its capacity for discovery" rather than an allergy to alterity. For Ricoeur this is not simply optimism or wishful thinking, but a necessary condition if the other is actually going to initiate responsibility in the ego; we must presuppose "a capacity of reception, of discrimination, and of recognition" if the self is to be able to hear the call of the other. The self requires the capacity to recognize the voice of the other to the degree that this call eventually becomes its own, in the form of a conviction (OA 339).

In Ricoeur's view, conscience plays a crucial role in this response, since conscience is the point where the external command can become an internal conviction. Ricoeur uses this definition to navigate his way through the opposition between Levinas and Heidegger, who take opposite positions regarding the ethical meaning of conscience. Contra Heidegger, Ricoeur insists that conscience cannot be stripped of all ethical or moral significance (OA 355). Ontology cannot be ethically neutral. But contra Levinas, Ricoeur insists that "the otherness of conscience" cannot be completely externalized and limited to "the otherness of other people." If the other is as wholly other as Levinas suggests, the self will never hear his or her call (OA 354–55). Instead of choosing between these two alternatives, Ricoeur proposes an ontology of selfhood whose structure is best characterized as "being enjoined to *live well with and for others in just institutions and to esteem oneself as the bearer of this wish*" (OA 352, 354). Conscience does not simply address our care for our ownmost Being; but neither is it limited to the naked prohibition against violating the other. If commands such as "Thou shalt not kill" are to find receptive ears, the self must already heed the broader call of conscience to this larger aim of the ethical life, which Ricoeur defines in terms of "living well with and for others."

Ricoeur's criticism of Levinas might seem to extend to Bonhoeffer as well. Both Levinas and Bonhoeffer depict responsibility in asymmetrical terms, in which a self-absorbed ego is decentered by the absolute demand of a radically transcendent other. This picture of responsibility involves a radical passivity on the part of the self, which Ricoeur sees as imbalanced. The passivity of the self needs to be balanced by an active component, which is necessary if the self is to receive and take up the call of the other as its responsibility. Ricoeur locates this dialectical interplay of activity/passivity, interiority/exteriority, in *conscience*. Setting aside the matter of a Levinasian response to Ricoeur, the question here and now concerns Bonhoeffer's vulnerability to a Ricoeurian critique: how, and to what extent, does Bonhoeffer affirm the conscience?

Bonhoeffer does indeed allow conscience a place in his account of ethical responsibility, but he continues to stress its deep ambiguity, which is endemic to our existence in the ambiguous middle between the primal state of creation and the eschaton. Before the fall, interpersonal relations were characterized by free giving. After the fall, this freedom for the other gives way to the isolation of ethical atomism: "Now everyone has their own conscience." And according to Bonhoeffer, this conscience is fundamentally ambiguous: "Conscience can just as well be the ultimate prop of human self-justification as the site where Christ strikes home at one through the law" (SC 108). In this "between," good and evil appear to us in the twilight (*Zwielicht*) (CF 104).

In the post-lapsarian twilight it is impossible to establish the absolute purity or goodness of our action. But conscience promises to purify our ethical existence: by scrutinizing our motives and feeling remorse over our misdeeds, we aim to establish the goodness and unity of our being. Yet the fallen human being is capable of a great deal of self-delusion in the name of conscience. There is therefore good reason to employ a hermeneutic of suspicion (to borrow Ricoeur's term) against conscience, since it is often more disposed to give voice to false consciousness than the call of the other. As Bonhoeffer writes in the working notes for *Ethics*, "Voice of the heart | in principle | self-deception" (E 321n77). However, even suspicion is insufficient to purge self-deception and overcome the ambiguity of conscience, since suspicion can be merely another tool for the fallen self to justify itself on its own terms. If Bonhoeffer sees the possibility of a retrieval of the conscience, it is not because suspicion is capable of purifying it. Bonhoeffer's sensitivity to the self-deception of conscience might even be instructive for Ricoeur in this regard. Before we outline Bonhoeffer's affirmation of conscience, we might ask: *Is Ricoeur sufficiently suspicious regarding conscience?*

Mark I. Wallace has argued that although Ricoeur's discussion of conscience is compelling overall, it lacks a sufficient appreciation for "the *war of the self with itself*" that takes place within the conscience, and the "plurality of *many different* voices" that sound out therein.[30] Granted, Ricoeur appears to allow for such conflict with his notion of "tragic action," which arises when circumstances force us to choose between competing goods, or the lesser of two evils. Such situations reveal the limits of universal rules as a guide for decision, since they demand difficult choices in the application of practice wisdom. But Ricoeur "eases the tensions inherent within tragic decision-making through an appeal to group process in moral judgment."[31] In tragic circumstances, practically wise judgments are made in dialogue with a larger social and communal group. Wallace objects that this social conception of conscience does not attend to those actions that conflict with the *Sittlichkeit* of one's present context, and cites Bonhoeffer as an example of just such a scenario. Bonhoeffer's own decision to act against the state, to the point of conspiring to commit tyrannicide, involved an undeniable conflict of loyalties and responsibilities—to himself, his family and fiancée, the state, those suffering from Nazi violence, and, ultimately, to God. It is this sort of isolating crisis of conscience, Wallace suggests, that Ricoeur's appeal to social dialogue does not sufficiently address, since it underestimates the turmoil that can characterize ethical and moral deliberation.[32] Insofar as Ricoeur is a bit too confident in the capabilities of conscience, Bonhoeffer's critique of conscience is an important corrective. Bonhoeffer not only exemplifies the inner conflicts of what Ricoeur calls tragic action, he also highlights the way conscience applies the soothing balm of self-deception. Moreover, Bonhoeffer's historical and political context exemplifies the ways in which self-deception can occur on an individual *as well as* a social level.

If Bonhoeffer says a sharp "No" to conscience, he also says "Yes." But on what basis? Bonhoeffer insists that conscience cannot purify itself, because every strategy of conscience—whether self-examination, introspection, suspicion, or another—remains an instance of the self trying to purify itself by itself. For this reason, the incurved self needs to be liberated by Christ. In Bonhoeffer's view, the intervention of Christ is crucial because it reveals what is really at stake in conscience: the justification of the human being. Conscience is unable to escape the influence of the human being's desire for self-justification. Thus Bonhoeffer points to "the moment when Christ breaks through the solitude" of the self-reflecting ego, and redirects its attention to Christ. This intervention is also important because it establishes Christ's mediating role between human beings and God, thereby overcoming the conscience and its aspirations to have an immediate relation with God on the basis of its own resources and on its own terms (AB 141).[33]

This is not to say that we should simply ignore conscience because it is fallen and unreliable. As Bonhoeffer observes, "it can never be advisable to act against one's own conscience." Considered in strictly formal terms, conscience is a call to the preservation of one's own being—that is, "unity with one's own self" (E 276). To act against conscience would be self-destructive, even suicidal. On this level, any violation of conscience "would indeed be reprehensible" (E 277). However, in probing deeper regarding the material content of this self-unity, Bonhoeffer proposes that conscience is the ego's attempt "to be 'like God'—*sicut deus*—in knowing good and evil." It is an attempt at autonomous self-justification. The self does not want to violate this inviolable law, lest it lose its autonomy, and *itself* (E 277). Consequently, the self-enclosed conscience needs to be decentered and turned outward in faith. This *alter*-ation occurs in the decisive moment when "the unity of human existence no longer consists in its own autonomy, but, by miracle of faith, is found in Jesus Christ, beyond one's own ego and its laws." There is a new unifying center in oneself, because the self surrenders its attempt to justify itself, and allows Christ to be the source of its justification. And with the justification of the sinner comes liberation of conscience: "conscience in the formal sense still remains the call, coming from my true self, into unity with myself. However, this unity can now no longer be realized by returning to my autonomy that lives out of the law, but instead in community with Jesus Christ." Thus the "godless self-justification" of the natural conscience is "overcome by the conscience that has been set free in Jesus Christ, calling me to unity with myself in Jesus Christ. Jesus Christ has become my conscience. This means that from now on I can only find unity with myself by surrendering my ego to God and others" (E 278). Rather than amounting to the abolition of conscience, this means its liberation. Since the self is no longer turned inward in self-scrutiny and self-justification, conscience is set free to serve God and the neighbor (E 279). Ethical responsibility is no longer a matter of my determining the ultimate goodness of my actions, but a matter of surrendering them to the justification of Christ.[34]

From a philosophical perspective, this liberation of conscience might sound like a *deus ex machina*—the sort of device that Bonhoeffer later criticizes so sharply in his prison letters, as though Christ enters the human scene and all problems subside. On the one hand, if ever there was a *deus ex machina,* an intervention that did not cohere with the immanent logic of a plot, it is Christ's incarnation in human history. But Christ's presence in the world does not diminish the very real anguish of making concrete ethical decisions. In fact, the liberation of conscience even extends to the possibility of taking *guilt* onto oneself as a result of one's responsible actions. Bonhoeffer puts this in very challenging terms in *Ethics,* writing that "those who act responsibly become guilty without sin; and only those whose conscience is free can bear responsibility" (E 282). The freedom of conscience to become guilty is possible, Bonhoeffer argues, only because the self surrenders its justification to Christ.

No doubt this portrait of ethical responsibility raises many questions. For instance, does Bonhoeffer's conception of ethical justification by faith mean that the concrete motives, means, and consequences of my action in the world are irrelevant, so long as I surrender them to Christ? In the words of the apostle Paul: May it never be! Nevertheless, Bonhoeffer does invite a number of objections. In the next section I will consider a few of the most salient ones, along with his response. This will also allow us to observe some important developments in Bonhoeffer's thinking about the self-other relation.

Bonhoeffer on the Possibilities and Limits of Ethical Responsibility

We have already discussed one possible objection to Bonhoeffer's position, stemming from Ricoeur's argument that conscience is necessary in order to hear and respond to the call of the other. According to Ricoeur, the call of the other is discernible because it is preceded by the enjoinment of conscience to live well with and for others, with all that entails. This conception of the self as being-enjoined provides the larger existential orientation that is necessary to make sense of a self capable of responding to others. One aspect that is important to acknowledge is the self's care for itself, which Ricoeur designates self-*esteem*. Ricoeur is particularly concerned that Levinas's emphasis on radical passivity and self-abnegation (taken to its extreme in *Otherwise Than Being*[35]) risks annihilating the sort of selfhood that would be capable of ethical responsibility (OA 339–41).

Despite his critique of the self-regarding subject as a symptom of sin, in *Ethics* Bonhoeffer clearly acknowledges the danger that extreme self-denial can destroy genuine ethical agency. Further, he identifies the Christological basis for a genuine Christian conception of self-affirmation and self-assertion. Christ overcomes the "dual morality" that polarizes the worldly and the Christian, political action and Christian action, self-assertion and self-denial. But "the reality of God's becoming human" overcomes this opposition and calls for a genuinely worldly understanding of Christianity, according to which Christian love requires political action and self-assertion. Christ opens up the ego that is curved in on itself for the sake of a truly Christian self-assertion. Equally interesting is Bonhoeffer's recognition of the role of conscience in this conception of ethical agency, since conscience helps to establish the limits of concrete, particular, responsible action: "[T]he conscience free in Jesus Christ still essentially remains the call to unity with myself. Acceptance of responsibility must not destroy this unity. Surrendering the self in selfless service must never be confused with destroying and annihilating the self, which would then also *no longer be able to take on responsibility*" (E 281, *emphasis mine*). This passage is full of implications for our discussion, but I will devote my attention to three that respond to some of the most pressing challenges for Bonhoeffer's position, and also illuminate key developments in Bonhoeffer's thought.

First, Bonhoeffer's critique of conscience does not eliminate the formal operations of the conscience as a call to unity with oneself. This means, among other things, that the moment of ethical responsibility is not an isolated instant of time with no relation to the unity and continuity of the self. The self is a temporal being, with a past and future. This is significant for Bonhoeffer, since he did not always put this emphasis on the continuity of selfhood. In *Sanctorum Communio,* his concept of the moment threatens to undermine the continuity of the person, particularly when he writes that the "*individual becomes a person again and again through the other, in the 'moment'*" (SC 55–56). But if the person is continually coming into being, personal identity is in danger of become a bundle of discrete "moments." When Bonhoeffer claims that "*the person ever and again arises and passes away in time,*" he wants to emphasize that personhood is a temporal phenomenon—that it is dynamic event rather than a static substance—existing "again and again in the perpetual flux of life" (SC 48). But Bonhoeffer does not explain what prevents the person from succumbing to an actualistic flux. This is a crucial question, because the notion of ethical responsibility is unintelligible without some measure of constancy over time.

Bonhoeffer became aware of this problem by the time he wrote *Act and Being,* where he discusses the continuity of "being in faith," criticizing Heidegger, Barth, and Bultmann along the way (AB 96–103). By the time Bonhoeffer writes his *Ethics,* he has clearly distanced himself from this earlier conception of the individual's existential moment of decision. Like the strictly formalist understanding of the ethical as derived from "innate universal human reason," this approach disintegrates life "into an infinite number of unrelated atoms of time, just as human community disintegrates into discrete atoms of reason" (E 373). Instead, Bonhoeffer insists that "[g]enuine ethical discourse involves more than a onetime pronouncement. It needs repetition and continuity; it demands time" (E 375). Without the continuity of historical existence, the ethical falls away from the concrete, into abstraction.

This raises our *second* observation regarding the passage. Bonhoeffer recognizes the necessity of *being able* to take on responsibility, which recalls Ricoeur's insistence on the need for ethical capabilities and resources. If Bonhoeffer were to write of *l'homme capable*, à la Ricoeur,[36] it would derive from his deepening recognition that the concreteness of the ethical injunction requires the larger context of one's real historical existence. "Vis-à-vis God's commandment, a human being is not Hercules standing in perpetuity at a crossroads," agonizing over conflicting duties and the need to make the right decision. "Nor does God's commandment show itself only in those momentous, turbulent, and utterly conscious moments of crisis in life." Instead, God addresses human beings while they are "on the way," in the midst of real life (E 385). God gives us freedom to live and to act as human beings: "God's commandment allows human beings to be human before God. It lets the flow of life take its course, lets human beings eat, drink, sleep, work, celebrate, and play without interrupting those activities, without ceaselessly confronting them with the question whether they were actually permitted to sleep, eat, work, and play, or whether they did not have more urgent duties" (E 384–85). This is not a license for hedonism, nor does it entail the ignoring of ethical responsibility. Instead, this picture of human life approximates Ricoeur's model of "being enjoined to *live well with and for others in just institutions and to esteem oneself as the bearer of this wish*." Bonhoeffer, like Ricoeur, recognizes that this larger framework of penultimate commitments and significations is what allows us to discern the call of the other as significant, as demanding our response. The danger of emphasizing moments of radical rupture is that of failing to do justice to human existence as a whole—what Bonhoeffer describes in his prison letters as the *polyphony* of life (LPP 303–306, 311).

Of course, moments of crisis are often necessary to jar us from our complacency, since they confront us with injunctions that we are usually happy to ignore. But our ability to recognize these as moments of crisis requires a horizon *against which* these moments stand out as crisis. We need the wish to live well, with and for others. Moreover, we need to recognize the way this wish requires just institutions to unfold. As Bonhoeffer argues, the ethical is "not a principle that levels, invalidates, and shatters all human order. Instead, it inherently involves a certain order of human community and entails certain sociological relationships of authority. Only in their context does the ethical manifest itself and receive the concrete authorization that is essential to it" (E 373).

Bonhoeffer also recognizes something like the need to "esteem oneself" as the bearer of the wish to live well, insofar as he challenges the "ethical" polarization of purely selfish and selfless motives.[37] This marks an important development for Bonhoeffer, whose earlier writings consistently identify sin with the self-centered, tyrannical ego. As Clifford Green observes, this conception of the ego led Bonhoeffer to shift away from the traditional Lutheran soteriology of the guilty conscience, toward the problem of the powerful ego that needs to be liberated from itself in order to regard God, self, and others truly.[38] The problem that Bonhoeffer discerns in modern humanity is the sinful ego that needs to surrender itself. Within this framework, salvation involves a surrender of the self and a submission to God and the neighbor. But if Bonhoeffer sees power as a temptation that requires self-submission, Green also demonstrates an important shift in Bonhoeffer's mature thought, in which he came to distinguish between egocentric power and legitimate strength. While egocentric power should be renounced, genuine human maturity, ability, and strength should be affirmed.[39] In Bonhoeffer's later thought one finds an increasing awareness—appearing in *Ethics* but emphasized most fully in the prison letters—that human strength and abilities are not in competition with God and others. Rather, they are gifts from God to be used with confidence, *for the sake of others*.[40]

Bonhoeffer discerns a Christological basis for this affirmation: "Christ is the life we cannot give ourselves, but which comes to us complete from the outside, completely from beyond ourselves." We are created, reconciled, and redeemed in Christ. As such, he is both a No and a Yes to our lives. In Christ we hear No to our falling away from the "origin, essence, and goal" of our lives, to our desire for aseity. But we also hear "Yes to what is created . . . to health, to happiness, to ability, to achievement, to value, to success, to greatness, to honor, in short the Yes to the flourishing of life's strength" (E 251). And in true dialectical style, Bonhoeffer insists that the No and the Yes can be said only together. But most significant for the present discussion is the way Christ's "Yes" makes room for the self to affirm and esteem its calling, along with the abilities that it has to fulfill this calling. This affirmation derives not from one's own immanent and autonomous resources, but from its being in Christ (E 249).

Bonhoeffer's affirmation of health and strength leads to my *third* observation, which concerns the limits of ethical responsibility. Lisa Dahill has argued that Bonhoeffer presents a dangerously imbalanced picture of ethical responsibility. This may be due to biographical reasons: as a white European male, from a wealthy family, with an excellent education, Bonhoeffer had first-person experience of how "the dominating self distorts all of reality into a mere projection of itself."[41] Thus Bonhoeffer understood the powerful ego from within, and his writings testify to his personal struggles with this sense of power. As Dahill observes, it is a testimony to Bonhoeffer's spiritual and ethical sensibilities that he could recognize these dangers and strive to counteract them. But in order to evaluate Bonhoeffer's account, she continues, it is important to keep the particularity of his perspective in mind. Bonhoeffer's emphasis on the "claimless" self responding to the absolute claim of the other can be misleading for those whose basic experience is not dominance, but powerlessness. Bonhoeffer's emphasis on surrendering to the claim of the other is not helpful for victims of abuse and violence, for instance. In fact, such advice can be destructive for those who are able *only* to hear the call of the other, and cannot see their own safety or well-being as a legitimate need. "In contrast to Bonhoeffer, who needed to turn down the volume of the self in order to hear the other, the person living with abuse needs to turn down the volume of the other (specifically, the abuser) in order to attend to herself."[42] In this regard, Dahill finds Bonhoeffer's conception of ethical responsibility (ironically) too abstract, because it describes his own experience of power and privilege while glossing over the experience of those who see from the "underside of selfhood."

Dahill's critique is important because it highlights the danger of carelessly using "undifferentiated language of 'selflessness,' 'self-renunciation,' or 'self-transcendence,'" which can "oversimplify the relative place of self and other in the Christian spiritual life."[43] But she also shows how Bonhoeffer's own writings provide resources to work against an extreme view of responsibility as self-abnegation—most notably in *Discipleship*'s description of Christ as *pro me*. In the case of "those who are *already* 'other,' whose lives are already poured out for many, Jesus as the one for 'others' provides tangible access to a God who is thus 'for me.'"[44] Moreover, Dahill shows that Bonhoeffer's own life undermines the notion of "passive acquiescence," given his very active engagement in his concrete ethical and political milieu.[45]

In light of what we have seen in *Ethics*, we should add that over time Bonhoeffer became more aware of the need for ethical strength—as distinct from sheer egocentric power—due not only to his sense of his own abilities, but to the strength and character he saw in the lives of those he encountered in the resistance movement.[46] We might also add that Bonhoeffer's *Ethics* clearly wants to distinguish between a *self-denial* that decenters the isolated, powerful ego, and a *selflessness* that destroys or annihilates the self. As Bonhoeffer observes, responsible action must not destroy the unity of the self. The conscience liberated in Christ sets limits to responsible action in this regard: "Surrendering the self in selfless service must never be confused with destroying and annihilating the self, which would then also no longer be able to take on responsibility" (E 281). Thus the limits of responsibility also have a Christological basis: just as Christ liberates the conscience for responsible action, so he limits responsibility by rendering it finite: "By grounding responsible action in Jesus Christ we reaffirm precisely the limits of such action. Because we are dealing with worldly action, this responsibility has a limited scope. No one has the responsibility of turning the world into the kingdom of God, but only of taking the next necessary step that corresponds to God's becoming human in Christ" (E 224–25). How does action "correspond" to the incarnation of Christ? Bonhoeffer sheds light on this suggestion in his letter "After Ten Years":

> We are certainly not Christ; we are not called on to redeem the world by our own deeds and sufferings, and we need not try to assume such an impossible burden. We are not lords, but instruments in the hand of the Lord of history; and we can share in other people's sufferings only to a very limited degree. We are not Christ, but if we want to be Christians, we must have some share in Christ's large-heartedness by acting with responsibility and in freedom when the hour of danger comes, and by showing a real sympathy that springs, not from fear, but from the liberating and redeeming love of Christ for all who suffer. (LPP 14)

When Bonhoeffer says that our action must "correspond" to the incarnation of Christ, he means that we live in response to the reality given in Christ. This response [*Antwort*] to Christ is the nature of responsibility [*Verantwortung*]. Responsibility is a matter of living—even risking—one's whole life in response to the life of Christ (E 254–55). Initially such a formulation might seem very abstract, but Bonhoeffer maintains that this understanding of ethical responsibility can only be concrete, because it does not rely on formal, a priori principles; instead, it requires a living faith in the person of Christ, and the trust that he is present and active in the real world.

One final point regarding the limits of responsible action: Just as victims of violence and abuse need to recognize the limits of their deference to the other, so it is necessary to practice *discernment* regarding the claims of the other. Ricoeur makes this point quite dramatically when he asks, "And what are we to say of the Other when he is the executioner? And who will be able to distinguish the master from the executioner, the master who calls for a disciple from the master who requires a slave?" (OA 339). On the one hand, Bonhoeffer argues that the ethical always involves risk and uncertainty, because it is fundamentally a matter of the concrete command of God. And contrary to our desires and expectations, no formal principle or ideology can provide an indubitable norm for responsible action (E 221, 234). A Christian ethic of responsibility must surrender the two basic ethical questions—"'How can I be good?' and 'How can I do something good?'" in favor of "the wholly other, completely different question: What is the will of God?" (E 47). This means that I cannot ensure the goodness of my actions on the basis of abstract, universal principles.[47] I am responsible for others, and it is "the concrete neighbor, as given to me by God" in a concrete situation, that is the norm (E 221). There is no a priori or formal rule that can guarantee absolute security and safety.

But this does not amount to sheer indeterminacy. Rather, Bonhoeffer recognizes the very real need to make wise decisions in this concrete situation. At one level the concrete situation calls for practical and particular judgments. But if this sort of wisdom seems to evoke Aristotelian *phronesis,* Bonhoeffer does not point to a *phronimos* whose ethical judgments are reliable in and of themselves. True, we need practical wisdom, and we need to heed our consciences when making decisions; "the point is to discern what is necessary or 'commanded' in a given situation. One must observe, weigh, and judge the matter, all in the dangerous freedom of one's own self" (E 221–22). But we live and deliberate "in the twilight that the historical situation casts over good and evil" (E 222). And since "the roots of human life and action are hidden in darkness" (E 385), such that the deepest motives of our action are inscrutable, we need to act with the faith that Christ can and will justify our actions. Action of this sort is not arbitrary. On the contrary, responsible action is that which "is most profoundly in accord with reality" (E 222). But responsible action is not in accordance with reality because of an autonomous or immanent source of justification. Rather, since "the most fundamental reality is the reality of the God who became human" (E 223), action is in accord with reality when it corresponds to the incarnation of Christ. This is a challenging claim, to be sure. What is so scandalous, so provocative, so difficult to come to terms with, and ultimately so promising, about Bonhoeffer's picture of ethical responsibility, is his insistence that our selves and our actions can be ultimately justified only by surrendering ourselves in faith to the living Christ.

†

We have cut a wide path across Bonhoeffer's thought, but much remains to be said. Taking a cue from Bonhoeffer's early indications regarding a "Christian social philosophy," I have considered the larger picture of his writings from a philosophical perspective, and have argued that Bonhoeffer's later writings flesh out that which is promising in his early account of ethical responsibility, giving a richer and more nuanced account of the self-other relation. One crucial development lies in Bonhoeffer's more robust conception of ethical agency, which we drew out in dialogue with Ricoeur's insistence on the need for ethical resources and capacities. We have discussed Bonhoeffer's Christological affirmation of concrete, historical existence, as well as conscience, and the goodness of human strength, ability, self-assertion, and so on. But a full account of his contribution to a Christian social philosophy would also require sustained discussion of ecclesiology, since the theme of Christian community remains prominent from his early work in *Sanctorum Communio* through to the claim in his prison writings that "the church is the church only when it exists for others" (LPP 382). For Bonhoeffer, any Christian discussion of the ethically responsible self presupposes the body of Christ, apart from which the Christian individual is an abstraction.[48]

Notes

1. The influence of Hegel on the French phenomenological scene is due in large part to Alexandre Kojève's famous lectures on Hegel's *Phenomenology of Spirit* between 1933 and 1939. Some of the notables who attended these lectures were Jean-Paul Sartre and Maurice Merleau-Ponty. See Kojève's *Introduction to the Reading of Hegel: Lectures on the Phenomenology of Spirit,* assembled by Raymond Queneau, ed. Allan Bloom, trans. James H. Nichols Jr. (Ithaca, N.Y.: Cornell University Press, 1969).

2. Martin Buber, "The History of the Dialogical Principle," in *Between Man and Man* (New York: Macmillan, 1965), 209.

3. Note well, however, that Levinas discerns an important difference between the Platonic and the biblical treatment of otherness. Where the *Sophist* concludes that otherness is always *relatively* other, Levinas insists that otherness is *absolutely* other, and thus utterly irreducible to the conditions and categories of sameness. See Richard Kearney, *Strangers, Gods, and Monsters: Interpreting Otherness* (London: Routledge, 2003), 14–15.

4. Husserl's challenge in this meditation is to refute allegations of solipsism by giving an account of intersubjectivity in which the Other truly transcends the immanence of the constituting subject, and thereby retains its genuine otherness. Edmund Husserl, *Cartesian Meditation: An Introduction to Phenomenology,* trans. Dorion Cairns (Dordrecht, Neth.: Kluwer Academic Publishers, 1991).

5. This theme is a constant throughout Levinas's writings, but it did develop gradually. One finds an important thematic breakthrough toward alterity in the culmination of *Existence and Existents* (trans. Alphonso Lingis [Pittsburgh, Pa.: Duquesne University Press, 1978], 94–98, 102), which Levinas opened up further in *Time and the Other* and *Totality and Infinity*.

6. Karl Barth praises Feuerbach not only for exposing the dangerous implications of liberal theology with his reduction of theology to anthropology, but also for his emphasis on human community. As Garrett Green observes, "Whereas Nietzsche represents for Barth the great champion of the isolated individual, of 'humanity without the fellow-man,' Feuerbach affirms the unity of the human bodily and spiritual reality 'in the relation of the I and the Thou.'" Garrett Green, *Theology, Hermeneutics, and Imagination: The Crisis of Interpretation at the End of Modernity* (Cambridge: Cambridge University Press, 2000), 90.

7. For example, see Feuerbach's preface to *The Essence of Christianity*, trans. George Eliot (New York: Harper and Brothers, 1957), xxxiv.

8. See Barth's essay on Feuerbach, included as an introduction to *The Essence of Christianity*, xiii–xxiv.

9. Robert E. Wood, *Martin Buber's Ontology: An Analysis of* I and Thou (Evanston, Ill.: Northwestern University Press, 1969), 5.

10. The most famous criticism comes from Karl Marx, who objects to the way previous materialism, such as Feuerbach's, conceives "the thing, reality, sensuousness" only as an object of contemplation, "but not as *sensuous human activity, practice*." Feuerbach's thought therefore stalls in abstract, theoretical contemplation rather than striking out into revolutionary, practical activity. "Concerning Feuerbach," in *Marx on Religion*, ed. John Raines (Philadelphia: Temple University Press, 2002), 182–83. Max Stirner objected that Feuerbach fails to discuss the individual human being, instead discussing "man in general," and attributing divinity to this abstraction rather than to "man as he is in reality." Karl Barth, *Protestant Theology in the Nineteenth Century*, new ed., trans. Brian Cozens and John Bowden (Grand Rapids, Mich.: William B. Eerdmans, 2002), 525. Barth's own criticism is that Feuerbach "does not seem sincerely and earnestly to have taken cognizance either of the wickedness of the individual, or of the fact that this individual must surely die. If he had been truly aware of this, then he might perhaps have seen the fictitious nature of this concept of generalized man. He would then perhaps have refrained from identifying God with man, the real man, that is, who remains when the elements of abstraction have been stripped from him. But the theology of the time was not so fully aware of the individual, or of wickedness or death, that it could instruct Feuerbach upon these points" (ibid., 526).

11. Paul Janz argues that Bonhoeffer actually poses a serious challenge to the phenomenological tradition. See his essay "Bonhoeffer, This-Worldliness, and the Limits of Phenomenology," in this volume.

12. Bonhoeffer studied phenomenology throughout his preparations for his next work, *Act and Being*, and in *Ethics* he undertakes a general phenomenology of the experience and limits of the ethical "ought" (E 366–76, and 376n45).

13. Again see E 376n45.

14. First, in the Aristotelian metaphysical model, the individual is subsumed within the species; "human beings only become persons insofar as they participate in the species reason" (SC 36). Second, in the Stoic model personhood is constituted by subordinating oneself to a universally valid imperative, which unites persons "in an order of reason."

When one obeys this imperative, one's soul "is of like nature with eternal reason and thus also with the soul of other persons" (SC 37). Third, the Epicurean concept of the person extends Democritus's atomism "to social and ethical life, asserting that human social formation [*Vergellshaftung*] only serves to heighten the pleasure of each individual." In this model persons remain fundamentally alien to each other, since each is oriented toward his own highest pleasure. Thus the only possible connection between persons must be one of utility, since persons are not intrinsically or essentially related. Bonhoeffer likens this to Hobbes's view of sociality as a "purely contractual" limitation of warfare—warfare being the Hobbesian man's natural state (SC 38–40).

15. However, in his next work (*Act and Being*) Bonhoeffer is more careful to distinguish Kant's "genuine transcendental philosophizing" from idealism. Whereas Kant preserves transcendence by distinguishing between the cognitive act and being, idealism is "self-contained"—i.e., it collapses this distinction and locates being within consciousness (AB 49–50).

16. This claim that God mediates between self and other distinctly echoes Kierkegaard. Cf. *Works of Love*, 107, where Kierkegaard argues that God is the middle term between persons (trans. Howard V. Hong and Edna H. Hong [Princeton, N.J.: Princeton University Press, 1995]). Bonhoeffer does not cite Kierkegaard to this effect, but other citations in *Sanctorum Communio* indicate that he was familiar with *Works of Love* (e.g., SC 170n28). There is more to be said about Bonhoeffer's account of Kierkegaard and Barth regarding the intersection between self, God, and other; I hope to say it in a future article.

17. Bonhoeffer's subsequent writings will emphasize the role of Christ as the mediator between self and other. But as Ernst Feil observes, *Sanctorum Communio* does not yet make this move. *The Theology of Dietrich Bonhoeffer*, trans. Martin Rumscheidt (Philadelphia: Fortress Press, 1985), 62.

18. Hans Ruin, "The Moment of Truth: *Augenblick* and *Ereignis* in Heidegger," *Epoché: A Journal for the History of Philosophy* 6, no. 1 (1998): 80.

19. Ibid. The term *exaiphnes* appears in Plato's *Parmenides*, where Socrates and Parmenides discuss the peculiarity that is the instant, which is situated between motion and rest but does not occupy any time itself (156d–e). It was translated into German by Luther and later Schleiermacher as *Augenblick*—the momentary "blink of the eye." *Kairos* also has a long history in Greek thought, starting as early as Homer's *Iliad,* and appearing in Greek philosophy and the rhetorical tradition as the "right" or "appropriate time," as distinguished from *chronos,* which is the uniformly ordered time of the cosmos. *Kairos* is also an important biblical term, designating most notably the fullness of time in Jesus' and Paul's references to the kingdom of God. See Phillip Sipiora's "The Ancient Concept of *Kairos,*" in *Rhetoric and Kairos: Essays in History, Theory, and Praxis*, ed. Phillip Sipiora and James S. Baumlin (Albany: SUNY Press, 2002).

20. The bibliography of *Sanctorum Communio* lists several of Kierkegaard's works: *Fear and Trembling, Repetition,* and *Works of Love.* But *The Concept of Anxiety* does not appear, even though this contains some of Kierkegaard's most important reflections on the moment. See *The Concept of Anxiety,* trans. Reidar Thomte (Princeton, N.J.: Princeton University Press, 1980), 86–93.

21. Karl Barth, *The Epistle to the Romans,* trans. Edwyn C. Hoskyns (London: Oxford University Press, 1933), 33, 109–12, 124–25, 202, etc.

22. Eberhard Bethge notes that Bonhoeffer did not study Heidegger seriously until he began research for his *Habilitationsschrift. Dietrich Bonhoeffer: A Biography,* rev. ed.,

rev. and ed. Victoria Barnett (Minneapolis, Minn.: Fortress Press, 2000), 129, 133. According to the editorial chronology listed in *Act and Being,* Bonhoeffer first read *Sein und Zeit* between February 1928 and February 1929 (AB 185). With Bonhoeffer having delved into Heidegger, the latter's presence in the second dissertation was significant. As Bethge observes, in *Act and Being* citations of Heidegger "took second place only to Luther—even before Barth" (Bethge, 133).

23. Martin Heidegger, *Being and Time,* trans. John Macquarrie and Edward Robinson (San Francisco: Harper and Row, 1962), 388. Cited hereafter in the text as BT.

24. If Heidegger does recognize something in the way of responsibility for others, it is on the basis of Dasein's prior response to its own call of conscience. Whether or not it is possible to develop an ethics on the basis of Heidegger's conception of *Mitsein,* as some commentators have suggested, is another question.

25. Bonhoeffer uses the linguistic similarity between response [*Antwort*] and responsibility [*Verantwortung*] to highlight their important ethical connection. See *Ethics,* 234n62, as well as 254–55.

26. "Human beings make themselves the defendant, they appeal to their better selves. But the cries of conscience only dull the mute loneliness of a desolate 'with-itself' [*'Bei-sich'*]; they ring without echo in the world that the self rules and explains" (AB 139).

27. Here we can only broach the deep difference between Bonhoeffer's Christian theological understand of the Fall and Heidegger's ontological understanding of *Verfallenheit.*

28. Heidegger wants to avoid such complications by suspending ethical and theological conceptions of conscience and limiting his analysis to the ontological level. But Bonhoeffer will not accept Heidegger's insistence that theological concepts of sin and redemption have no jurisdiction at the ontological level. For a discussion of Bonhoeffer's critique of Heidegger in this regard, see my essay "Formal Indication, Philosophy, and Theology: Bonhoeffer's Critique of Heidegger," *Faith and Philosophy* 24, no. 2 (April 2007): 185–202.

29. Paul Ricoeur, *Oneself as Another,* trans. Kathleen Blamey (Chicago: University of Chicago Press, 1992), 331, 336. Cited hereafter in the text as OA.

30. Mark I. Wallace, "The Summoned Self: Ethics and Hermeneutics in Paul Ricoeur in Dialogue with Emmanuel Levinas," in *Paul Ricoeur and Contemporary Moral Thought,* ed. John Wall, William Schweiker, and W. David Hall (New York: Routledge, 2002), 88–89.

31. Ibid., 89.

32. Ibid., 90–91.

33. We should also note that elsewhere Ricoeur presents a more theological treatment of conscience as a crucial "organ of reception" that allows the self to hear the kerygma and the call of Christ to discipleship. Apart from this "anthropological presupposition," the event of justification by faith would be "marked by a radical extrinsicness." "The Summoned Subject in the School of the Narratives of the Prophetic Vocation," in *Figuring the Sacred,* trans. David Pellauer, ed. Mark I. Wallace (Minneapolis, Minn.: Fortress Press, 1995), 271–75. Ricoeur's presentation of conscience as a theological point of contact demands further analysis, but would unfortunately fill the present paper beyond its bursting point.

34. As Bonhoeffer writes, "human historical action is good only insofar as God draws it into God's own action and as the human agent completely surrenders all to God's action without claiming any other justification" (E 227).

35. For Ricoeur's extended engagement with this text, see his essay "Otherwise: A Reading of Emmanuel Levinas's *Otherwise than Being or Beyond Essence*," trans. Matthew Escobar, Yale French Studies, no. 104, pp. 82–99.

36. See Ricoeur's essay "Ethics and Human Capability: A Response," in *Paul Ricoeur and Contemporary Moral Thought*.

37. "The motives of actions are inscrutable, everything we do is interwoven with something conscious and unconscious, natural and supernatural, with inclination and duty, with the egotistical and the altruistic, the intended and inevitable, the active and passive" (E 384). God's commandment sets us free from the "self-tormenting and hopeless question about the purity of one's motives, suspicious self-observation, the blazing and wearisome light of ceaseless conscious awareness" (E 385).

38. Clifford Green, *Bonhoeffer: A Theology of Sociality*, rev. ed. (Grand Rapids, Mich.: William B. Eerdmans, 1999), 136–37.

39. Ibid., 175–78.

40. In *Ethics* Bonhoeffer even uses the word "power" to designate this notion of ability: "Political action means taking on responsibility. This cannot happen without power. Power is to serve responsibility" (E 245).

41. Lisa E. Dahill, "Reading from the Underside of Selfhood: Dietrich Bonhoeffer and Spiritual Formation," *Spiritus* 1 (2001): 189.

42. Ibid., 193.

43. Ibid., 199.

44. Ibid., 195.

45. Ibid., 198–99.

46. This awareness of the strength and "goodness" of his co-conspirators, many of whom were not Christians, informs his discussion of Christ and "good people" (E 339–51).

47. Bonhoeffer rejects this approach, citing Kant's "grotesque conclusion" that it is better to tell a murderer the truth about his intended victim's whereabouts than to lie. This is self-righteousness "escalated into blasphemous recklessness" (E 279–80).

48. Given the deeply Christological orientation of Bonhoeffer's thought, there is also much to be said regarding the prospects for a give-and-take relationship between Christian and non-Christian philosophy. Bonhoeffer's discussion of the relation between the ultimate and the penultimate is particularly helpful for thinking through this important issue. For a discussion of the ultimate/penultimate distinction as it pertains to philosophy and theology, see our introduction to this volume, as well as chapter 8 in Paul D. Janz, *God, the Mind's Desire: Reference, Reason, and Christian Thinking* (Cambridge: Cambridge University Press, 2004).

TEN

"At the Recurrent End of the Unending": Bonhoeffer's Eschatology of the Penultimate

JOHN PANTELEIMON MANOUSSAKIS

> On this ground alone, I regard the common practice of explaining
> things in terms of their final causes to be useless in physics: it would
> be foolish of me to think that I can discover God's purposes.

DESCARTES, MEDITATION IV

With this remark of pseudo-modesty Descartes dismissed a tradition that was held from the times of the Presocratics to the era of High Scholasticism, according to which what a thing is, its real essence, lies in its purpose, that is, in its future. Descartes's timing was rather opportune: the rise of the scientific spirit favored efficient causality, and this preference would in subsequent years become a monopoly. It is only over efficient causes that science (*that* type of science anyway) could have control: it could observe them, measure them, and even reproduce them for the sake of experimentation. Thus the past was to be allotted an importance disproportional to that of the future, and the "how" of things was to take a definite priority over the "whys"; for example, it is easier to explain how a mountain was formed, but what purpose it serves, what it was made for, becomes now, even as a question, inadmissible.

The epistemological exclusion of the future has had some repercussion on the epistemic modesty that prevailed over the theological discourse on eschatology. Only in the twentieth century, following the critique of science and technology, did eschatology slowly reassume its rightful place. That way, however, theologians became aware of more pressing questions regarding the church's expectation regarding the last things. It seems that modernity did not simply rearrange the emphasis between two kinds of causality, but also changed our worldview altogether to such an extent that the very beliefs of the church became questionable, if not incredulous, once the old cosmology that had supported them was discredited. The new task for the theologians of the last century was, then, to rearticulate the articles of faith to make them again meaningful. It is against such a task that Bonhoeffer's contribution to eschatology should be appraised.

The importance of Bonhoeffer's thought for contemporary theology is well attested and does not need to be reiterated here. Since the present volume, however, has chosen as its objective the point of convergence between Bonhoeffer's thought and philosophy, as well as their mutual relations, we must attempt to show why and in what ways Bonhoeffer's eschatology constitutes, in our opinion, the most promising fruit of such an encounter.[1]

The Context of Bonhoeffer's Eschatology

"[T]he question of good," writes Dietrich Bonhoeffer, and thus of ethics, "can only find its answer in Christ" (E 49). The first section of his *Ethics* leaves no doubt about this: ethics is to be subordinated to and grounded in Christology. The reason for this bold reduction is to be found in Bonhoeffer's criticism of the doctrine of the two realms [*Räume*] (E 55–66) or two kingdoms [*zwei Reiche*] (E 60).[2] Bonhoeffer traces this distinction back to the High Middle Ages and post-Reformation Lutheran theology, although one could extend its genealogy as far back as the early Christian literature and the gospels themselves.[3] These two realms have assumed many names throughout the ages—Church and State; nature and grace; the kingdom of God and the kingdom of Man—whatever their form, however, Bonhoeffer insists that it is a distinction eventually untenable. What follows might surprise the modern reader, used as we are in the post-Enlightenment to divorce between the sacred and the secular:

> There are not two realities, but *only one reality,* and that is God's reality revealed in Christ in the reality of the world. Partaking in Christ, we stand at the same time in the reality of God and in the reality of the world. The reality of Christ embraces the reality of the world itself. The world has no reality of its own independent of God's revelation in Christ. It is a denial of God's revelation in Jesus Christ to wish to be "Christian" without being "worldly," or to wish to be worldly without seeing and recognizing the world in Christ. Hence there are not two realms, but only *the one realm of*

Christ-reality, in which the reality of God and the reality of the world are united. . . . There are not two competing realms standing side by side and battling over the borderline, as if this question of boundaries was always the decisive one. Rather, the whole reality of the world has already been drawn into and is held together in Christ. History moves only from this center and toward this center. (E 58)

This is indeed an important passage. The emphasis on Christology is underlined not only by its content (there is only one reality, Christ's) but also by the forms around which this passage is structured (the symmetry of "being worldly in Christ" and "Christian in the world"; the chiasmus formed by the unity between God and world in Christ). Bonhoeffer seems to deny the distinction between God and world as either monophysite or arianistic. In other words, he understands the implications of this distinction in terms of the church's age-old Christological debates against the denial of Christ's divinity (Arianism) or against the denial of His humanity (monophysitism).[4] For Bonhoeffer, then, God and world are indeed united in a way similar and parallel to the hypostatic union of the two natures in Christ as declared by the Council of Chalcedon "without division" (ἀδιαιρέτως) and "without confusion" (ἀσυγχήτως). A clear echo of the Chalcedonian formula can be heard later in Bonhoeffer's text when he writes, "There are two kingdoms, which, as long as the earth remains, must never be mixed together, yet never torn apart" (E 112).[5]

Alongside this Christological character, the ethical assumes also a eucharistic dimension. This is a less evident development in Bonhoeffer's text. It is, nevertheless, an implicit image occupying a central position, since it is the very image which Bonhoeffer chooses in order to replace the inadequate model of the two realms. So he writes, "It is hard to give up an image that we have customarily used to integrate our thoughts and concepts. Yet we must get beyond this two-realms image. The question is now whether we can replace it with another image that is just as simple and plausible." And his answer: "Above all we must turn our eyes to the image of Jesus Christ's own body—the one who became human, was crucified, and is risen" (E 66). The association of the body of Christ with the Eucharist is of course obvious and needs no further explanation. Suffice, perhaps, to note how the three-fold explication attached to the introduction of Christ's body is none other than that of Eucharist's memorial acclamation: "Christ has died, Christ is risen, Christ will come again."[6] Furthermore, Bonhoeffer invites us to see through this new paradigm not only the church (which was spoken of as the body of Christ already in Paul's letters) but also the world itself: "Like all of creation, the world has been created through Christ and toward Christ and has its existence only in Christ" (E 68). This is a litany repeated in various formulations throughout the remaining section (the world "expects Christ, is directed toward Christ, is open for Christ and serves and glorifies Christ" [E 71]). It is fundamentally in the offering of the eucharistic gifts, the bread and the wine, that creation is affirmed and accepted precisely because through this eucharistic thanksgiving we come to see the world "through him, with him, and in him" (to use another eucharistic formula echoed by Bonhoeffer).

This eucharistic affirmation of the world, however, does not become forgetful of the evil in our actions and the pain in our lives. In other words, Bonhoeffer's kataphatic approach to creation and its creaturely character is not on account of some naïve optimism (far from it—this manuscript is written, after all, as Europe and the world are torn apart by war), but rather on account of his consistency with the church's eschatological vision. The introduction of the eschatological into a discussion of the ethical (or rather the casting of the ethical in terms of the eschatological) completes Bonhoeffer's radical departure from previous treatments of Christian ethics. The initial—indeed, inaugural— position of his *Ethics* was to deny the splitting of reality into a Gnostic dualism of good and evil, sacred and profane, and so on—and by doing so, to rescue the Christian believer from the "schizophrenia" of a dual citizenship (being, at the same time, a citizen of heaven and earth). As we have already seen, his reasons for this denial were Christological and eucharistic. The link between them is, as it will become more explicit in later sections of the *Ethics*, eschatology.

His, however, is an eschatology quite different from what a student of systematic theology might be used to: the emphasis here lies not on some beyond-this-world, end-of-times utopia but on the quiet and unnoticeable unfolding of the eschaton through the ephemeral and the everyday. Thus we are to find "the 'supernatural' only in the natural, the holy only in the profane, the revelational only in the rational," and yet the natural is not identical with the supernatural or the revelational with the rational (E 59). The eschaton is in the present but not of the present, as Christ's kingdom is in the world but not of the world (Jn 18, 19). The precise relationship between the "two kingdoms" will be further elucidated in the following development of the relation between the penultimate and the ultimate. In fact, Bonhoeffer's treatment of the latter is prefigured in the former in such a way that the reader is forced to think the association that connects the political with the eschatological. As "in Christ we are invited to participate in the reality of God and the reality of the world at the same time, the one not without the other" (E 55) so one cannot participate and live in the temporal without also participating in the eternal—"the one not without the other." It is this association that will lead Bonhoeffer to the criticism of the so-called orders of creation. The reference here is to the Lutheran doctrine of the "orders of creation" (*Schöpfungsordnungen*), which regarded worldly institutions such as nations and states and civil conventions such as marriage as belonging intrinsically to the creation and thus "good." This doctrine gave rise to a *Theologie der Ordnungen* that did not hesitate to support Nazi ideology (since the Third Reich could be seen as part of God's creation). Bonhoeffer criticized such theories by changing the terminology from "orders of creation" (which would imply a permanent validity) to "orders of preservation," making them, thus, part of the transient scheme of this world that has its justification only in relation to the eschaton (CF 140). In *Ethics* we meet them under the terminology of the "mandates" (E 68–75). The four mandates (work, marriage, government, and church) derive their meaning and validity from God and thus stand toward God as the penultimate toward the ultimate. If considered "in themselves" they become, instead of divine, demonic, as the penultimate "in itself"—without the constant reference to the ultimate for whose sake it exists—becomes sin. The crucial question, however, is: will the mandates survive, that is, continue to exist in the kingdom or will they become abolished? From the kingdom's perspective, that is, seen eschatologically, Bonhoeffer's grouping of the four mandates becomes problematic, as it is inconceivable that the first three (work, marriage, government) will continue to exist in the kingdom, while it is equally inconceivable that the fourth (church) will not. Work was a consequence of the fall (Gn 3:17–19); as for marriage, "when people rise from the dead, they neither marry nor are given in marriage" (Mt 22:30). Besides, the association of marriage with death (see John Chrysostom's "where is death, there is marriage" from *De Virginitate*, PG 48, 543) makes marriage an unlikely participant of the kingdom. Conversely, the church pre-existed the creation of the world: "she was created before all things and for her sake the world was formed" (*The Shepherd of Hermas*, 8) and her existence will continue in the age to come (Rv 21). Secondly, Bonhoeffer thinks that the mandates are also mandatory: "God has placed human being under all these mandates, not only each individual under one or the other, but all people under all four" (E 69). This is a rather radical view, incompatible with the example of Christ who fulfilled some of these mandates but not others (e.g., marriage).

Penultimacy

This novel understanding of eschatology required a new concept: the term employed by Bonhoeffer is the "penultimate." Its purpose is not so much to indicate the sequential precedence of the temporary world over the kingdom—in other words, the penultimate is *not* a *temporal* indicator but rather a *relational* one: it does not express the arrangement between the world and the kingdom (in terms of a before and an after), but rather it exposes the inner relation—a relation of *interdependence* and *reciprocity*—between God's creation and God's kingdom. Etymologically as well as conceptually, the penultimate presupposes the concept of the ultimate. In *Ethics,* we are presented with penultimacy not simply prior to the ultimate—as if in succession—but as impregnated by the ultimate things-to-come, which, since they are already to be found in the penultimate, that is, in the things-themselves, are not only to-come but also *already* here. It is precisely this Johannine tension between the *not-yet* and the *already* (Jn 4:23, 5:25) that Bonhoeffer is interested in preserving and uplifting by his discussion of the eschatological.

However, the very poles of this fragile balance exercise an irresistible attraction that threatens to dissolve their harmony as either the *already* takes over and thus compromise is the order of the day, or one surrenders to the enthusiasm of the *not-yet* and its ensuing radicalism. Put otherwise: the world is pregnant with the kingdom (cf. creation's "birth pangs" in Rm 8:22), but neither "abortion" nor "premature birth" can be the solution. Bonhoeffer identifies the former with a stance of compromise that rejects the ultimate for the sake of the penultimate and the latter with the radical or enthusiastic tendencies that reject the penultimate for the sake of the ultimate. For Bonhoeffer both positions are equally monistic and thus culpable of the same crime, that is, of attempting to manipulate the kingdom either by delaying or by hastening its coming. "Both solutions," he writes, "are extreme in the same respect. . . . One absolutizes the end, the other absolutizes what exists" (E 154). Only their chiastic intertwining can bring about and maintain their accord: the ultimate *in* the penultimate and the penultimate *for* the ultimate. This chiasm, as we will see, is Christological through and through. "The relationship between the ultimate and the penultimate is resolved only in Christ" (E 157). Bonhoeffer then proceeds to demonstrate their unity by means of a Christological triptych: incarnation, crucifixion, and resurrection. He skillfully adopts the same idea into those three registers (dedicating one paragraph for each) like a composer who sets the same melody into different keys. In their structural unison, however, their thematic differences can be heard all the more clearly: Christ's incarnation (living "in deepest poverty," "unmarried," and dying "as a criminal") pronounces the condemnation of this world and of its "orders"; Christ's crucifixion mediates between the rejection of the world on the one hand—now brought to its utter conclusion as assumed by the "beaten, bleeding, spat-upon face of the crucified"—and the acceptance of the ultimate that breaks through the salvific efficacy of Christ's cross; finally, Christ's resurrection realizes the ultimate already in the here and now of the penultimate as "it breaks ever more powerfully into earthly life and creates space for itself within it." It becomes thus clear that any monism introduced in the reciprocity between the ultimate and the penultimate jeopardizes the core of the church's Christological confession.

It is precisely this conviction that makes it so difficult to accept Bonhoeffer's modification of the ancient doctrine of *theosis,* a doctrine that is equally grounded on Christology and on the church's eschatological expectation. As early as Athanasius, the Fathers understood the incarnation of the Son as having a twofold effect: first, that "the Word became flesh" as the Gospel of John had declared and secondly, that flesh will participate in the divine life as the ascension had indicated. To expect the latter meant to believe the former, just as belief in the former suggested the latter. Athanasius phrased the symmetry of this doctrine thus: "He became man [ἐνηνθρώπησεν] so that we can be made gods [θεωποιηθῶμεν]" (*De Incarnatione Verbi,* PG 25b, 192).[7] Bonhoeffer, however, seems to fall prey to an unbecoming humanism when he repeats Athanasius's formula, only with the following twist: "God changes God's form into human form in order that human beings can become, not God, but human" (E 96).[8] One appreciates the paradox of the humans who are called to become humans (meaning, I suppose, that only in Christ humanity regains its proper image), as one wonders whether Bonhoeffer—and with him all of us today—could espouse the radical implications that Christ's incarnation has had, and is to have, on our human state without stopping short a step—the crucial step!—before *theosis.* If Christ's incarnation is to leave us essentially unchanged (only now restored to some alleged dignity) then, perhaps, we sell short the church's hope (a "cheap" hope, so to speak, analogous to "cheap" grace). What is at stake here is nothing less than our understanding of God's kingdom. If we believe in a minimalist (humanistic) eschatology that feels compelled to allegorize (or, worse, moralize) the church's expectations because it secretly deems them incredulous, then the most we can expect is the alleviation (or even perfection) of our human condition. But if we are willing to embrace a maximalist eschatology, then Athanasius's daring formula should not cause any trepidation; participation in God's life, deification by grace is indeed our future—this *is,* after all, what we have been promised (cf. 1 Jn 3:2 and even more importantly 2 Pt 1:4). Our choice between these two kinds of expectations reflects our position with regard to Christ's person: a minimalist eschatology is complementary to an equally minimalist Christology: if the result of God's salvific economy were to be nothing more than the perfection of man, it makes sense to require only that much of Christ, that is, a perfect man and nothing more. But if it was God who became man in Christ, then, one should not expect anything less than man becoming god in the kingdom.[9]

What is the precise relationship, however, between the eschatological and the ethical? Bonhoeffer's understanding of eschatology creates a certain ethos of expectancy and patience that can be viewed both negatively and positively.

Negatively: The disclosure of the world as penultimate keeps at bay our possessive desires while it reveals that the worldly elements of our lives lack validity in themselves, that they are but transient schemes that should not be despised but recognized for what they are: precursors of the ultimate. In other words, the goodness of the world is not to be found in itself, in self-isolation, in independence, in autonomy, but in relation to the ultimate (in all these cases, where the world is cut off from the ultimate and becomes its own value, goal and purpose, the world becomes demonic and sinful because it sets itself up against the ultimate and its coming—in the traditional language of the New Testament we could say that that world becomes the anti-Christ). The goodness of the world then is precisely drawn from this relationship to the ultimate. The more explicit their relation the more joyous the sojourn in the world. Under this light, sin can be redefined as the forgetfulness of this relationship; sin is nothing more than treating the penultimate as ultimate, as what is *not*. To take what-is-not as something that is—better yet, to mistake the non-being as being, this is sin. It should make sense now why some early Fathers defined sin not simply as an ethical category but also as an ontological deficiency, a lack of being, a "death" much more "essential" than our biological death (cf. Kierkegaard's concept of sin as "sickness unto death").

One feels tempted at this point to go through the traditional list of sinful actions and show how each and every one of them exemplifies this failing in recognizing the ultimate beyond the penultimate, that is to say, failing to recognize the penultimate as penultimate. St. Augustine has done already the work for us, and we only have but to copy his words:

> For thus *pride* imitates high estate, whereas Thou alone art God, high above all. And what does *ambition* seek but honors and renown, whereas Thou alone art to be honored above all, and renowned for evermore? The *cruelty* of the powerful wishes to be feared; but who is to be feared but God only, out of whose power what can be forced away or withdrawn—when, or where, or whither, or by whom? The enticements of the *wanton* would fain be deemed love; and yet is naught more enticing than Thy charity, nor is aught loved

more healthfully than that, Thy truth, bright and beautiful above all. *Curiosity* affects a desire for knowledge, whereas it is Thou who supremely knowest all things. *Ignorance* and *foolishness* themselves are concealed under the names of ingenuousness and harmlessness, because nothing can be found more ingenuous than Thou; and what is more harmless, since it is a sinner's own work by which he is harmed? And *sloth* seems to long for rest; but what sure rest is there besides the Lord? *Luxury* would fain be called plenty and abundance; but Thou art the fullness and unfailing plenteousness of unfading joys. *Prodigality* presents a shadow of liberality; but Thou art the most lavish giver of all good. *Covetousness* desires to possess much; and Thou art the Possessor of all things. *Envy* contends for excellence; but what so excellent as Thou? *Anger* seeks revenge; who avenges more justly than Thou? *Fear* starts at unwonted and sudden chances which threaten things beloved. And is wary for their security; but what can happen that is unwonted or sudden to Thee? Or who can deprive Thee of what Thou lovest? Or where is there unshaken security save with Thee? *Grief* languishes for things lost in which desire had delighted itself, even because it would have nothing taken from it, as nothing can be from Thee.[10]

Positively: The positive relation between the penultimate and the ultimate is that of the particular to the universal. The reference of the particular to its universal is manifold, and not all of the ways are helpful or even appropriate to serve as an analogy for the correspondence of the penultimate to the ultimate. Nevertheless, and in a certain way, the particular belongs to the penultimate: it is in its realm that we encounter the concreteness of the everyday. On the other hand, the eschaton could be envisioned as the realm from where the manifoldness of the everyday world draws its unity and therefore its intelligibility. This analogy, however, is not applicable to eschatology insofar as it comes from the logical or cognitive schema. In other words, the eschaton cannot be made the "universal" of the penultimate in the same way that a concept is the universal of a particular object (although this tendency is indeed to be found, no matter how implicit, in the eschatologies influenced by Neoplatonism, such as those of Dionysius, Maximus, and, later on, Hegel). The eschaton can be only an *indeterminable* "universal," to which the penultimate refers (otherwise it would not be possible to recognize the penultimate as such), but its reference remains open-ended. Indeed, there is such a category where the particular refers to a universal that one cannot determine but needs somehow to provide. Let me offer an example: Galileo's law of acceleration of falling bodies is a particular law of physics that, at the time of its proposition, was lacking its universal—that came about a hundred years later with Newton's law of universal gravitation. This relation, of a particular to an indeterminable universal, is employed by Kant in the analysis of aesthetic judgments. The object of an aesthetic judgment (e.g., this rose) is a particular that refers to a universal that cannot be determined (it is not, for example, the concept of the "rose," or that of a flower and so on, as in the case of understanding).[11] On the other hand, the particular rose in its aesthetic manifestation (i.e., as a *beautiful* rose) needs to be recognized, that is, to be subsumed under a universal. Could the beautiful itself be that concept? Kant's answer might come as a surprise: the beautiful is not a concept and therefore cannot serve as the universal of the particular beautiful rose.[12]

Similarly, the penultimate is a particular that refers to an indeterminable universal, that is, the ultimate. The latter cannot be determined or known, but it can only be awaited and anticipated. It is not that the ultimate lacks reality, intelligibility, or content. Its indeterminability—its unknowableness as we would say in theological language—is due not to its emptiness nor to its transcendence but to its mode of manifestation, which is none other than *surprise* (Mt 24:27, 50, Mk 13:36, Lk 12:40, 17:24).

Eschatology and Philosophy

Eschatology, we would like to argue, follows a similar logic (indeed, it is not an accident that Kant pairs aesthetic judgments with teleology). The universal a priori idea of aesthetic judgments is for Kant purposiveness, that is, as we would see, an eschatology. Of course, for Kant eschatology is only teleology, that is, an eschatology without recourse beyond the creaturely character of nature within which it exhausts itself. Regardless, however, of such a Kantian gesture that hails toward transcendence while at the very same time finds itself obliged to deny it, Kant's basic insight should be allowed to stand. In the beautiful, indeed, we recognize a purpose—by means of purpose we see *now* an aspect that the thing will come to have only *at the end*. Purpose foresees; it previews the future and affords us a view that no here and now could furnish, not even at the final state of things. Naturally, if we understand beauty as symmetry or proportion, as harmony of color or sound, it would be difficult, indeed impossible, to explain the catholicity of the beautiful as the call that calls through the visible, even when it is not a question of harmony or symmetry. These "scientific" explanations, as Socrates somewhat scornfully calls them in the *Phaedo*, are descriptive at best of the ways in which beauty is perceived; that is, they explain only the "mechanics" of the aesthetical phenomenon, but fail to answer why we call something beautiful or, worse, what beauty is in itself.

For Plato "what is beautiful is beautiful by the beautiful" (100d, 7–8). Of course, such a statement is heavily in need of interpretation. One has learned to see in this answer Plato's so-called theory of forms. The beautiful, then, by which anything becomes beautiful, is taken to be the form of beauty. This already implies that what makes something beautiful is not itself, that is, it is not to be found in the thing itself, but rather comes from beyond; it is other than the thing that one perceives as beautiful. As we have seen, Kant gives a very similar answer when he refuses to assign beauty as the property of a thing. For him, too, beauty is external and a sign of exteriority. Both Plato and Kant seem to converge on another point: that beauty is teleological. Plato's treatment of the beautiful takes place within a certain historical and semi-biographical context: it is the famous episode where Socrates gives a brief account of his philosophical autobiography and of his encounter with Anaxagoras's teleology in particular. Socrates believes that in Anaxagoras he has found the only tenable answer as to the cause of things, that is, perfection ("for if one wished to know the cause of each thing . . . one had only to find what was best for it"—97c). His later disillusionment with Anaxagoras leads Socrates to the famous "second sailing" that consists of an investigation into the *logoi* of things, the latter being, as it is made clear in the dialogue, a *final* causality.[13] For the remaining pages of the dialogue, Plato singles out one particular form, that of beauty, which, by calling everything to itself, makes everything that heeds its call—and everything to some degree is—beautiful. Indeed, what else can the beautiful be than what calls? And how else is one to understand the ability of the call to call if not by means of beauty? Language tells us that much when it indicates that the derivation of "the beautiful" (τό καλό) comes from the verb "to call" (καλέω, καλεῖν).

Dionysius is situated in the middle of the distance between Plato and Kant. His beautiful is no longer as impersonal as Plato's form, nor has it yet been depersonalized as Kant's a priori idea of purposiveness. For Dionysius the beautiful is a person, God himself:

> The beautiful [καλὸν] that is beyond all being is called beautiful [κάλλος] on account of its own beauty that it transmits to each and every thing and for being accountable for the harmony and brilliance of all as the light that shines to every thing its radiating rays and for calling [καλοῦν] everything to itself and gathering everything and in every respect, for which reason it has been called beautiful [κάλλος].[14]

Therefore, if the beautiful is recognized as beautiful it is because it renders itself visible (i.e., it "calls" to itself) and, by the same token, what is visible, what appears and by appearing "calls" to itself, is only the beautiful. Dionysius's passage distinguishes between these two (simultaneous) movements clearly: the beautiful radiates "like the light"—thus it renders everything visible; indeed it is the condition of visibility—but also recollects everything to itself, now strictly in its capacity as the "beautiful"—that is, as a call from the future.[15] It is not, therefore, that through the dioptra of beauty we can get a glimpse of what lies ahead but rather that the finality of perfection "opens" the present by adding along with the incomplete state of the present thing the image of its completion, that is, of its perfection.

If, indeed, only the end (in the double sense of *telos* as finality and purposiveness) makes things perfect (*teleia*), then purpose keeps reminding us of such perfection amidst incompletion and imperfection. It is as if the human mind were indeed made in such a way as to understand only the perfect and the complete. For even if this is lacking in the present state of things (and it can only be lacking) then it feels compelled to supply it by itself. Memory and anticipation are both mediums of idealization, that is, of bestowing a perfection upon the thing remembered or expected that, once present, the thing lacks. Hence the disenchantment that follows every realized expectation.

How are we to understand this ability of the mind? It is precisely at this point that we need to turn to a phenomenological inquiry of the eschatological. It would seem that the first (that is, the most fundamental and the most readily available) intuition of eschatology is that of awaiting or expecting. But what would such an intuition have been without the idea of purpose, that is, of fulfillment of one's anticipation, even if we were to know not what or whom we are waiting for? More fundamental, then, than waiting is this waiting-for, that is, the structure of a purpose. Whence can we phenomenologically derive such a structure? First of all, from the very character of intending. Intentionality, even prior to intending this or that, always intends a purpose; in fact, it *is* purposive. In every fulfillment, in every filled intention, one can observe the structure of the eschatological. Kant spoke of pleasure precisely on these terms,[16] and we believe that it is the joy of the kingdom to come that is foreshadowed in the feeling of satisfaction that every filled anticipation yields. The very passage from an empty intention to a filled one (that is, the passage from absence to presence) is such an eschatological indication, for in all these common structures of anticipation the absolute anticipation, that is, the anticipation of the absolute, is reflected.

But by speaking of anticipation we have already entered the realm of imagination, of which anticipation is one of its modes. The association of imagination with the eschatological deserves a more attentive study that exceeds the limitations of the present essay. We could, however, say that such a connection is indeed to be discovered in imagination's ability to posit things otherwise without allowing presence to fully collapse into the present. One should, however, distinguish between *imagination* (as our sole capacity to envision the eschata) and *fantasy* (as what hinders our vision of the eschaton by "binding" us down to the things-themselves). What fantasy does is to present things as our only possibility precisely by presenting us with the phantasmagoria of their (infinite as it would seem) possible transformations.

Without imagination (in its broad, existential sense) there can be no freedom. Man is thus engulfed in the inertia of his nature, unable to expect or wait for what comes beyond the natural. Eschatology in a very fundamental sense is counterintuitive—by that we mean to say that that for which the church waits cannot be given empirically as present-at-hand; if it were, the waiting would have been canceled out. That for which the church waits cannot be presented to us except by means of hope and expectation, that is, of imagination. At the same time, one needs to stop imagination before it completes its work, for the risk in that is canceling out surprise as the mode of eschatological manifestation. This can be done by realizing that one's imagination would never succeed in representing the ultimate (lest it becomes an idol), and, therefore, the proliferation of images in which imagination takes comfort is nothing but the very indication of its inability in capturing the singular.

If, in other words, we leave ourselves only to perception and cognition we deprive ourselves of the possibility of the eschatological. If, on the other hand, we indulge in our imagination's infinite possibilities we have somehow already given ourselves the eschaton, and, therefore, we need no more wait for its coming. Biblical language trod down the middle path between these two extremes by providing prophecy and parable. Imagination is indeed employed (e.g., "the kingdom of heaven is likened unto . . .") but also left undone by its very resources, that is, the biblical imagery of the kingdom is so imaginative that it becomes prohibitive to imagination's own attempt to appropriate it.

Conclusion

The penultimate is indispensable for our effort of reaching for the ultimate; even more, the penultimate is indispensable in order for the ultimate itself to reach us. Indeed, through this reciprocal relationship we come to realize the indispensability of the created world for our salvation. We are not saved apart from this world or to the extent that we succeed in living by leaving the world behind us, by withdrawing from it or by denying it, but our salvation passes through and depends upon the world as well as our bodies with which we are bound to the world. It is by working through corporeality and worldliness that little by little the penultimate becomes more and more diaphanous and the ultimate shines through. Thus the invisible is glimpsed through the visible, the spiritual achieved by means of the material, the supersensible becomes experienced in the tangible and the concrete. It is in front of this scandal for our thought that we stand perplexed: how indeed can the eternal give itself through our daily routine, through our mundane concerns? The penultimate as the precursor of the ultimate, as ultimacy's vehicle, appears before our eyes with a dignity that no philosophical system or thought had granted it before. There is no place here for Plato's world as prison, for the Gnostic world as punishment, for Plotinus's progressive degeneration, for Origen's necessity of evil. Indeed, "all shall be well, and/All manner of thing shall be well."[17] Philosophy has a great deal to learn from such a theologically informed vision of eschatology.

But what perhaps is more important than all of this is that this penultimate world will not be left behind when the ultimate arrives, that this insufficient and incomplete world will not be discarded like a ladder that one needs no more once the ultimate has been reached, that our efforts and our failures, our anticipations, empty or fulfilled, will not be lost, that our past will not be erased, that the ultimate will preserve and uplift every little moment of penultimacy, every passing thought and every fragment of feeling. Indeed, "Christ gives up nothing that has been won, but holds it fast in his hands" (E 66).

Appendix: The Penultimate and the Precursor

I would like to append to the foregoing discussion of Bonhoeffer's eschatology a story—providing, as if it were, a more phronetic understanding to the theoretical exposition that preceded it. If we were to speak of the penultimate using "everyday words"—what kind of language, what metaphor or simile, might we employ? What figure or character might be said to embody and exemplify the eschatological awaiting of the penultimate? I would like to suggest the story of St. John the Baptist or, as he is also known since ancient times, St. John the Forerunner. It is precisely this epithet, "the forerunner" or "the precursor," that, I think, makes him the paradigm through which the penultimate is to be best explained.

From the outset, we understand that John is to Jesus what the penultimate is to the ultimate. John is introduced in the gospel narrative by the verse from the prophet Isaiah: "prepare the way of the Lord" (Mt 3:3, Is 40:3). He is to go before Jesus, in anticipation of him, announcing the good news of his coming. Indeed, John's kerygma consists of the proclamation of the kingdom's imminent coming. "The ax is laid to the root of the tree" (Mt 3:10).

As a result of this role, John lacks a proper identity—he himself by himself makes no sense; without him to whom he constantly refers, John is no one. Thus the perplexity of those who insisted asking after his identity: "Who are you?"

> When the Jews sent priests and Levites from Jerusalem to ask him, "Who are you?" he confessed, and did not deny, but confessed, "I am not the Christ." And they asked him, "What then? Are you Elijah?" He said, "I am not." "Are you the Prophet?" And he answered, "No." Then they said to him, "Who are you, that we may give an answer to those who sent us? What do you say about yourself?" He said: "I *am the voice of one crying in the wilderness.*" (Jn 1:19–23)

John has to deny, one by one, all the identities that the crowds are willing to attach to him. Some think he is the Messiah, others Elijah, and others yet the Prophet. These are all different attempts to normalize the penultimate in a recognizable category. Furthermore, they indicate the danger of degenerating the penultimate into what precisely it is *not*: the fulfillment of an expectation instead of its reminder. This is why John had to efface himself, turn himself into no one (*personne*), into a person who lacks a proper identity, the shadow of a person, a voice without a body: "I am the voice of one crying in the wilderness." Those who were frustrated with John's elusiveness, and understanding that John does nothing in his own name, demand now to know in whose authority he is acting: "If you are not the Messiah, nor Elijah, nor the Prophet, why do you baptize?" (Jn 1:25). At this point we can see most clearly John as a deferral, as a pointer to someone else beyond himself: "I baptize in water. There is one among you one whom you do not recognize—the one who is to come after me—the strap of whose sandal I am not worthy to unfasten" (Jn 1:26–27). So John has given an answer: he is the shadow of one-whom-you-do-not-recognize, the one who-is-to-come, the one who-is-not-expected—thus John spoke of the ultimate, and he established once and for all the relationship between himself, the figure of the penultimate, and the ultimate One: "after me is to come a man who ranks ahead of me because he was before me" (Jn 1:30).

It is of utmost importance to grasp this conundrum: the ultimate comes after the penultimate and ranks higher than it *because* (here logic trembles) it, the ultimate, was before the penultimate and it is for the sake of the former that the later exists (thus, teleologically, the things-to-come precede the things-themselves).

At the banks of Jordan the old creation encounters the new. John stands on the threshold between the Old Testament, being the last of the prophets, and the New, of which he is the first witness. In John we see the last priest in the lineage of Aaron (John inherits the priesthood from his father Zechariah, Lk 1:5, 13) and in Jesus we recognize the "fulfillment" of the priestly office in assuming a new priesthood "in the order of Melchizedek" (Psalm 110; Heb 5:6), who, "without a father or mother, without genealogy, without beginning of days or end of life, like the Son of God he remains a priest for ever" (Heb 7:3).

In Grünewald's *Crucifixion*, we meet John by the foot of the cross. Here one sees most evidently how the artist becomes the theologian by altering historical accuracy in order to render explicit a theological claim: according to the gospels it was John the beloved disciple (later called the "theologian") that became the only of Jesus' disciples to witness his Lord's death. Grünewald substitutes one John (the Theologian) with the other (the Forerunner). This substitution is most telling. The role of this John is not merely to witness the passion ("and he who has seen has testified and his testimony is true," Jn 19:35) but to "preach Christ crucified" (1 Cor 1:23) even now, all the more now, at the moment of his utter disparagement and, at the same time, of his glory. John is wholly transformed into this pointing finger that Grünewald depicts in the most dramatic fashion—all his life and ministry has been nothing else but this pointing, this *ecce homo*—or, as the lamb in Grünewald's painting reminds us, into this cry: "behold the lamb of God that takes away the sin of the world" (Jn 1:29). For Karl Barth, John's pointing finger (pointing toward Christ and, at the same time, away from himself) exemplifies the theologian's task.[18] Thus, in Grünewald's interpretation it is not John the Theologian who is the preeminent theologian but John the Forerunner.

In the famous fresco of Christ's *Resurrection* (in the style of the *Descent into Hades* or the *Harrowing of Hell*) from the Monastery of Chora in Constantinople we meet John once more, and this time too he is next to the triumphant Christ, pointing at Him as he did earlier by the foot of His cross. According to the Church's tradition (reflected in his *apolytikion*) St. John descended into Hades before Christ in order to preach His coming even among those in the underworld. Thus his ministry as the forerunner extends from the time *before his birth* (when he leaped in joy for having met his Lord already in the womb of his mother Elizabeth) to the time *after his death* when he awaits his Lord's coming even in the underworld. Being Christ's forerunner exceeds the limits of one's life.

All of this is rather eloquently indicated by John's role in Christ's baptism. The descent into the waters of Jordan became the visible sign of Christ's two other, mystical descents: into the virginal womb of Mary and into the "belly" of Hades—that is, his birth and his death respectively. Since John was undoubtedly present into the former event, so he ought to be at the latter ones. Christ's baptism at John's hands looks back in the past, reaffirming His birth, and, at the same time, forward in the future, foreshadowing His death.[19] As at the theophanic moment of Christ's baptism both past and future are recapitulated in the present, so too at the kairological moments of the eschaton's intertwining with the present, the present carries the past as well as the future.[20]

Thus, we come to recognize in the figure of John the Forerunner the tripartite structure around which Bonhoeffer builds his treatment of ethics, that is, *Christology*, contained in John's witness to Christ's birth, death, and resurrection; *Eucharist*, expressed by John's words "behold the lamb of God"; and, of course, *eschatology*, indicated by John's role as the figure for the penultimate, a role that he fulfils in both his life and his death.

Notes

The title of this chapter is from T. S. Eliot, "Little Gidding," in *Four Quartets* (New York: Harvest Books, 1968), 80.

1. The most fruitful appropriation of Bonhoeffer's eschatology by philosophy is that of Jean-Yves Lacoste in his *Experience and the Absolute: Disputed Questions on the Humanity of Man*, trans. Mark Raftery-Skehan (New York: Fordham University Press, 2004). The author expresses his gratefulness to Bonhoeffer by these words from the introduction: "Two names do not appear in this text, those of Dietrich Bonhoeffer and John of the Cross. To the former, I am indebted not only for the term 'next to last' but also for an entire part of its treatment" (3). The "next to last" (Lacoste's translation of the penultimate) is indeed given a four-page treatment (137–40), but its presence is continuously felt throughout Lacoste's book under a variety of names: as the "provisional" (seemingly a slightly different concept than that of the penultimate, but as Lacoste indicates on p. 145, ultimately united with it), as the "chiaroscuro" or as "liturgy" (perhaps the most central term in Lacoste's analysis).

2. At other times, the example used is that of the two swords.

3. For example, Bonhoeffer does not discuss the famous line "render to Caesar the things that are Caesar's and to God what is God's" (Mt 22:21), which would appear to contradict what he is trying to establish.

4. Bonhoeffer warns against such ideologies as "denying the body of Christ" (E 67) in the literal sense.

5. The acknowledgment here of "two kingdoms" does not contradict what Bon-

hoeffer has emphatically denied earlier, as he adds immediately, "but the lord of both kingdoms is God revealed in Jesus Christ. God rules the world by the office of the word and the office of the sword" (E 112).

6. The eschatological expectation ("Christ will come again") is missing from Bonhoeffer's formula—an interesting lacuna—but its lack, as we will see, is made up by the eschatological discussion that follows.

7. "To become gods" (i.e., the doctrine of *theosis*) does not mean that we will cease being humans. The change implied here concerns the *how* of our being, not the *what*. As Irenaeus makes clear, deification results in a change not of essence, nature, or form but of the *way* we experience and manifest our being. Irenaeus uses the following metaphor: "[A]s the engrafted wild olive does not certainly lose the substance of its wood, but changes the quality of its fruit, and receives another name . . . so also, when man is grafted in by faith and receives the Spirit of God, he certainly does not lose the substance of flesh, but changes . . . and receives another name" (*Adversus Haereses*, V, x, 2). This transformation begins, little by little, already with the Eucharist, for in eating the body of Christ we become "digested" into his body (i.e., the church); "I am the food of full-grown men," Christ says to Augustine. "Grow and you shall feed on me. But you shall not change me into yourself, as you do with the food of your body. Instead you shall be changed into Me" (*Confessions*, VII, x).

8. See also the editor's introduction, 6–7.

9. Despite the modern aversion to such language, the tradition's witness (in both East and West) to the doctrine of *theosis* is overwhelming and hard to ignore (for the evolution of the doctrine see Jaroslav Pelikan, *The Christian Tradition*, 4 vols. [Chicago: University of Chicago Press, 1971–84], 2:10–12 for its inception with the Greek Fathers; 4:66 for its treatment by Nicholas of Cusa after scholasticism; and 4:359 for its reception by Martin Chemnitz after the Reformation). A future task will be, perhaps, to refine the meaning of *theosis* and to place it in context with the corresponding concepts of justification, sanctification, and salvation.

10. Augustine, *Confessions*, II, vi., trans. Whitney J. Oates, in *Basic Writings of Saint Augustine*, 2 vols. (New York: Random House, 1948), 1:25–26 (emphasis added).

11. "Judgment in general is the ability to think the particular as contained under the universal. If the universal (the rule, principle, law) is given, then judgment, which subsumes the particular under it, is *determinative*. . . . But if only the particular is given and judgment has to find the universal for it, then this power is merely *reflective*." Immanuel Kant, *Critique of Judgment*, trans. Werner S. Pluhar (Indianapolis: Hackett, 1987), 18–19 (emphasis in the original). All aesthetic and teleological judgments are reflective.

12. "*Beautiful* is what, without a concept, is liked universally" (Kant, *Critique of Judgment*, 64, emphasis in the original). Furthermore, "beauty is not a characteristic of the object [as, say, the redness of the rose] when taken in its own right" (221). That means that a thing is never beautiful *in itself*, as if beauty were a quality, but its beauty lies with the feeling aroused in the subject. So, "apart from a reference to the subject's feeling, beauty is nothing by itself" (63). Of course, this does not imply a subjectivism along the lines of "beauty is on the eye of the beholder." The whole purpose of the third Critique is to establish the universality of aesthetic judgments.

13. Here we have another idea that would come to play a decisive role in Christian philosophy: the Platonic idea of the *logoi* of beings is inherited by Dionysius (as *proorismoi* or exempla), amended according to a Christian metaphysics (since the

logoi are now "in God," DN V.8 842C), and via Dionysius, received by St. Maximus the Confessor (*Ambigua* in *Patrologia Graeca* 91, 1081A–1085A; a particular reference to Dionysian *logoi* as *proorismoi* is made at 1085A, 5). It was this Dionysian exemplarism that helped the medieval West navigate away from the rock of crude realism (incompatible with Christian doctrine) and the whirlpool of nominalism.

14. Dionysius (the Areopagite), *De Divinis Nominibus* IV 7, 701C. In *Corpus Dionysiacum,* vol. 1, ed. Beate Regina Suchla (Berlin: De Gruyter, 1990). The translation is mine.

15. The teleological character of the beautiful (and, for Dionysius, its eschatological character as well) do not allow us to imagine the attraction that the Beautiful itself exercises as vertical (contemporaneous) but rather as horizontal (diachronic), that is, as coming from the future (*telos*) in order to gradually perfect the present (*teleiosis*). Jean-Louis Chrétien, commenting on the very passage from the Divine Names that we have quoted, writes: "God's call gathers back, the origin calls insofar as it also constitutes itself as the end. This luminous dispensation does not communicate beauty as an inert property but as a power of radiation rekindled from being to being. What it sends out to the extremity of diastole and effusion is the same as what makes the creature turn around toward the source. Creation is here inseparable from a vocation for beauty; the call takes on its biblical meaning of election, which is what distinguishes Dionysus [*sic*] from Platonism. To call is to create, to bestow being and beauty, but also to save" (*The Call and the Response,* trans. Anne Davenport [New York: Fordham University Press, 2004], 15–16).

16. "The very consciousness of a merely formal purposiveness in the play of the subject's cognitive powers, accompanying a presentation by which an object is given *is* that pleasure" (Kant, *Critique of Judgment,* 68, emphasis added). "For the basis of this pleasure is found in the universal, though subjective, condition of reflective judgments, namely, the purposive harmony of an object (whether a product of nature or of art) with the mutual relation of the cognitive powers (imagination and understanding) that are required for every empirical cognition" (31).

17. T. S. Eliot, "Little Gidding," in *Four Quartets,* 168–69, echoing Dame Julian of Norwich's *Revelations of Divine Love.*

18. Eberhard Busch, *The Great Passion: An Introduction to Karl Barth's Theology,* trans. Geoffrey W. Bromiley (Grand Rapids, Mich.: William B. Eerdmans, 2004), 6. I am indebted to Brian Gregor for this reference (see also his discussion of Grünewald's *Crucifixion* in his forthcoming "Thinking through Kierkegaard's Anti-Climacus: Art, Imagination, and Imitation," *Heythrop Journal* 50 [2009]). For a theological appreciation of John the Forerunner see Sergei Bulgakov's *The Friend of the Bridegroom* (Grand Rapids, Mich.: William B. Eerdmans, 2003).

19. In Byzantine iconography, the body of Christ at his baptism is made to resemble closely the dead body of Christ on the cross (an allusion to Rom 6:4).

20. For *kairos* as the moment of divine manifestation and as the unfolding of the eschaton see my "The Anarchic Principle of Christian Eschatology," *Harvard Theological Review* 100, no. 1 (2007): 29–46.

Frits de Lange is Professor of Ethics at the Protestant Theological University, Kampen, The Netherlands. He is author of *Waiting for the Word: Dietrich Bonhoeffer on Speaking about God*.

Brian Gregor is a doctoral candidate in the Department of Philosophy at Boston College. In addition to his work on Bonhoeffer, he has published several essays on Continental philosophy of religion and ethics.

Jean Greisch is enseignant-chercheur at the C.N.R.S. (U.R.A 106, Phéno-ménologie et Herméneutique = Archives Husserl). His most recent books include *Paul Ricœur: l'itinérance du sens; Le Buisson ardent et les Lumières de la raison* (3 vols.); *Entendre d'une autre oreille: Les enjeux philosophiques de l'herméneutique biblique;* and the forthcoming *Qui sommes-nous? Chemins phénoménologiques vers l'homme*.

Kevin Hart is Edwin B. Kyle Chair of Christian Studies in the Department of Religious Studies at the University of Virginia. His most recent books are *The Dark Gaze: Maurice Blanchot and the Sacred* and *Counter-Experiences: Reading Jean-Luc Marion*.

Paul D. Janz is Senior Lecturer in Philosophical Theology, King's College London. Recent publications include *God the Mind's Desire* and *The Command of Grace: A New Theological Apologetics*.

John Panteleimon Manoussakis is Visiting Assistant Professor of Philosophy at the College of Holy Cross. He is author of *God after Metaphysics: A Theological Aesthetic* (Indiana University Press, 2007) and the editor of a number of works, including *Heidegger and the Greeks: Interpretive Essays* (with Drew Hyland, Indiana University Press, 2006).

Paul Ricoeur was one of the leading philosophers of the twentieth century. Among his many influential works are the three-volume *Time and Narrative; Oneself as Another; Memory, History, Forgetting;* and *The Course of Recognition.*

Christiane Tietz is Visiting Professor at the University of Mainz. She is author of *Bonhoeffers Kritik der verkrümmten Vernunft: Eine erkenntnistheoretische Untersuchung,* and one of the executive editors of the Dietrich Bonhoeffer Yearbook.

Ralf K. Wüstenberg is Director of the Institute for Protestant Theology and Visiting Professor for Systematic Theology/Christian Ethics at the Freie Universität Berlin. His publications include *A Theology of Life: Dietrich Bonhoeffer's Religionless Christianity; Theology in Dialogue: The Impact of Arts, Humanities and Sciences on Contemporary Religious Thought;* and *The Political Dimension of Reconciliation.*

Jens Zimmermann holds a Canada Research Chair in Interpretation, Religion and Culture at Trinity Western University. He is author of *Recovering Theological Hermeneutics* and *The Passionate Intellect: Incarnational Humanism and the Future of University Education.*

INDEX